"ALL IN ALL"

"ALL IN ALL"

Unity, Diversity, and the Miltonic Perspective

Edited by

Charles W. Durham and Kristin A. Pruitt

SUP

Selinsgrove: Susquehanna University Press
London: Associated University Presses

Associated University Presses
440 Forsgate Drive
Cranbury, NJ 08512

Associated University Presses
16 Barter Street
London WC1A 2AH, England

Associated University Presses
P.O. Box 338, Port Credit
Mississauga, Ontario
Canada L5G 4L8

The paper used in this publication meets the requirements
of the American National Standard for Permanence of Paper
for Printed Library Materials Z39.48-1984.

Library of Congress Cataloging-in-Publication Data
All in all : unity, diversity, and the Miltonic perspective / edited
by Charles W. Durham and Kristin A. Pruitt.
    p.   cm.
  Includes index.
  ISBN 1-57591-016-0 (alk. paper)
  1. Milton, John, 1608–1674—Criticism and interpretation.
2. Christian poetry, English—History and criticism.   3. Epic
poetry, English—History and criticism.   4. Whole and parts
(Philosophy) in literature.   5. Milton, John, 1608–1674.   Paradise
lost.   6. All (Philosophy) in literature.   I. Durham, Charles W.
II. Pruitt, Kristin A., 1945–   .
PR3588.A79   1999
821'.4—dc21   98-28760
                                                                              CIP

PRINTED IN THE UNITED STATES OF AMERICA

To Diane Kelsey McColley, whose "gracious words"
have contributed so much to Milton scholarship and
whose "graceful acts" have supported our efforts to
augment Milton's "fit audience."

Contents

Acknowledgments

We wish to thank the Middle Tennessee State University Faculty Research Committee, the Middle Tennessee State University English Department Research Committee, and the Christian Brothers University Sabbatical Committee for grants that made possible our editing of this volume; Kevin J. Donovan, John T. Shawcross, and Donald Peter McDonough for their help in organizing the 1995 Conference on John Milton, the Virginia Peck Foundation Trust Fund for financial support, and all the participants for making the event a success; our colleagues, whose continued support sustains our efforts; Janie, Elliott, Carrie, and Andrew for their love and enthusiasm for our projects; and, most especially, the sixteen contributors, without whom *"All in All"* would not exist.

"ALL IN ALL"

Introduction

In describing the building of the temple of the Lord in *Areopagitica,* Milton draws attention to the energizing diversity that characterizes the search for ultimate Truth:

> there must be many schisms and many dissections made in the quarry and in the timber, ere the house of God can be built. And when every stone is laid artfully together, it cannot be united into a continuity, it can but be contiguous in this world; neither can every peece of the building be of one form; nay rather the perfection consists in this, that out of many moderat varieties and brotherly dissimilitudes that are not vastly disproportionall, arises the goodly and gracefull symmetry that commends the whole pile and structure.[1]

That Milton recognized the impossibility, in this world, of constructing a perfect, whole, and consistent Truth out of the dissimilar stones that are laid together, however artfully, is itself a truth contiguous to another truth, that however impossible the task, Milton's works are a testament to his attempts.

Andrew Marvell, in his dedicatory poem, "On Paradise Lost," records his response to one such attempt when he wonders in verse how Milton will avoid ruining "The sacred Truths," how find his way "Through that wide Field" comprised of such diverse elements as "Messiah Crown'd, God's Reconcil'd Decree, / Rebelling Angels, the Forbidden Tree, / Heav'n, Hell, Earth, Chaos, All."[2] Yet in the course of Marvell's poem, his "surmise[s]" are rendered "causeless": Milton's "slender Book," with its tapestry so "vast" and so varied, nonetheless is controlled by a unity, a "Design," and the "Mighty Poet" Milton is hailed for his gift of "Prophecy."

The issue of diversity and unity that Milton raises in *Areopagitica* and that Marvell reacts to in relation to *Paradise Lost* is one apropos of the Miltonic canon generally and one that has continued to engage critics of a poet who, like Shakespeare, transcends his age. Thus Diane Kelsey McColley, in "'All in All': The Individuality of Creatures in *Paradise Lost*," considers the claim that Milton may well be the poet for the upcoming millennium through examining the prediction in *Paradise Lost* that, apocalyptically, "God shall be All in All," especially its significance for seventeenth- and twenty-first-century concepts of individualism, freedom, conscience, and environmental responsibility. She, like Marvell centuries earlier, sees the magnitude of Milton's accomplishment as indelibly inscribing his poetic creation with individuality and diversity while anticipating the ultimate oneness of the "All in All."

The sixteen essays in this volume were included on the program of the 1995 Conference on John Milton at Middle Tennessee State University, and because they were judged particularly significant and stimulating, their authors were invited to expand and revise their works for the present collection, which is intended to reflect the individuality and diversity of varied ideas and approaches to Milton scholarship. Nonetheless, readers will no doubt discern correspondences among the essays. For example, several essays investigate sources—literary, pictorial, architectural—and Milton's use of those sources in his poetry. Others view Milton from the perspective of his age and other writers such as Michael Drayton and Aemilia Lanyer. Still others use the twentieth-century methodologies of transformational grammar, deconstruction, and chaos theory to *re*read Milton's works and assess their prophetic potential.

In the first essay, McColley argues that Milton's vision of transcendent unity need not involve loss of uniqueness, that, quite possibly, "those whom God shall be *in* are not reduced from an 'All' meaning a communicating congregation of lives to an 'All' that digests them, but may retain the distinctions that the process of creation proliferates." To illustrate her point, McColley describes Raphael's account of the creation of earthly species, an account that reveals his delight in "beings wildly unlike himself" and consonant with "The God who invented otherness." God creates particular voices, and each, McColley concludes, paradoxically "gets a separate hearing and is an indispensable part of the whole. It seems likely that a God already fused through all would do no less when all are dynamically fused in him."

For Albert C. Labriola, the "All in All" passages provide the basis for a laserlike investigation of the implications of Milton's uses of the word "all" throughout *Paradise Lost*. Drawing on "linguistic analysis, notably Latinate grammar, Renaissance rhetorical figures, and finally transformational grammar," Labriola focuses on the earliest event in the poem, the begetting of the Son, and the earliest utterance by the Father explaining that event to the angels, who are for the first and only time in the poem all together. Here Labriola locates the "origin . . . of the language and behavior of obedience and disobedience, which recur with variation in numerous later episodes, especially when the word 'all' is used." This word, he maintains, is a "crucial" one, and its study helps to illuminate "the process by which *Paradise Lost* as a linguistic artifact is created."

Diana Treviño Benet, like McColley, sees the concept of God as "All in All" to be illustrative of the character of the deity and descriptive of "the total union of the blessed with God at the end of time." However, Benet explores potentially ominous ramifications of this union that "hints at the erasure of separate identities" in Milton's poem. Citing Sin's birth and Eve's creation, both "images of physical separation," Benet cautions that union and separation are "morally inconsistent" and are not necessarily indicative of "spiritual states." The problem, she contends, is "that the ideal of 'All in All' was common to the different traditions of spiritual and romantic love" and that a confusion of these ideals results in the "terror in love" experienced by Satan and by Eve, who view the "unity proposed or assumed by their superior Others" as seeming "to threaten the diminishment or obliteration of their identities." According to Benet, Milton's use of these "disparate religious and romantic traditions . . . [exposes] as spiritually dangerous the romantic notion that love makes two into one heart, mind, or soul."

In reopening the much-debated question of the hero of *Paradise Lost,* John C. Ulreich maintains that "Eve embodies more fully and perspicuously than any other character those qualities that Milton explicitly identifies as crucial to the new and greater heroism appropriate to a Christian epic" and that in sinning, Eve "initiates the properly human action of the poem by fulfilling God's intention that she and Adam should become 'Authors to themselves.'" Proposing that Eve becomes her own author by experiencing the limits of her own authority, Ulreich suggests that she realizes selfhood "only by an act of self-annihilation." Resolution of the two seemingly incongruous "heroic ideals" represented by Eve "can be defined by a structural paradox: 'whosoever will save his life, shall lose it: and whosoever will lose his life for my sake shall find it' (Matt. 16.25)."

Also considering the role of Eve in Milton's poem, Elizabeth Mazzola regards her as "apocryphal text" in three major ways: first, she appears and disappears repeatedly in *Paradise Lost;* second, she is connected to the apocryphal character Lilith; and third, she possesses hidden potential and "assumes a large part of the burden of memory." Mazzola argues that Milton's personal "'di-

vorce issue' forces Eve . . . to become the idol Milton smashes,"
that he "fastens on [her] as hermeneutical catastrophe and in this
way is able, repeatedly, to let her go." The Eve of Mazzola's essay,
then, is marginalized, "produced as supplement and obstacle,
buried prize and secondhand fiction."

Kari Boyd McBride and John C. Ulreich read the "marginalized"
author Aemilia Lanyer in relationship to "major" author Milton,
both of whom "share an interest in theorizing womankind through
biblically based poetic narrative" and read both authors in relationship "to the larger debate about women," the sixteenth- and
seventeenth-century *querelle des femmes*. In Lanyer's defense of
Eve in "Salve Deus Rex Judaeorum," the idea that Eve's deception
by the serpent "serves to extenuate [her] trespass" is a reversal
of the logic of the biblical text in 1 Timothy. Lanyer's position
suggests that she was familiar with Henricus Cornelius Agrippa's
work *De nobilitate et praecellentia foeminei sexus* and raises the
possibility that she influenced later translations of Agrippa. Although "there is no evidence that [Milton] knew of either Agrippa
or Lanyer," in *Paradise Lost* "he seems to be responding to those
very argumentative points about the relative culpability of Adam
and Eve that are unique to Lanyer, showing him to be . . . closer
to Lanyer than to Agrippa and others."

In disputing the critical position that Satan's punishment entails
a curtailment of his freedom, Claude N. Stulting, Jr., invokes
"Jacques Derrida's description of language as a field of *differance*
and free play" in order to "comprehend Satan's predicament" and
in turn uses that predicament "as a . . . heuristic device to illuminate the theological ramifications of the Derridean project." Stulting believes that Satan's fate "is a radical *lack* of containment," that
because, as Derrida would have it, "Satan rejects stable presence,
centered meaning, and self-limitation, he is condemned to free
play, indeterminacy, and, essentially, deconstruction." God, Stulting goes on to argue, "does not so much deconstruct Satan; rather,
as the *deus absconditus*," or hidden deity, "God opens up a limitless space within which Satan deconstructs and disseminates
himself." From a theological point of view, Derrida's representation of God as an "absolute presence in the history of Western
thought" is, ultimately, a misreading of the God who "is never
present in the fully determinable way that Derrida thinks the tradition claims he is."

Lawrence F. Rhu focuses on Satan's wandering and solitary ad-
venturing as paradigmatic markers of romance, which Milton
"demonizes" by associating it with evil. These "generic signals"

reappear at critical points in the poem "to indicate the continuing fallibility of human nature before and after the Fall." Rhu considers the Spenser/Milton and Ariosto/Tasso relationships, which are "not unlike . . . from the perspective of genre." Like Tasso, Milton rejects Ariosto's multiple plot lines in favor of structural unity. Moreover, "in this demonic romance Milton decisively employs the language of anti-Catholicism in ways that bespeak as much his own polemic against the established Church of England as his condemnation of the Church of Rome."

Richard J. DuRocher's essay explores the "demonization" of architecture, as it were. He regards Milton's presentation of the building of Pandemonium in Hell as an exposition of the essential architectural principles of Vitruvius Pollio, Roman author of *De architectura* (circa 28 B.C.) and a "central and primary" influence on Milton's picture of the devils' palace. Further, DuRocher suggests that Pandemonium is meant to convey more than Milton's anti-Catholic sentiments. Rather, it "stand[s] as an image of both good and bad building," since it also "reflect[s] sound aesthetic and architectural principles." Because of this, the description of Pandemonium highlights the poet's "daring narrative strategy, inviting readers to marvel at demonic echoes of the architectural achievements of the high Renaissance."

Also concerned with Milton's visual imagination in *Paradise Lost* is Cheryl H. Fresch's essay, which challenges denunciations of Milton's "'pictorialist conventions.'" Concentrating on the Expulsion scene in book 12, Fresch notes how late seventeenth- and eighteenth-century illustrators of Milton's poem appropriated its visual details, and she describes the "remarkably different tone" of Blake's early nineteenth-century paintings. Fresch then looks to earlier artistic conventions of the Anastasis tradition, in which Christ leads Adam and Eve from Hell, that in all probability influenced Milton's "extraordinarily new image of the Expulsion from the Garden of Eden." By "Collapsing the Last Judgment and the Expulsion into apocalyptic simultaneity," Milton infuses the conclusion of his poem with an image of "deliverance and restoration." Subsequently, Blake "made visible precisely this vision" in his illustrations of the scene.

Stella P. Revard, in analyzing the hymns and anti-hymns to light in *Paradise Lost,* finds literary models in the classical hymn tradition, a tradition ranging from ancient Homeric hymns to Renaissance works in imitation of the classical types. In particular, Revard sees Satan's address to the Sun in book 4 not simply as "an extended soliloquy" but also as an anti-hymn "that inverts many of

the traditions of classical hymn and in so doing contrasts with the
Hymn to Light in book 3 that precedes it and Adam and Eve's
Morning Hymn in book 5 with its salute to the Sun that follows
it." Satan's "parody" of the formulas also contrasts with Neoplatonic and humanist hymns to Apollo-Sun familiar to Milton and
reveals how, "even as [Satan's] Evil has subverted Good and his
Darkness the Light, [his] anti-hymn subverts the worship of the
true hymn."

David J. Bradshaw also examines the relationship between a
classical genre and *Paradise Lost* in his discussion of Milton's use
of Virgil's *Aeneid* in books 11 and 12. Bradshaw claims that "Milton
learned from Virgil the importance and the techniques of emulating
his epic predecessors, but it may well have been from Augustine
that he acquired the strategy for adapting Virgil himself to Christian apologetics." That strategy involved using "what was worthwhile [Egyptian gold] in the classical tradition"; however, the
seventeenth-century poet was aware of the risks of "infection"
from "tainted" sources. Bradshaw shows how Milton adapts such
Virgilian materials as the call of Aeneas to leave Troy and the epic
prophecy, and he points out "telling differences in the views of
history that are offered within the poems," a telic view in the
case of the *Aeneid* and a cyclic view in *Paradise Lost*. Michael's
prophecy, Bradshaw concludes, "reveals Milton's redefining of the
conventional Christian conception of history," since "Salvation
. . . always lies not really at the conclusion of a providentially
controlled segment of history, but, rather, beyond or apart from
history altogether."

In the first of the essays dealing with a work other than *Paradise
Lost,* Louis Schwartz argues that the relative lack of critical attention devoted to "Epitaph on the Marchioness of Winchester" belies
the poem's "ambitiousness and originality" based on its generally
overlooked historical context: the high rate of childbirth deaths in
seventeenth-century London and among middle and upper classes
in various parts of England. With this context firmly established,
Schwartz considers why maternal mortality was rarely a subject
for poetry, examines an elegy by Michael Drayton, which may
have influenced Milton's "Epitaph," that reveals the difficulty of
dealing with this topic, and demonstrates how Milton employed in
this occasional poem "allusions to the ritual forms and poetry of
funeral and wedding" in an effort to resolve social, theological, and
psychological difficulties, addressing issues of decorum through
"mythopoeic abstraction." Thus, the "Epitaph on the Marchioness
of Winchester," Schwartz claims, "pushes at the boundaries of its

genre to produce an aesthetic conciliation with maternal mortality" and is, in its attempt to achieve such resolution, "significant."

The debate between Comus and the Lady in the 1637 version of *Comus* is the focus of J. Martin Evans's essay, which addresses the inconsistency between the Lady's initial praise of temperance, a position congruous with "the Aristotelian concept of virtue . . . as a mean between two opposing extremes, one of defect, one of excess," and later, in response to Comus's temptations to drink of the cup, and to seduction, her espousal of virginity, itself the opposing extreme to licentious indulgence. The problem, Evans contends, is that "At one moment virtue is being defined as a mean between extremes; at the next it is being defined *as* one of the extremes." Evans locates the source of the contradiction "in a deep-seated tension within the concept of temperance itself." In another, qualitative, sense, the mean itself constitutes an extreme, and in a choice between good and evil, "the middle of the road is neither the best nor the safest place to be." Evans closes his argument on *Comus*'s argument by asserting that while the Lady's movement from defender of temperance to defender of abstinence may appear logically inconsistent, "psychologically and morally the shift from one to the other is entirely plausible."

In her investigation of Milton's *Areopagitica* in light of twentieth-century chaos theory, Mary F. Norton defines conscience as "both a principle of order and a force for disorder." She contends that, like chaos theory, Milton's epistemology allows for disorder and change "and thus, as does chaos theory, interprets 'disorder and order not as antitheses but as complements.'" Consequently, "Milton's moral system based on free will" corresponds to "nonlinear" chaotic systems, which possess patterns but are unstable. With regard to the attempt to reassemble dismembered Truth described in *Areopagitica*, Norton draws parallels to "fractal generation," and she views conscience as a "strange attractor," the point at which a chaos system "attracts systemic action." Finally, Norton maintains that "Milton's epistemology of chaos is implicit and fundamental" and that *Areopagitica* reveals a world in which "free will and choices make new civic orders possible, and multidimensionality is a form of freedom that will lead us closer to reassembling fractured Truth."

The final essay in the collection seeks to discern the spirit, or truth, in Milton's portrayal of Samson and Dalila in *Samson Agonistes*. Alan Rudrum takes issue with revisionist views of recent years, views that defend Dalila's behavior and regard Samson "as deluded and . . . acting willfully," and argues for a more "traditional interpretation" of Milton's poem as "the drama of Samson's regeneration." To support his belief that Dalila was not within her rights to betray Samson, despite his earlier hostile actions toward her people, Rudrum argues, first, that in the Hebrew context, a wife "renounced her god and society and owed fealty to" her husband's, and second, that the contrast between the true, transcendent God of Israel and the non-transcendent Dagon, whose will is "coterminous with that of the priests and elders of Philistia," obviates the rightness of Dalila's betrayal. In contending that Samson destroyed the Temple of Dagon because he was divinely impelled, not because he was self-motivated, Rudrum demonstrates that "Words that are meant to be interpreted by the Philistian lords in their common sense" can ironically refer "to Samson's own individual empowerment through reconciliation with God."

Overall, these essays demonstrate the continued scholarly commitment to a search for truths in and about Milton's works, a process that began in the seventeenth century and promises to continue unabated into the next millennium.

Notes

1. John Milton, *Areopagitica,* in *Complete Prose Works of John Milton,* 8 vols., ed. Don M. Wolfe et al. (New Haven: Yale University Press, 1953–82), 2 : 555.

2. Andrew Marvell, "On *Paradise Lost,*" in *John Milton: Complete Poems and Major Prose,* ed. Merritt Y. Hughes (New York: Odyssey, 1957), 209.

"All in All": The Individuality of Creatures in *Paradise Lost*

DIANE KELSEY McCOLLEY

At the 1993 Conference on John Milton in Murfreesboro, Tennessee, Joseph Wittreich concluded his keynote speech with the view that *Paradise Lost,* with its ability to host "conflicting systems of thought" and so liberate the mind, is a poem "uniquely poised for global challenges," and that "Milton, with his future gaze, may prove to be . . . the poet for the twenty-first century." I want to respond to that summons by considering what "systems of thought" might be held in suspense by the prediction that at the end of time "God shall be All in All." The question touches on problems of the seventeenth century that are also problems for the twenty-first: the relations of liberty and justice, of external and internal tyrannies, of identity and community, and of the natural and the spiritual parts of creation that merge in Milton's monism. What might the All-in-Allness of God mean in view of the energetic individualism, the insistence on liberty of conscience and of creative genius, and the abundance of entity and identity that overflow Milton's works? How does this apparently transcendent beatific vision relate to Milton's attitudes toward freedom and conscience and toward human responsibility for the natural world—a twenty-first-century emergency already emerging in the seventeenth, with Milton the poet-prophet of its present urgency? And what might it mean in view of Milton's call for the renewal of "the fair music that all creatures made"[1] and of the apocalyptic vision of a heaven where "all nations, and kindreds, and people, and tongues" stand before the throne, and join with "every creature which is in heaven, and on the earth, and under the earth, and such as are in the sea" in the hymn to the Lamb that was slain (Rev. 7.9 and 5.13)?[2]

The proclamation that "God shall be All in All" is in a root sense totalitarian; taken as a political metaphor, it appears to foreclose debate and submits Milton's Heaven to the charge that the internalization of conscience—traditionally, God's voice—is the subtlest prison, because the prisoner does not recognize his bondage. By intimating, possibly, an end to singularity, the proclamation bears on our discussion of Milton's artistic practice in view of postmodern challenges to the integrity of the self, and hence to respect for Milton's claim in *Areopagitica* that "a good book is the precious life-blood of a master-spirit."[3] It pertains to Milton's place in the critique of cultural imperialism because a model of a homogeneous heaven requiring assent to a particular religion offers little incentive to respect other cultures and can be used as an excuse for persecution. And it relates to his environmental ethic because if he believes that the ultimate goal of being is for differences to be dissolved, he offers little incentive to preserve species other than our own.

The phrase "All in All" first appears in book 3 when, in response to the Son's offer, "Account mee man . . . on me let Death wreck all his rage" (3.238, 241)[4] the Almighty proclaims "all Power / I give thee, reign for ever, and assume / Thy Merits" (317–19). He adds that after the Last Judgment,

> Hell, her numbers full,
> Thenceforth shall be for ever shut. Meanwhile
> The World shall burn, and from her ashes spring
> New Heav'n and Earth, wherein the just shall dwell
> And after all thir tribulations long
> See golden days, fruitful of golden deeds,
> With Joy and Love triumphing, and fair Truth.
> Then thou thy regal Sceptre shalt lay by,
> For regal Sceptre then no more shall need,
> God shall be All in All.
>
> (332–41)

Immediately, of course, "all / The multitude of Angels"—political wimps, as some would have them—with "loud Hosannas fill'd / Th' eternal Regions" (344–45, 348–49). Marshall Grossman calls this harmony "a final, implicit metaphor for the dialectic of the individual and the community to which he or she is joined by the measured rule of an internal law ('Umpire Conscience') and the shared 'light after light' in which that law is read." But he also finds that "The ultimate resolution of the historical process is understood as the abolition of all difference. . . . When the process of internalization is complete, rhetorically projected relationships, indeed, language itself, will collapse as the will of God establishes a homogeneous community of the Godly."[5] William Empson thinks that even the good angels are resistant to the "ideal of total union" that precipitated the rebel ones out of Heaven in the first place, and that "God can gobble them up as soon as look at them, which would make him an alarming employer."[6] For Stanley Fish, "the prospect of merging in an undifferentiated union with a God who shall be 'all in all' (III.341) turns into the horror of a uni–verse in which all distinctions will have been effaced and the landscape will be reduced to a 'universal blanc.'"[7] Versions of this assumption of anagogical monotony derived from Marx, Freud, and Foucault suggest that Milton's depiction of Heaven promotes a masochistic subjection to an internalized higher power. Robert M. Myers maintains that the "erasure of hell" mirrors a historical shift away from belief in damnation in the seventeenth century and implies a lessening of freedom; since Hell is not a successful deterrent, the external threat of it is less controlling than a socially constructed conscience.[8] Rational consent does not constitute liberty; Francis Barker identifies "self-discipline" as the principle of censorship in *Areopagitica,* because it is "ideological control implanted in the new subjectivity."[9] If the internalization of conscience, instead of being a way to civilized freedom, is an insidious imposition of power, Milton scholarship, along with the rest of Western civilization, has come to a literal crisis of conscience.

Myers raises a corollary problem:

> [I]f hell is "full" and "forever shut", there is apparently no possibility of a new rebellion against God's reign, and it becomes difficult to conceive how free will could be maintained for the saints. Accordingly, the erasure of hell subverts God's justification of his willingness to permit Satan's temptation, for if the final result of the divine plan is beings who love God freely but are immune from any possible inclination to sin, it becomes difficult to understand why God did not create man with this capability in the first place.[10]

This conundrum, like Grossman's "homogeneous community of the Godly," assumes that free choice is limited to the choice between good and evil. But what does it mean to be "the Godly" if the "All" that is in them devised the different potentialities of each being and species? Might a world cured of evil still have abundant choice of creative activities producing interesting individuality? It is evil that destroys individuals and species and imaginative processes, after all. A will obsessed with power erases distinctions, as it is personified in a despotic Satan or practiced by a dictatorial Hitler or Stalin, or anyone who desires power without desiring the well-being of each creature.[11] The God of Genesis and Job, and of books 7 and 8 of *Paradise Lost,* delights in dissimilarity, and evil resents or effaces it. In book 1, John Peter Rumrich notes, the rebel angels have become "nonentities, strictly from nowhere, and beyond recognition because of 'thir hideous change.' . . . The identity of a thing with itself is the basis of all reason, all assurance, all happiness, but the only hope the devils have is the complete loss of their created identities and the establishment of new ones." Yet they have become "fixed like stone, artifacts of their own discontent."[12] So I would rephrase the problem: If God is to be "All in All," why admit the history of sin and suffering by making creatures with a capacity for creativity and diversification in the first place? Why create opportunity to participate in our own creation if identity is to be erased?

Taken as a model for human government, then, as Robert Fallon and Mary Ann Radzinowicz have warned us *not* to do, the heavenly theocracy appears to give warrant for oppression.[13] Taken as an argument that blessedness means the loss of personality, vagary, eccentricity, dissonance, debate, and differentiation of species, the prediction that "God shall be All in All" raises the questions of what earthly life was for, and who, after it, will consent to become "the saints."

The relation of the multiplicity of creatures to the One and the Good was seen by Plotinus as a temporal condition of souls whose purpose was reunion with God; but for him that reunion is a purely spiritual process, entailing the turning away from sensible things. Multiplicity is inconsistent with perfect unity of the soul with the One to be sought: "This," he says, "is the life of gods and of the godlike and blessed among men, liberation from the alien that besets us here, a life taking no pleasure in the things of earth, the passing of solitary to solitary."[14] There is no place in such blessedness for a communion of creatures, because com-union requires more than one, and number inheres in the particular, which it is the soul's business to transcend.

Milton, in contrast, believes that it is "by orderly conning over" of those sensible things that we can "know God aright."[15] His biblical source for the "All in All" passages is 1 Cor. 15.28, "And when all things shall be subdued unto him, then shall the Son also himself be subject unto him that put all things under him, that God may be all in all." All of the "alls" in this 1611 version translate the Greek neuter plural *panta*, which is usually rendered "all things."[16] In *De Doctrina Christiana*, the statement "*ut Deus sit omnia in omnibus*"[17] makes the plurality clearer, but omits the interesting syntactic reversibility that the less inflected English version permits.[18] These plurals assure the possibility that those whom God shall be *in* are not reduced from an "all" meaning a communicating congregation of lives to an "All" that digests them, but may retain the distinctions that the process of creation proliferates. The phrase "All in All" not only brings divinity into the multiplicity of creatures but counters Neoplatonic ideas of the inadmissibility of multiplicity into the unity of Transcendent Being.

However, the question remains of what it might mean for God to be "All" in the creatures. According to the evidence of *Paradise Lost*, the more a being made in God's image admits God, the more it loves the other beings God has made, and the more it is itself, because God is a God of differentiation who gives creatures made in his image the ability to participate in the divine imaginative freedom that is one of his attributes.[19] That respect for selfhood and for the creative activity of free agents seems to me implicit in Milton's conception of creation *ex deo,* in which creatures are made out of the very stuff of God and innumerably diversified. For rational and intuitive beings, reentry into the All is a chosen entry, or entry of the All into each an invited one, since the freedom of their will is one of God's few immutable decrees. The desire for mystical transcendence is among those ideas Milton holds in suspension, but it is the communion of creatures rather than the transcendence of creaturehood that his epic sets before us.

Arthur E. Barker finds in all of Milton's work "[t]he integration of the natural and the spiritual" and "the perfecting of the [natural] by the [spiritual] with the increase, not the loss, of its peculiar glory."[20] If God is "All in All," the individuality of creatures in both senses—as indivisible selves who are also indivisible from their shared creaturehood—can fully unfold. In this process, each degree of the hierarchy of creatures is raised up, without loss of its "peculiar glory," by those "more refin'd, more spiritous, and pure" (5.475)—plants and animals by Adam and Eve, human beings by angels.

The Father's elevation of the Son in the "All in All" speech of book 3 echoes and enlarges his previous speech-act in book 5, later in the text but earlier in the action, "your Head I him appoint; / . . . Under his great Vice-gerent Reign abide / United as one individual Soul / For ever happy" (606, 609–11). One seraph's disinclination to be "happy" in this particular way begins the dramatic conflict. Mary Ann Radzinowicz writes that by the Son's appointment "Milton rejects the Son's hereditary right" for a "political reason": "to instate the Son as Son on the grounds of merit . . . he insists on a vicegerency rather than kingly inheritance in order to wash out the political inference that kingship on earth mysteriously resembles or is sanctioned by kingship in Heaven."[21] However, in the "All in All" speech the Son is promoted to "universal King" (3.317) because of his offer to suffer death on humankind's behalf; *therefore* "all knees . . . shall bow" (321) in Heaven, Earth, and Hell. Here, too, Stevie Davies finds, "God . . . explicitly repudiates hereditary rule in favor of elective rule on a meritocratic basis. . . . Here also, the anointing of the king is stressed, in close relation to the anointing of humanity, God's youngest sons."[22] I suggest also that God's love of identity and differentiation motivates the begetting of the creative Son into the body of creatures: he condescends to headship over the angels and so unites with creaturehood, as he will do further in the Incarnation. By that descent down the scale of being for which he is exalted, divinity unites itself with angelhood and later with all flesh without violating the holiness of the Godhead or the selfhood of each being.

As we consider the kingship by which the Son will put all things, including Death, under his feet, it is useful to remember that the phrase "All in All," while spoken first by the Father in book 3 of the text, is spoken first by the Son (in book 6) in the chronological action, following the Father's commission to end the war: the angelic combatants are at an impasse because, the Father says,

> Equal in thir Creation they were form'd,
> Save what sin hath impair'd, which yet hath wrought
> Insensibly, for I suspend thir doom.
>
> (6.690–92)

He therefore sends the Son to intervene in "this perverse Commotion" (706). The Son replies that in order to fulfill God's will,

> Sceptre and Power, thy giving, I assume
> And gladlier shall resign, when in the end
> Thou shalt be All in All, and I in thee
> For ever, and in mee all whom thou lov'st.
>
> (731–34)

The timely *resignation* of power, which the Son himself identifies as the conclusion of his mission, *is* the model for the purposes of all who wield it. Once evil—the power of those who deny their own creaturehood and make war on their fellow creatures—has been cast out, all who do not choose evil will be "in" the Son and he "in the Father" who will be "All in All"; the thought is expressed liturgically in the communion prayer "that we may evermore dwell in him and he in us."[23]

There are, then, three steps in the Son's exaltation: his appointment as vicegerent, his commission to stop the war, and his elevation to kingship on the basis of his merciful humility and willingness to suffer for his people. Each of these ascents is a kind of descent on behalf of the beings created by the Son's agency. Although the casting out of evil is often used in human governments as an excuse to seize power and commit further oppressions, the Son, on his own, sees that it is part of his mission to cast out *that* evil—the evil of replacing one form of oppression in particular. Once he has put under his feet Death and the unjust will to power that engendered it, the community of the "All in All" is specifically one from which the satanic desire to transcend creaturehood with its differentiations has been expelled.

"[A]ll whom thou lov'st," like the predication "I love you," distinguishes persons, suggesting a retention of identity. The process of creation by division and diversification in book 7 gives strong evidence that Milton's God promotes specificity and differentiation; and the point of this multiplicity is the increase of love, since to love others requires some degree of otherness.

The "Individuality" of my title is one of those words that means the opposite of itself—being numerically and indivisibly one, and also being inseparable from another, as in "individual solace dear" (4.486). Eve gives a spirited and, in my view, politically alert argument (9.273–89, 322–41) that being "individual" in the sense of indivisibility in love does not mean loss of individual identity and mission. The angels, though already united under the vicegerent Son "as one individual Soul," also have separate identities and missions. When asked about angelic love, Raphael tells Adam with a glow—not a blush—of seraphic joy that when angels embrace, "Total they mix" (8.627). This ability is evidence not of the sexuality of angels, since they are not in these embraces adopting gendered form, but of their interimmersibility without loss of identity.[24] Unity and difference co-inhere. This doubly "individual solace" predicts the manner in which God may be "All in All."

Milton's God creates by a process of partition and parturition that proliferates diverse species and distinct selves within an organic community. He conceives that the more choice, and even struggle in choosing, reasoning beings have, the more they will become selves. And the more they are surrounded by other selves, and by other species different from themselves, the more opportunities for delighted apprehension of others they will have. In this process, selfhood is not a state but an activity, as it is for Gerard Manley Hopkins: each "Deals out that being indoors each one dwells; / Selves—goes itself."[25] When the Judge receives his faithful, as Michael says, "into bliss, / Whether in Heav'n or Earth, for then the Earth / Shall all be Paradise" (12.462–64), is there any reason to think that Milton's God would not still be in them in ways that Gardner Campbell has eloquently suggested that we see as provocative?[26] Would he not continue to call forth their selving by continuing to be, though in all, nevertheless the eternally amazing Other? We are not to suppose that *all* of God will be in each, only that divinity will be in them according to their capacities. Beyond that, would God not continue to be the *mysterium tremendum* and startle his creatures in stimulating ways?

In the *Christian Doctrine* we read, "since all things come not only from God but out of God, no created thing can be utterly annihilated. . . . All entity is good: nonentity, not good. It is not consistent, then, with the goodness and wisdom of God, to make out of entity, which is good, something which is not good, or nothing."[27] The chapter on "Perfect Glorification," with the Dantesque number of 33, begins, as Milton's chapters often do, with an individual person: Enoch, who was translated to glory before the Law; and then another, Elijah, who was translated after the Law. Following the principle that salvation is a covenant—a willing agreement on both sides, hence between parties with separate wills—the author declares that "the covenant with God is not dissolved by death," and he assents to the resurrection of the body: "It appears that each man will rise with the same identity as he had before. . . . If this were not so we should not be like Christ. He entered into glory with that very same body, that very same flesh and blood, with which he had died and risen again" (6:620–21). In sorting out those to be glorified, "The standard of judgment will be the individual conscience itself, and so each man will be judged according to the light which he has received" (623): not only an escape hatch from outer darkness but a warning against conformity and intolerance.[28] The tractate's dispassionate description of the torments of Hell, dismissively ending "So much for the punishment of the wicked" (630), is open to the kind of critique brought forward by Foucault, but it mitigates the idea of eternal punishment by introducing gradation in "severity and duration" (628), and neither tractate nor poem, unlike the *Commedia,* consigns particular human beings to everlasting fire. According to the *Christian Doctrine,* the Judgment "will not last for one day only but for a considerable length of time, and will really be a reign, rather than a judicial session," and the whole human race will be judged after "The judgment of the evil angels and of the chief enemies of God" as in

the cases of the Judges of Israel (625), suggesting equity and perhaps an opportunity to receive more light before the final sentence.
After the Judgment, the blessed will "possess the kingdom" made
ready for them (626: Matt. 25.34), and the Son "shall hand over
the kingdom to God the Father, after annihilating all domination,
authority and power . . . so that God may be all in all" (626: 1 Cor.
15.24–28). Apparently, God's way of being all in all is not one of
domination, authority, and power, those methods of the powers of
darkness that will have been abolished. The abolition of domination
does not mean removing all distinctions of persons, since "It appears that the saints will not all be equally glorified in heaven"
(631–32).[29] The chapter concludes: "Our glorification will be accompanied by the renovation of, and our possession of, heaven
and earth and all those creatures in both which may be useful or
delightful to us" (632). The statement that some kinds of nonhuman
earthly creatures will be included in the renovation, not only for
use but for delight, supports the poem's promise that the Son will
"raise / From the conflagrant mass, purg'd and refin'd, / New
Heav'ns, new Earth" (12.547–49) and surely clinches the case
against a featureless afterlife: the "Elephant . . . [will wreathe] His
Lithe Proboscis" (4.345–47) for "Ages of endless date" (12.549).

But what about the statement that nothing will be lost that is
useful or delightful to *us?* John Muir writes,

> No dogma taught by the present civilization seems to form so insuper-
> able an obstacle in the way of a right understanding of the relations
> which culture sustains to wildness as that which regards the world as
> made especially for the uses of man. Every animal, plant, and crystal
> controverts it in the plainest terms. Yet it is taught from century to
> century as something ever new and precious, and in the resulting
> darkness the enormous conceit is allowed to go unchallenged.[30]

The Milton of *Paradise Lost* did challenge that conceit, not by
abolishing the hierarchy of creatures but by educating the reader's
delighted consciousness of other creatures' lives and human responsibility for them. This education in creature-awareness is one
of the ways the poem is an improvement over the tractate; the
process of writing a poem often refines an author's sensibilities.
But even the tractate affirms "the renovation of . . . heaven and
earth, and all those creatures in both which may be useful or delightful to us," liberated from death and corruption; by analogy
with Eden, the creatures would nourish human affections and
moral wisdom and delight the mind and senses simply by being
themselves and living their lives. The creatures delightful to Adam

and Eve and Raphael in the *poem* do not exclude those whose usefulness for predatory fallen man is usually in being eaten or worn. Given the abolition of death, lovers of wildness and scientific accuracy will wonder how an eagle who is not a raptor can truly be an eagle; one can only suppose that God's imagination can project employments of an eagle's talents and talons of which our imaginations fall short.[31]

But what about "our possession of heaven and earth"?[32] A primary meaning of "possess" (from *potis* and *sedere*) is "inhabit." The *Oxford English Dictionary* uses as its proving quotation the words Milton gives Adam about the "power and rule / Conferr'd upon us" (4.429–30), which he calls "Dominion giv'n / Over all other Creatures that possess / Earth, Air, and Sea" (430–32). Since Adam is speaking to Eve, she is included in the "us" who receive "Dominion." But it is the *creatures* who "possess" their habitats. In the poem these habitats bring forth and belong to the creatures: "out of the ground," Raphael reports, "up rose / As from his Lair the wild Beast where he wons / In Forest wild, in Thicket, Brake, or Den" (7.456–58); "Air, Water, Earth, / By Fowl, Fish, Beast, was flown, was swum, was walkt / Frequent" (502–4). Adam and Eve do not "possess" the animated creatures—whom Milton calls "living souls"—but govern them beneficently. They do not enslave, tease, or butcher them; they do not dig up or sell or pollute their habitats.[33] The dominion or lordship over them given to Adam and Eve, who were made in the image of the God who created the animals and blessed them and called them good, is to be, Raphael says, the rule of a creature "endu'd / With Sanctity of Reason" (507–8) who will

> Govern the rest, self-knowing, and from thence
> Magnanimous to correspond with Heav'n,
> But grateful to acknowledge whence his good
> Descends.
>
> (510–13)

To the extent that Adam and Eve do possess the *Earth*, they do so for the benefit, not the exploitation, of other creatures. They dress and keep the habitat they share with animals *in* whom they delight and *whom* they delight. Care of this habitation is the center of human work: given in the beginning, practiced gladly, acknowledged by Eve when she proposes to Adam that their vocation of earth keeping might be hampered by too much "Casual discourse" (9.223) and reiterated by Adam at the vision of the Ark, from which he gladly—if over-optimistically—learns that "Man shall live / With *all* the Creatures, and thir seed preserve" (11.872–73; emphasis mine). Contemplating the promise of the Seed of woman, he calls Eve "Mother of all things living, since by thee / Man is to live, and all things live for Man" (160–61). Anthropocentric as it may be, his statement implies that through her the Incarnation offers salvation to all living things.

The God who invented otherness, who made such individual creatures as human beings are, who delights in the untamable crocodile whose "eyes are like the eyelids of the morning" (Job 41.18) and sends springs to give drink to the wild asses (Ps. 104.10–11), likes diverse entities. That the good angels in *Paradise Lost* share this attitude may be seen in Raphael's account of the creation of earthly species and of the responses of the angelic choirs, for Raphael is confirmed in blessedness. He is one in whom God is all, yet he speaks in a distinctive style, a language of nature exquisitely observant of the particularities of each creature and empathetic with it, responding, through Milton's mimetic prosody, to each one's form and motion and describing each one's activity from within. He imagines how it feels to be an oyster or a crane and makes *us* feel it sensuously and kinetically, in our nerves and muscles and breath and organs of speech as we shape the words. He is attentive to and delighted by the distinctive properties of beings wildly unlike himself. His empathetic delight is part of what blessedness is. New creations increase it. When God is "All in All," Heaven will be replenished by the visitation or immigration of those creatures who until then are confined to Earth, since then "Earth [will] be chang'd to Heav'n, and Heav'n to Earth" (7.160). This state of blessedness, which Raphael inhabits wherever he goes, is exhibited by the quality of his consciousness, and it also illuminates the problem of the tyranny of conscience. The intuitive angel does not need to be told not to kill, covet, or bear false witness; he does not need laws, principles, theoretical isms, or a culturally constructed conscience, because for him conscience is the same as consciousness. He is fully conscious of the creatures he encounters as fully experiential others, and, by virtue of being God's works, as worthy of their lives. He responds with unintrusive but observant pleasure to each creature he encounters. That kind of conscience is not the tyrannical invasion of external power into subjectivity, but the sympathetic awareness of the fullness of the lives of other beings and the conditions in which they thrive. The kind of God whom Milton shows creating numerous species transmits this kind of consciousness to conscious beings and so

proliferates sympathies. This is one of the ways God is in them
without consuming them.

   In book 7, Raphael describes the life of each animal from *its*
point of view, giving equal attention to varied creatures from the
largest to the smallest, in prosody that itself provides us with a
kinetic experience. "And God created the great Whales" (391), he
begins, in the spacious and weighty consonance of the 1611 version
of Genesis; and later, "part of huge bulk / Wallowing unwieldly,
enormous in thir Gait / Tempest the Ocean" (410–12): as we experience the unwieldliness of enormity on our lips and tongues, the
creature suddenly springs dangerously alive; we experience its being in our breath as Leviathan "at his Gills / Draws in, and at his
Trunk spouts out a Sea" (415–16). Fish "Glide under the green
Wave, in Sculls that oft / Bank the mid Sea" (402–3)—and the
enjambment imitates the banking. When the shorebirds hatch their
numerous brood, "from th' Egg that soon / Bursting with kindly
rupture forth disclos'd / Thir callow young" (418–20), the energy
produced by the trochaic reversal on "Bursting," the double meaning of "kindly rupture"—according to kind, as well as merciful—
and the pun on "disclos'd" let us share the moment of liberation
for the young and recognition by the parents, and the literalness of
"callow," or unfledged, shows their vulnerability and the humorous
sympathy of a fully fledged angel. As Raphael goes on, "but
feather'd soon and fledge / They summ'd thir Pens, and soaring th'
air sublime / With clang despis'd [literally, looked down on] the
ground, under a cloud / In prospect" (420–23), he gives Adam the
birds' point of view, even to the clang, or resonant sound, by which
flocks keep together. When the land birds

                       set forth
        Thir Aery Caravan high over Seas
        Flying, and over Lands with mutual wing
        Easing thir flight . . .
                              the Air
        Floats, as they pass, fann'd with unnumber'd plumes;
                                                    (427–32)

the airy assonance and the alliteration of fricatives in Raphael's
description make us feel the sensation of flight. At "the grassy
Clods now Calv'd" (463), the relation of earth to offspring is recorded in the alliteration; and the syntax kinetically inscribes the
effort and energy of participatory birth when

                              now half appear'd
        The Tawny Lion, pawing to get free

His hinder parts, then springs as broke from Bonds,
And Rampant shakes his Brinded mane.

(463–66)

Next, before man, come creeping and winged things, the aerators
and pollinators essential to life and provident of ethical lessons:[34]
insects, earthworms, ants, and bees. But instead of merely gauging
their usefulness, Raphael imagines their experience. At God's creating voice, "At once came forth whatever creeps the ground, /
Insect or Worm; those wav'd thir limber fans / For wings" (475–
77)—and the sibilants and aspirated consonants imitate the soft
sensation of air passing across their limber lineaments.

> First crept
> The Parsimonious Emmet, provident
> Of future, in small room large heart enclos'd,
> Pattern of just equality perhaps
> Hereafter, join'd in her popular Tribes
> Of Commonalty.

(484–89)

The vowels swell spaciously at "in small room large heart en-
clos'd," while the p's and t's patter through the passage like a quick
heartbeat or minute provident feet. Of the worms he says in one
unbroken line "These as a line thir long dimension drew" (480),
and we feel on our tongues their long bodies extend liquidly in
the repeated l's and contract tactilely with the harder dentals of
"dimension drew."

In contrast, Satan, the first environmental predator, refuses to
acknowledge his own creaturehood and exploits other creatures;
he appears as a cormorant and a toad, usurps the body of a snake,
and then complains of having to mingle with "bestial slime" (9.165).

Raphael's observation of the creatures tells us much about the
attitudes of the epic's blessed spirits—after all, he is one—toward
God's creativity. You would think that angels had enough to love
already, in God and their millions of selves. Even so, Raphael also
loves and enters into, actually or imaginatively, the peculiar beings
of the new creation, however different from himself. He would be
a disappointed archangel if biodiversity should disappear in the
new Heaven and Earth when "God shall be All in All."[35] In his
love of diverse creatures and in his monism, Raphael has much in
common with John Muir, who carried *Paradise Lost* in his pocket

on a thousand-mile walk from Indianapolis to the Gulf of Mexico, and writes:

> I have never yet happened upon a trace of evidence that seems to show that any one animal was ever made for another as much as it was made for itself. Not that Nature manifests any such thing as selfish isolation. In the making of every animal the presence of every other animal has been recognized. Indeed, every atom in creation may be said to be acquainted with and married to every other, but *with* universal union there is a division sufficient in degree for the purposes of the most intense individuality; no matter, therefore, what may be the note which any creature forms in the song of existence, it is made first for itself, then more and more remotely for all the world and worlds.[36]

Muir seems to me much in accord with Milton's creation story, and with Adam's now ironically glad cry: "I revive . . . assur'd that Man shall live / With all the Creatures, and thir seed preserve" (11.871–73).

And what about the diversity and individuality of readers in the imaginary gardens, with their real toads, of poems? The critiques offered by cultural materialism and deconstruction of the impositions of logocentricity are salutary against literary and political complacency. But the bloodless procedure of consigning the creations of imagination and conscience to the material past commodifies the reader, too, into a culturally material being dessicated of imaginative inner life. Milton's poetry—any poetry worth the name—is too open and subtle to become trapped in an ideology and springs away from categorical cages by its nature. "The squirming facts," as Wallace Stevens said, "exceed the squamous mind."[37] I think that Milton, not only cultural constructs, crafted his work, though those constructs are questioned within it, and that he takes care not to conform his characters to cultural icons, but rather invites readers to grant passionate entity to them and imagine and debate their lives on the basis of observation as careful as Raphael's. To appropriate the "life-blood of a master-spirit," or even a literary scholar, into an ism is to usurp the attentiveness of the reader. A writer, as John T. Shawcross has argued,[38] is a person with intentions, although we cannot presume that we fully discern them and although the process of poetry overflows them and creates mysteries; these are the gifts of whatever the muse is, perhaps some fusion of personal genius and that *creator spiritus* whom both Milton and his father invoked in song, which becomes the poet's experience of the "All" in him. Proportionally, Milton's creation epic creates a communing creativity in his readers. He gives them practice in experiencing that kind of "All in All."

I would like to conclude with the last two lines of William Shullenberger's rendering of Milton's epigram, "To Leonora Singing at Rome," which he sent me in an envelope rubber-stamped with his motto, "Do Theology": "If God, through all things fused, himself is all, / In just one, you, he speaks; all else turns still." Perhaps Milton addresses not only the famous singer, but each reader as the only one, at some times, in whom God speaks. Milton's God grants each creature a particular voice. These voices do not always sing solos; both nature and Heaven are choral societies; but as in the English verse anthem and the *stile concertante* in which his angels sometimes sing, each voice both gets a separate hearing and is an indispensable part of the whole. It seems likely that a God already fused through all would do no less when all are dynamically fused in him; and Milton, in turn, grants each of us a particular voice in the community of readers.

Notes

1. John Milton, "At a Solemn Music," in *John Milton: Complete Poems and Major Prose*, ed. Merritt Y. Hughes (New York: Odyssey, 1957), 81–82.

2. All biblical references are to the King James Version and are cited parenthetically in the text.

3. *Areopagitica*, in *The Student's Milton*, ed. Frank Allen Patterson (New York: Appleton-Century-Crofts, 1933), 625.

4. John Milton, *Paradise Lost*, in *Paradise Lost: A Poem in Twelve Books*, ed. Merritt Y. Hughes (New York: Odyssey, 1962). All references to *Paradise Lost* are to this edition and are cited parenthetically in the text.

5. Marshall Grossman, *Authors to Themselves: Milton and the Revelation of History* (Cambridge: Cambridge University Press, 1987), 66, 64. Grossman continues, "Restored man will assent intuitively to the Law and thus experience its prohibition as his own affirmation" (65), and he appends a note that reads the Son's scepter in line with

> Lacan's rewriting of Oedipal resolution as the acquisition of the name of the Father and the gaining of access to the signifier of the self. . . . The apocalyptic identification of Father and Sons suggests the infinitely deferred fulfillment of Oedipal desire (displaced into an appropriate object after a latency period envisaged by Milton as human history). The "subjection" of the angels to the Son, which precipitates Satan's rebellion, may be understood as the primal repression through which the Son surrenders the object of desire so as to gain access to its signs. (213 n. 31)

6. William Empson, *Milton's God* (London: Chatto and Windus, 1965), 138–39.

7. Stanley Fish, "Wanting a Supplement: The Question of Interpretation in Milton's Early Prose," in *Politics, Poetics, and Hermeneutics in Milton's Prose*,

ed. David Loewenstein and James Grantham Turner (Cambridge: Cambridge University Press, 1990), 67.

8. Robert M. Myers, "'God Shall Be All in All': The Erasure of Hell in *Paradise Lost*," *The Seventeenth Century* 5 (1990): 43–53.

9. Francis Barker, "*Areopagitica* and the Moment of Censorship," in *John Milton*, ed. Annabel Patterson (London: Longman, 1992), 69.

10. Myers, "'God Shall Be All in All,'" 51.

11. Satan does allow debate by the senators of hate, greed, and debauchery, but by appeal to these interests he easily extracts consent to the plan presented by Beelzebub but "first devis'd / By Satan" (2.379–80).

12. John Peter Rumrich, *Matter of Glory: A New Preface to "Paradise Lost"* (Pittsburgh: University of Pittsburgh Press, 1987), 88, 91, 92.

13. Mary Ann Radzinowicz, "The Politics of *Paradise Lost*," in *John Milton*, ed. Patterson, 120–41; Robert Thomas Fallon, *Divided Empire: Milton's Political Imagery* (University Park: Pennsylvania State University Press, 1995), xiii–ix.

14. Plotinus, *The Enneads*, trans. Stephen MacKenna, 2nd ed., rev. B. S. Page (London: Faber and Faber, 1956), 625.

15. *Of Education*, in *The Student's Milton*, ed. Patterson, 726.

16. The same is true of 1 Cor. 8.6, from which Milton also draws: "there is but one God, the Father, of whom are all things, and we in him; and one Lord Jesus Christ, by whom are all things, and we by him."

17. *De Doctrina Christiana*, in *The Works of John Milton*, 18 vols., ed. Frank Allen Patterson et al. (New York: Columbia University Press, 1931–38), 16:366, hereafter cited as Columbia Milton.

18. That is, "God shall be All in All" may be interpreted as both "God shall be in all things" and "All things shall be in God." The latter interpretation makes it clear that all creatures could be within the divine "All" without losing their distinction. But that statement alone might compromise God's transcendence and privilege his immanence more than is allowable in a monotheistic theology. Milton keeps the distinction between creator and created. But this distinction is not simply one of transcendence. All potential being was originally *in* God and becomes differentiated in the process of creation; for God to be in all or for all to be in God is a re-union in which the entities proliferated in the creation remain distinct.

19. Albert W. Fields ("The Creative Self and the Self Created in *Paradise Lost*," in *Spokesperson Milton: Voices in Contemporary Criticism*, ed. Charles W. Durham and Kristin Pruitt McColgan [Selinsgrove, Pa.: Susquehanna University Press, 1994], 157) writes that "The importance of the Self's rational resemblance to God . . . cannot be disengaged from . . . his representation as creator of entities external to himself."

20. Arthur E. Barker, *Milton and the Puritan Dilemma* (Toronto: University of Toronto Press, 1942), 8.

21. Radzinowicz, "The Politics of *Paradise Lost*," 126.

22. Stevie Davies, *Images of Kingship in "Paradise Lost": Milton's Politics and Christian Liberty* (Columbia: University of Missouri Press, 1989), 152–53.

23. *The Book of Common Prayer, 1559*, ed. John E. Booty (Washington, D.C.: Folger Books, Folger Library, 1976), 263.

24. Contemporary angelologists believed that each angel is a different species, individually created, not generated.

25. Gerard Manley Hopkins, "As kingfishers catch fire," in *The Poems of Gerard Manley Hopkins*, ed. W. H. Gardner and N. H. MacKenzie (Oxford: Oxford University Press, 1970), 90.

26. Gardner Campbell, "Paradisal Appetite and Cusan Food in *Paradise Lost,*" in *Arenas of Conflict: Milton and the Unfettered Mind,* ed. Kristin Pruitt McColgan and Charles W. Durham (Selinsgrove, Pa.: Susquehanna University Press, 1997), 239–50.

27. John Milton, *Complete Prose Works of John Milton,* 8 vols., ed. Don M. Wolfe et al. (New Haven: Yale University Press, 1953–82), 6:310–11; all references to *Christian Doctrine* are to this edition and are cited parenthetically in the text. My thanks to Annabel Patterson for opportunely producing this reference.

28. One problem of interpretation for a multicultural society is that a model of heaven based on a form of Christianity may be unacceptable to some readers and has sometimes been used to abet coercion. However, *Areopagitica* warns that the imposition of human power over conscience is tyranny and assent to such an imposition is idolatry. In *Paradise Lost* Adam and Eve repent and begin their journey of regeneration before Michael has spelled out the conditions of the prophecy that the Seed of woman should bruise the serpent's head, exercising what Jason Rosenblatt in *Torah and Law in "Paradise Lost"* (Princeton: Princeton University Press, 1994), 156, calls, with regard to Raphael's account of creation in book 7, "forbearance" in Milton's use of Christology. As Christianity takes its place in the English-speaking world as a religion among many and none, *Paradise Lost* in its complexity may be a less divisive expression of it than either religious conservatism or secular liberalism's simplified perceptions of it have to offer.

29. At the end of chapter 33 the author comes to his dry definition: "Complete glorification consists in eternal and utterly happy life, arising chiefly from the sight of God" (6:630), though it does not consist in equality (as Piccarda in *Paradiso* also holds)—a point of difference hard to envision without individuality. Perhaps the author deems inequality an effect of the doctrines of free will and the covenant between individual and creator; the saints will retain the identities that they have attained and be judged by the conscience of each; they will each, however, attain "perfect happiness."

30. John Muir, *Wilderness Essays,* ed. Frank Buske (Salt Lake City: Peregrine Smith Books, 1980), 235–36; first published in *Overland Monthly,* April 1875.

31. The raptor is a figure of Christ and of rapture in Hopkins's "The Windhover."

32. The passage reads, "Glorificationis nostrae comes erit coeli et terrae rerumque in iis creatarum, quae quidem nobis usui aut oblectationi esse possint, renovatio et possessio" (Columbia Milton, 16:378).

33. Commonly in Reformation commentaries on Genesis, when permission is given to eat flesh after the greed of men and the purging Flood have vitiated the natural world, this eating of flesh is granted limitedly and to be undertaken temperately, with gratitude, and only at need. Andrew Linzey discusses the history of interpretation of biblical passages relating to treatment of animals in *Animal Theology* (Urbana: University of Illinois Press, 1995).

34. On insect ethics, see Timothy Raylor, "Samuel Hartlib and the Commonwealth of Bees," in *Culture in Cultivation in Early Modern England: Writing and the Land,* ed. Michael Leslie and Timothy Raylor (Leicester: Leicester University Press, 1992): 91–129.

35. On animal salvation, see Alan Rudrum, "Henry Vaughan, the Liberation of the Creatures, and Seventeenth-Century English Calvinism," in *The Seventeenth Century* 17 (1989): 33–54.

36. Muir, *Wilderness Essays,* 236.

37. Wallace Stevens, "Connoisseur of Chaos," in *The Collected Poems of Wallace Stevens* (New York: Knopf, 1955), 215.

38. See John T. Shawcross, *Intentionality and the New Traditionalism: Some Liminal Means to Literary Revisionism* (University Park: Pennsylvania State University Press, 1991).

"All in All" and "All in One": Obedience and Disobedience in *Paradise Lost*

ALBERT C. LABRIOLA

I intend to analyze one word in *Paradise Lost*—"all"—as it recurs in numerous phrases and as it is implied in countless others. Explicit or implied uses of "all" in Milton's epic will drive my presentation, even to the extent that I will alternate between various modes of linguistic analysis, notably Latinate grammar, Renaissance rhetorical figures, and finally transformational grammar, in order to account for the signification of this crucial word in *Paradise Lost*. This one word, in the contexts where it variously appears or when it is conceptually implied, is crucial to the language and behavior of obedience and disobedience—in effect, the essence of *Paradise Lost*.[1]

In 1 Cor. 15.28, Paul's apocalyptic vision—"that God may be all in all"[2]—describes the society in the heavenly hereafter. When Milton refers to Paul, he does so at times through the mouth of God the Father, who in book 3 of *Paradise Lost* states that "God shall be All in All" (341).[3] This echo of Paul occurs, however, in the broader context of the celestial dialogue that elaborates on the process leading to the consummate union of the faithful and the Godhead. First, the Son, anticipating his ultimate triumph over the "powers of darkness" (256), forecasts that he, "with the multitude of [his] redeem'd" (260), "Shall enter Heav'n long absent" (261). Together they will view the "face" (262) of the Father, in whose presence they will experience "Joy entire" (265). Then the Father's reply complements our understanding of the Son's role at the Second Coming, which will eventuate in the formation of heavenly society:

> The World shall burn, and from her ashes spring
> New Heav'n and Earth, wherein the just shall dwell
> And after all thir tribulations long
> See golden days, fruitful of golden deeds,

> With Joy and Love triumphing, and fair Truth.
> Then thou thy regal Sceptre shalt lay by,
> For regal Sceptre then no more shall need,
> God shall be All in All.
>
> (334–41)

In later books of the epic, similar accounts recur. When in book 7 the Father empowers the Son to create, even before the process begins, he foresees how the Creation will ultimately end. In this instance, the Father frames his prescient view of "One Kingdom . . . and Union" (161) in language that conceptually underscores his apocalyptic dictum that "God shall be All in All": "And Earth be chang'd to Heav'n, and Heav'n to Earth, / One Kingdom, Joy and Union without end" (160–61). Such accounts and others like them in *Paradise Lost* are suffused with political implications, ostensibly benign and felicitous. Not to be overlooked, however, is the threatened or actual military might—somewhat muted in the Father's phrase in book 3 ("Joy and Love *triumphing*"; emphasis mine)—crucial to the process of forming the final society.

To drive home my point, I will cite a further reference to "All in All" but in another rendition of celestial dialogue, this time at the outset of the War in Heaven. Having empowered the Son to "Go . . . thou Mightiest in thy Father's might" (6.710), the Father enjoins him to "bring forth all my War" (712). The Son who replies that fulfillment of the Father's will "is all my bliss" (729) adds:

> Sceptre and Power, thy giving, I assume,
> And gladlier shall resign, when in the end
> Thou shalt be All in All, and I in thee
> For ever, and in mee all whom thou lov'st.
>
> (730–33)

The Son further affirms: "But whom thou hat'st, I hate, and can put on / Thy terrors, as I put thy mildness on" (734–35). The Father's reference to "all my War" and the Son's threefold iteration of "all"—"all my bliss," "All in All," and "all whom thou [the Father] lov'st"—develop the contrast between the "terrors" meted out to all disobedient angels and the "mildness" shown toward all others.

Virtually the same contrast informs the earliest episode in the epic, the so-called begetting of the Son, whose kingship over the angels is declared by the Father. In choosing to be with the Son "as one individual Soul" (5.610), each and every obedient angel (the most notable example being Abdiel) will incorporate with "all whom [the Father] lov'st." The paradoxical wordplay on "one" and "all" proliferates, even to the extent that "all" is "one" with and within another word, namely "shall"—"to *him* sh*all* bow / *All* knees in Heav'n, and sh*all* confess *him* Lord" (607–8; emphasis mine). Thus, "shall," used twice to express the Father's issuance of a command that *all* sh*all* worship the Son, interacts with "him," also twice used as a reference to the Son. These words appear in a chiastic arrangement, at the center of which, appropriately, is the word "All."

After this chiastic arrangement, the Father's command divides itself neatly into the options and consequences of obedience and disobedience:

> Under his great Vice-gerent Reign abide
> United as one individual Soul
> For ever happy.
>
> (609–11)

Midway in line 611 (after "For ever happy"), rather than at the outset of the succeeding verse, the Father heightens the contrast between obedient and disobedient angels by threatening military retribution against the latter: "him who disobeys / Mee disobeys" (611–12). From one perspective, the denunciation means that whoever disobeys the Son also disobeys the Father; from another, whoever disobeys the Father also disobeys the Son. From both perspectives, the word "him," consistent with third-person usage earlier in the Father's command, refers to the Son while the word "who" (which I have glossed as "whoever") glances at any one angel and all such angels disobedient toward the Godhead, whether any Divine Person or all Divine Persons.

But the inverted word order—"him who disobeys / Mee disobeys"—creates a Latinate grammatical construction in which "him" before "who" indicates that the personal pronoun is the antecedent of the relative pronoun. The juxtaposition of "him" and "who" as elements of a clause, whose predicate is "disobeys," and the placement of "Mee" at the outset of the next line create an enjambment. Intonationally, the enjambment shall (or must) be read in the following way—"him who disobeys mee"—so that "him" and "who" have the same referent, any one angel and, by implication, all such angels who disobey the Father. Latinate grammatical construction, enjambment, and intonation converge to produce an utterance in which the word "him," which actually designates the Son, comes to signify "him who" disobeys "him," the Son. This is perhaps the most graphic example of a single word,

"him," operating on two levels, designating simultaneously (1) the
Son under whose headship all obedient angels incorporate and (2)
any one disobedient angel, "him," who incorporates with all others
against "him," the Son.

To be sure, the paradoxes embedded in the Father's utterance—
"him who disobeys / Mee disobeys"—may be explained by reference to traditional grammar and its terminology and to rhetorical
figures (and their variations) commonplace in Renaissance and
seventeenth-century England. One might argue, for instance, that
the Father's utterance combines inversion and chiasmus, not to
mention inventive modifications of zeugma, syllepsis, and other
figures. But the fuller import of the Father's utterance emerges
when analysis proceeds in accordance with the idiom and ideology
of transformational grammar. In line with that outlook, the Father
frames his discourse on disobedience as a deep structure, a linguistic universal, a kernel sentence, or as intuitive syntax. While lin-
guists would and should differentiate among the foregoing terms,
for our present purposes treating them more or less synonymously
is useful. In short, I contend that the Father's utterance is a deep
structure that generates, among others, both interrogatory and de-
clarative surface structures, a linguistic universal implying any
number of particular reformulations, a kernel sentence to be unbundled by the application of rewrite rules, and intuitive syntax
furnishing the potential for discursive and interpretive paraphrase.
For example, readers of the Father's utterance—"him who disobeys / Mee disobeys"—may apply interrogatory rewrite rules
with the following outcomes: Does one who disobeys the Father
also dis-obey "him who" was begotten by the Father? Does the
Father denounce "him who" disobeys his command to worship the
Son? Will the Son punish "him who" disobeys the Father? If one
disobeys "him" (the Son), will he (the Son) punish "him who" does
so? Or the Father's utterance may be treated as a kernel sentence
whose potential for transformation when unbundled will yield numerous declarations. Accordingly, to disobey "him who" was begotten by the Father equates with disobedience toward the Father.
And who(ever) disobeys "him" begotten by the Father is disobedient toward the Father.

The foregoing transformations, while interrelating syntactics and
semantics, not to mention intonation, all issue from the Father's
one generative utterance and in their expatiation return to it discur-
sively and interpretively. This phenomenon is nowhere more suc-
cinctly described than by Raphael, who aptly uses the words "one"
and "all": the "*one* Almighty . . . from whom / *All* things proceed,

and up to him return" (5.469–70; emphasis mine). In addition to unfolding what were intuitively and potentially enfolded in *one* of the Father's utterances, *all* such transformations become linguistic and behavioral deliberations concerning (what may be called) a divine command to obey, if not a divine prohibition that one not disobey.

For "him who disobeys"—for him, that is, who "breaks union" (612) with all the obedient angels—the Father announces the retribution as he continues his utterance: to be "Cast out from God and blessed vision" (613). A disobedient angel, consequently, "falls / Into utter darkness" (613–14). The phrase "utter darkness," which for Milton is virtually homophonous with "outer darkness," indicates where the disobedient angels, after their exclusion from Heaven, will be relegated. Figuratively, the same phrase—"utter darkness"—implies how the disobedient angels will suffer another form of obscurity—namely, the anonymity of having their names "ras'd" (1.362) from the Book of Life. One may liken the performative role of the Son, whose right-handed onslaught in the War in Heaven defaces the visages of the disobedient angels and diminishes their glory, to that of a scribe who erases names from parchment and reinscribes differently thereon or who blots a word by a strikeover and adds anew alongside, atop, or below the previous inscription, which is still evident though defaced. If a strikeover juxtaposes defaced and new inscriptions, a more profound paradox in *Paradise Lost* is that erasure, seemingly tantamount to obliteration or annihilation, begets indelible memory. This process occurs because the language and behavior of "him who disobeys" unfold only by reference to the language and behavior of obedience. As a result, a character may remember what he himself or even another character once was. Satan's perception of Beelzebub on the burning lake is a case in point, as is Abdiel's perception, then Michael's, of Satan during the War in Heaven. The most poignant example involves Satan's self-perception at the outset of book 4, when he is transformed from obdurate sinner to prospective penitent. Though his changeover from sinner to penitent—from disobedience to obedience—is not to be actualized, the potential to have done so and to do so, linguistically and behaviorally, can never be forgotten.

If the begetting of the Son is the earliest event in *Paradise Lost,* then the Father's discourse explaining it, recounted and interpreted above, is the first utterance. Accordingly, the very first words of the Father—"Hear all ye Angels" (5.600)—that herald his discourse on obedience and disobedience comprise the genesis of the epic.

Aptly, the word "all" (without a comma either before or after it) is used ambiguously. From the perspective of Latinate grammar, "all" may be adjectival or pronominal. Adjectivally, it modifies "ye Angels," all of them. In such circumstances, "all" would be preceded by a comma to signal the direct address that follows; but in the absence of grammatical punctuation, the reader may insert a pause before "all," the equivalent of rhetorical punctuation to demarcate the intonation and thus to interpret the intent of God the Father. Pronominally, "all" designates "all" that the angels are to hear; as such, it is the objective complement after "Hear." Whether "all" is adjectival or pronominal, "Angels" is a form of direct address—what in Latin is called the vocative.

Enriching the Father's syntactic and semantic implications is the homonymic wordplay on "Hear": All who are to "hear" are "here," the latter signifying both the current time and present location. This is the first and last occasion—or the earliest and only time in *Paradise Lost*—at which all the angels are in one place, only to be imminently disintegrated by the language and behavior of obedience and disobedience. This divergent reaction whereby "all" the angels are no longer all together—or not all in one community— is anticipated by Milton's trifold use of "all" in one line: "*All* seem'd well pleas'd, *all* seem'd, but were not *all*" (617; emphasis mine). Encompassing the foregoing verse are two additional uses of *all,* which also appears in the medial position as part of a two-word construction, "*all* seem'd." This two-word construction divides one half of the line from the other, each half composed of four words (each word a monosyllable).

This tripartite structure—with the medial construction composed of two monosyllabic words—becomes a veritable mathematical equation, though rendered linguistically. In other words, the reader who anticipates the impending War in Heaven will learn from the very structure of the verse the numerical composition of the opposing forces, good versus evil angels. By merging the medial construction with the first half of the line, the reader will combine two-thirds of the words (or of the syllables in the decasyllabic verse), from which the remaining one-third is dissociated. The linguistic merger to which I refer occurs because of *repetitio*—i.e., the repetition of "All seem'd," which occurs at the head of the verse and again at the outset of the medial construction. In this linguistic maneuver, the reader succeeds in drawing together two cohorts of angels, whereas Satan who claims the other cohort "Drew after him *the third part* of Heav'n's Host" (710; emphasis mine). No verses in the epic epitomize more effectively the mutually exclusive effects of obedience and disobedience, with the reader functioning as a unifying agency, on the one hand, and Satan as a divisive agency, on the other. The complementary interaction of these processes not only prefigures the numerical disposition of the good and evil angels in the War in Heaven but also anticipates the duration of the three-day War and the expulsion of one-third of the angels or all of the disobedient ones.

The foregoing accounts of the earliest event in the epic, the earliest utterance, the earliest and the one occasion for the togetherness of all the angels, and of their "first disobedience" redefine the genesis of the epic. By "genesis" I mean the origin in *Paradise Lost* of the language and behavior of obedience and disobedience, which recur with variation in numerous later episodes, especially when the word "all" is used. When pursued systematically, this linguistic methodology will identify not only traces but also transformations in later events of (what may be termed) the originative episode of *Paradise Lost*. Viewed, therefore, as originative, the earliest episodes in the epic are the kernels whose potential is progressively unfolded and whose potency is thereby acknowledged throughout the epic. Viewed as originative, moreover, these episodes provide a new perspective on the language and behavior in the epic or, to put it differently, on the process by which *Paradise Lost* as a linguistic artifact is created.

To support the foregoing views, I will elaborate on one example but suggest a few others, particularly when the words "all" and "one" are interrelated. The one example involves the narrator's assertion concerning "him who" continues to disobey, as well as all others who are continuously disobedient: "hope never comes / That comes to all" (1.66–67). The fallen angels, having previously heard the Father's threat of "utter darkness" (5.614) as a punishment for disobedience, come to experience "utter darkness" (1.72) when they are cast into Hell. Indeed, the narrator iterates the Father's very phrase only after having elaborated on the psychological and spiritual experience of "utter darkness": For the fallen angels in Hell, "hope never comes / That comes to all." The reader exfoliates, in turn, the narrator's paradoxical commentary. One linguistic transformation after another strives to unpack the paradox. For example, as a consequence of their disobedience, hope never comes to *all* of the fallen angels, though (or while or because) it comes to *all* others. The foregoing transformation of the narrator's utterance, generating the former "all" as pronominal and the latter as adjectival, resolves the paradox. The same transformation uses conjunctive adverbs ("though," "while," "because") to designate concessive, temporal, or causal relationships, respectively. Such relationships, which involve various means of subordination, accommodate the paradox to discursive modes of interpretation.

By rewriting the narrator's utterance in other ways, the reader participates in a comprehensive interpretation of the fallen angels' experience of hopelessness. If the rewrite involves a nonrestrictive clause, the interpretation implies a distinction between the unstated "ever" and the forcefully asserted "never": Hope, which (ever) comes to all, never comes to all of the fallen angels. The repetition and parallelism in the foregoing transformation—(ever) comes to all, never comes to all—likewise unfold through the use of a restrictive clause and rhetorical punctuation: Hope that never comes to all, comes to all others. If the contrast between "never" and "ever" continues to come into play, then the rewrite, with the restrictive clause, reverses the order occupied by these words in the nonrestrictive construction. Thus, "(ever) comes to all, never comes to all" becomes "never comes to all, (ever) comes to all." While these transformations and (all) others that can be generated beget seemingly inconsequential distinctions, the import of the linguistic filiations that emerge syntactically and semantically highlight the unfathomable richness of the Father's utterance, which itself begets interpretations that enact the fusion of obedience and fission of disobedience. At the same time, the nuances that unfold from the linguistic filiations enrich the reader's discursive reasoning. Are obedience and disobedience contrary or contradictory? How are the states of being ever-hopeful and never-hopeful different? How different is ever-hopeful from hopeful, or never-hopeful from unhopeful? How, why, and when do variations in negativity come into play in defining the implications of the word "all"?

Other examples that can and should be pursued include Satan's utterance—"All is not lost" (1.106) after the expulsion from Heaven. The homophonous wordplay on "not" and "naught" urges the reader to engage the satanic paradox also in the following way: All is naught (or nothing) lost. From such a rewrite, various interpretations will emerge, one of which is the following—what *is not* (or never?) lost *is* the capability to disobey and to exercise disobedience in any one or all ways. Or what is ever maintained is the capability not to obey. From this perspective Satan generates the discourse of the "everlasting nay." Another example occurs in *Paradise Lost*, toward the mathematical center of the epic, when the obedient angels are "Under thir Head imbodied all in one" (6.779), namely the Son. Perhaps the semantic affinity of "imbodied" and "imbedded" encourages the reader to intuit that the discourse of the Son in the epic will exfoliate the kernel utterances of the Father with clarity, authority, and cogency, in contrast to the multifarious and discursive processes enacted by the reader and even the narrator. After all, the narrator in seeking to "express . . . unblam'd" (3.3) the relationship of the Father and the Son likens the former to a lamp and the latter to a ray emanating therefrom, the former to a fountain and the latter to the effluence thereof. Framed at the outset of book 3, these metaphors suggest not only the interrelationship of the Father and the Son but also the role of the latter as an expositor; in other words, the linguistic filiations of the latter consummately articulate the intentionality of the former.

In sum, it is not overstatement to argue that all of *Paradise Lost* engages one question in the epic, posed by Adam to Raphael:

> But say,
> What meant that caution join'd, *if ye be found Obedient?*"

> (5.512–14; emphasis in the text).

When this interrogatory is engaged in manifold ways and by various characters within the epic, not to mention a major character without (notably the reader), the language and behavior of *Paradise Lost* are created.

Notes

1. In general, the intensive, almost microscopic, study of Milton's language in *Paradise Lost* has not been undertaken in the manner exemplified in the present essay. Nevertheless, there are numerous excellent studies of Milton's language, though their various emphases differ from mine. See, among other recent studies, the following: Christine Avery, "*Paradise Lost* and the Power of Language," *English* (Oxford) 19 (1970): 79–84; Ann M. Banfield, "Stylistic Transformations: A Study Based on the Syntax of *Paradise Lost*" (Ph.D. diss., University of Wisconsin, 1973), abstract in *Dissertation Abstracts International* 34 (1973): 1265A-66A; Peter Berek, "'Plain' and 'Ornate' Styles and the Structure of *Paradise Lost*," *PMLA* 85 (1970): 237–46.

2. King James Version.

3. John Milton, *Paradise Lost*, in *John Milton: Complete Poems and Major Prose*, ed. Merritt Y. Hughes (New York: Odyssey, 1957). All references to Milton's poetry are to this edition and are cited parenthetically in the text.

"All in All": The Threat of Bliss

DIANA TREVIÑO BENET

Paradise Lost continually moves between, or refers to, the opposite poles of union and separation. The poem seems to celebrate unity and wholeness: faith and eternal bliss are states of union with God; sin and damnation, states of separation. Two statements in the poem refer explicitly to union with God at the end of time. The Son's assertion in book 6 that God shall be "All in All," echoing the Father's in book 3, especially illuminates the nature of deity, implying that, the Son's individuation notwithstanding, eventually he will be incorporated into the greater Father. "All in All" also describes the total union of the blessed with God at the end of time and hints at the erasure of separate identities.

> Sceptre and Power, thy giving, I assume,
> And gladlier shall resign, when in the end
> Thou shalt be All in All, and I in thee
> For ever, and in mee all whom thou lov'st.
>
> (6.730–33)[1]

As William Empson remarked, the idea of eternity as the mystical melding of all into the "All" was known to the early moderns in the popular writings of authors like Christopher Marlowe and Sir Thomas Browne, whose *Hydriotaphia* draws to a close with such a vision of heaven:

> And if any have been so happy as truly to understand Christian annihilation, extasis, exolution, liquefaction, transformation, the kiss of the Spouse, gustation of God, and ingression into the divine shadow, they have already had an handsome anticipation of heaven; the glory of the world is surely over, and the earth in ashes unto them.[2]

As bliss is union with God, damnation is separation.

But, finally, *Paradise Lost* as a whole does not allow so uncomplicated a moral significance to unity or separation. Although the poem includes great images of physical union, the most entrancing being Raphael's description of angel merging with angel, the commingling that Satan visits upon the serpent—the parody of heavenly sex—is an equally striking vision. Besides, the poet matches the science-fiction or horror-movie frisson of these bodily unions with equally spectacular (and morally inconsistent) images of physical separation: the issue of Sin from Satan's head is as impressive as the creation of Eve from Adam's side. While Eve's creation demonstrates the power of divine goodness, Sin's birth attests to the power of evil. Obviously, union and separation do not, in themselves, indicate spiritual states.

But unity and division are stages in the biblical (and Miltonic) mode of creation, in which two characters are created from originary males. Milton imitates the Bible when he invents, after the Zeus-Athena myth, a third case of a procreative Oneness dividing to form an Other. From the perspective of this kind of creation, the erasure or merger of separate identities in bliss seems a less bizarre possibility. Moreover, throughout the poem, Milton sometimes blurs the separateness of the Father and Son, Satan and Sin, and Adam and Eve so that the boundaries between them seem permeable, and the cognate beings act as one. Such apparently seamless unions seem to figure and valorize the promise of "All in All."

But the stories of these paired characters themselves apprise us that the ideal of "All in All" was common to the different traditions of spiritual and romantic love. Milton uses the characters joined in the first place by creation to raise questions about love, identity or independent being, and will, matters complicated by the fact that some of his characters have conterminous wills. Because of the confusion of the romantic and spiritual ideals, Eve's volition and agency become contested zones, areas in which who determines what is willed and what is done are open to question. William Kerrigan and Gordon Braden have argued persuasively that "Milton's *agon* with love poetry is considerably richer and more extensive" than has been generally recognized.[3] By intertwining the strands of the disparate religious and romantic traditions, Milton interrogates a major poetic theme, finally exposing as spiritually dangerous the romantic notion that love makes two into one heart, mind, or soul.

Though unity remains, in general, the ideal celebrated by the poem, Milton nevertheless demonstrates how it collides with the freedom required for moral choice. For union between entities of persons, while seemingly desirable, may have negative or fearful implications: sometimes, the possibility of disunity motivates sin;

sometimes the prospect of union seems a prospect of diminished selfhood or an omen of personal obliteration. And the poem never overcomes lingering images of union as a frightening reabsorption of creature into originary being. Finally, the prospect of eternal or romantic bliss in *Paradise Lost* is at once promise and threat, evoking delight and terror in almost equal measure.

I

The phrase "All in All" has two sources, ancient philosophy and the Bible, and two areas of signification, spiritual and romantic. Raymond B. Waddington has discussed "All in All" as the soul-in-body topos that had reached the early Fathers through Plotinus from Plato and Aristotle; in the early modern period, the phrase was a commonplace used in discussions of the soul by historians, theologians, and poets.[4] In this context, "All in All" refers to the quality of the soul that it inheres in every part of the body, though the body parts are different and separable.

Given the extensive Greek influence on the New Testament, it is not surprising that the terms employed in philosophical discussions of the soul-in-body were used to describe God-in-creation in the biblical text. Milton's "All in All" in books 3 and 6 comes specifically from I Cor. 15.28: "And when all things shall be subdued unto him, then shall the Son also himself be subject unto him that put all things under him, that God may be all in all."[5] But the idea pervades the book of John, where Jesus prays, for example: "That they [his disciples] all may be one; as thou, Father, art in me, and I in thee, that they also may be one in us. . . . And the glory which thou gavest me I have given them; that they may be one, even as we are one: I in them, and thou in me, that they may be made perfect in one" (John 17.21–23). Jesus' exploration of his filial relationship with the Father is most thorough in John. The Son's incarnation by the Maker using human "material" parallels the myth of Eve's creation from Adam's rib. The Son of God is "born, not of blood, nor of the will of the flesh, nor of the will of man, but of God" (John 1.13). In John, also, Jesus links his progenitor's will and his own most emphatically: "I can of mine own self do nothing . . . because I seek not mine own will, but the will of the Father which hath sent me" (5.30); "For I came down from heaven, not to do mine own will, but the will of him that sent me" (John 6.38). The Son is "one" with his living source (John 10.30).

The radical union indicated by "All in All," Empson suggested, was an ideal common to both spiritual and romantic love, inasmuch as both held out the promise of "interpenetration."[6] Raphael's account of angelic lovemaking describes the shared desideratum of sacred and profane love:

> Easier than Air with Air, if Spirits embrace,
> Total they mix, Union of Pure with Pure
> Desiring; nor restrain'd conveyance need
> As Flesh to mix with Flesh, or Soul with Soul.
>
> (8.626–29)

The merger of two angels is a "step away from making 'one individual soul' with God,"[7] a foreshadowing of the total union of all the blessed with God at the end of time. But poets like John Donne and others before him claimed that the same kind of merger was possible for "ideal human lovers [who] make one soul by interpenetrating completely."[8]

The romantic "All in All" maintains that love makes two different and separable beings one heart or one soul. Sexual union is the physical manifestation of two become one, an idea with roots in the Hebrew Bible. Though Milton's "All in All" in books 3 and 6 alludes specifically to I Corinthians, the idea of a primary One who can combine or recombine with or absorb an Other refers, in the first place, to Genesis. Practically the instant the myth of human creation is articulated, it becomes colored by sex to form a new and potent myth about the male-female relationship. Adam declares that Eve, made from his rib, "is now bone of my bones, and flesh of my flesh. . . . Therefore shall a man leave his father and his mother, and shall cleave unto his wife: and they shall be one flesh" (Gen. 2.23–24).[9] In *Paradise Lost,* Adam and Eve's common flesh, their unique nature in the world, and their love combine to create Adam's heightened sense of oneness with Eve, expressed in his assertion that she is "my Self / Before me" (8.495–96). Though love poets like Donne and Shakespeare gave new currency to the possibility of becoming one with an Other through love, the absorption of one into an Other (or of the many into the One), was familiar in the seventeenth century from various sources, including Marlowe and Browne, the ancients, and the Bible.

II

Creation pairs and unites the main characters in *Paradise Lost.* The Father and the Son, Satan and Sin, Adam and Eve: the first of each pair is the originary, complete entity from whom the Other is created. The male plenitude in each instance expresses itself as, or somehow divides itself into, an Other. The fundamental relationship between the two beings produces an emotional, hierarchical, and relational frame of reference that Milton uses to raise questions about love, essence (or independent being), and will. Obviously, the most significant and mysterious unity in *Paradise Lost* exists between the Father and the Son. The Father—not Satan—inaugurates difference in Heaven, when he "begets" the Son in the Exaltation. The Son's manifestation as an angel is an act of individuation. Albert C. Labriola explains that "the Father's 'begetting' does not mean that the Son's divine nature is being created. It means simply that the Son in the presence of the angels has assumed their nature and form."[10] On the simplest level, the Son's visibility differentiates him from the Father. The Father and the Son are not identical, though the difference or space between them seems almost imperceptible:

> Begotten Son, Divine Similitude,
> In whose conspicuous count'nance, without cloud
> Made visible, th' Almighty Father shines,
> Whom else no Creature can behold; on thee
> Impresst th' effulgence of his Glory abides,
> Transfus'd on thee his ample Spirit rests.
>
> (3.384–89)

"Substance" and "essence," theological concepts discussed some time ago by William B. Hunter, help describe the Father's and the Son's identity and difference: on the one hand, "substance is the substratum or stuff of God the Father which underlies the Son. It is not common to both but derives only from the Father." Essence, on the other hand, is "individuality or individual being. The persons of Father and Son are two; they receive their individuality from the fact that they are different essences."[11]

The paradoxical identity and difference between the Father and the Son, characteristic of the triune God, also obtains in will and agency. The Son expresses the Father, who calls the Son "My word, my wisdom, and effectual might" (170). As the Father's "effectual might," he performs such particular tasks as the Creation and the defense of Heaven, in which he is instructed to "bring forth all [his Father's] War" (6.712). But the Son's willing enactment of the Father's will and power is joined to filial independence. As events in Heaven unfold, the Son's distinctiveness becomes more apparent, confirming his individuality as separate (however mysteriously) from the Father's: the Son "debates" with the Father in book 3[12] and, subsequently, freely answers the Father's challenge to become "mortal to redeem / Man's mortal crime" (3.214–15). If nothing else had done it, his voluntary humiliation alone would render him a unique being. Clearly, the Father and the Son rejoice in their union *and* in their difference. The Father delights in the Son, and never more than when the Son thinks or acts independently; the Son delights in praising and expressing the Father:

> this I my Glory account,
> My exaltation, and my whole delight,
> That thou in me well pleas'd, declar'st thy will
> Fulfill'd, which to fulfil is all my bliss.

(6.726–29)

Judging the rebels by his own feelings, the Son wonders at their abandonment of the Father, "Whom to obey is happiness entire" (741). The Son, both the efficacy of the Father and a free individual, expresses the Father's will and his own simultaneously. The Father does not overpower or subsume the Son: they have confluent wills, so that the Son acts from both his own will and the Father's.

The creation of Sin parodies the Son's creation. Like the Father, Satan is the originary, complete entity from whom an Other is generated. Whereas the Father brings the Son into being deliberately, however, Satan gives shape to his evil thought spontaneously. Springing from Satan's head, Sin externalizes his mind and, as the exact image of her radiant father, inspires his lust. But while they are apart, Sin grows different. Unrecognizably ugly to Satan at the Gates of Hell, she manifests his spiritual condition. Later, Sin demonstrates unbroken union with her father when she intuits his success in the Garden:

> [something] draws me on,
> Or sympathy, or some connatural force
> Powerful at greatest distance to unite
> With secret amity things of like kind
> By secretest conveyance.

(10.245–49)

Following Satan's tracks to the Earth, Sin and Death merely pave the path he blazed. Sin's altered appearance suggests that she is individuated. But she denies individuation when she describes herself as Satan's mere efficacy, insisting that Satan, not she or Death, is the doer of the "magnific deeds . . . which thou [Satan] view'st as not thine own" (10.354–55). Because he "impow'r'd" (369) them, he is the "Author and prime Architect" (356) of the bridge to the world—he is, in other words, the will whose motions Sin and Death express. Sensibly enough for an allegorical figure, Sin denies independent being. Both Satan's substance and essence, Sin shows forth his mind and will, and, ultimately, he acknowledges the identity between himself and the hideous mother when he makes her and their Son his "Substitutes . . . Plenipotent on Earth, of matchless might / Issuing from mee" (403–5). Like the Father and the Son, Satan and Sin are one.

Like the Father and Satan, Adam generates the Other from his plenitude. Though the Creator forms Eve from Adam's wholeness, she is left in no doubt about the origin of her substance. The Maker sends her to Adam, "Whose image thou art" (4.472). Throughout their unfallen existence, Milton highlights this identity of image, perhaps to suggest to the reader that, like the Son, Eve is the image of her generative Other without being identical to him. Adam, however, seems unable to credit any difference or space between Eve and himself. In their first moments together, he exclaims: "of [me] thou art, / [My] flesh, [my] bone . . . an individual solace dear; / Part of my Soul! I seek thee, and thee claim / My other half" (4.482–83, 486–88). To Raphael, Adam says that Eve's "sweet compliance," her love and obedience, "declare unfeign'd / Union of Mind or in us both one Soul" (8.601–4). Adam believes Eve is the obedient body permanently attached to his guiding head.

Only the infernal and celestial pairs share certain similarities. The infernal infusions of glory and power from one to the other parody the heavenly relationship. As the Son reigns at the right hand of the Father, Sin expects to "Reign / At thy right hand voluptuous" (2.868–69). But the history of all these related characters dictates their relative status: in general, the creators lead, the creatures follow; the "fathers" are greater than their creatures, and so on. Milton's Adam is Eve's better also by virtue of the superior nature his Maker gives him. As above, so below, it seems: the creatures' love and gratitude inspire obedience, making them the efficacies of their makers. The Son and Sin do not simply acknowledge their fathers' primacy; they love (according to their natures) and, therefore, will as their creators do. Though the Son possesses and Sin lacks an independent will, both creatures are the efficacies of their primaries. The Son continually acknowledges being the Father's efficacy:

> Father Eternal, thine is to decree,
> Mine both in Heav'n and Earth to do thy will
> Supreme.
>
> (10.68–70)

Sin links her obedience to her creation, saying to Satan:

> Thou art my Father, thou my Author, thou
> My being gav'st me; whom should I obey
> But thee, whom follow?
>
> (2.864–66)

For the human couple, however, the relation between creation, love, and will is problematic. Adam's acknowledged superiority initially allows him to assume that Eve is his efficacy. Early on, Eve herself considers their union so essential that it encompasses essence as well as substance, mind and will as well as flesh:

> My Author and Disposer, what thou bidd'st
> Unargu'd I obey; so God ordains,
> God is thy Law, thou mine: to know no more
> Is woman's happiest knowledge and her praise.
>
> (4.635–38)

Eve's compliance encourages Adam to see her, as he is already inclined to do, as his efficacy. She has at first no occasion or desire to express anything but her Author-husband's will. This extraordinary sense of oneness is based, at least in part, on sexual love. Adam and Eve have predecessors in Satan and Sin in their double relationship, filial and sexual. Especially because Eve, like Sin, is her father-lover's image, these assumptions and parallels might persuade the reader that Eve, too, is her parent's efficacy.

III

Empson, Waddington, Kerrigan and Braden have discussed the ancient and early modern poetic fantasy about the merger of lovers' bodies and souls.[13] Even early authors of domestic advice preached the desirability of oneness, specifying what it meant in practical terms. In what was surely an effort to subvert the popular notion of a passionate fusion of lovers as well (of course) as to promulgate the Pauline view of marriage, they described the wedded union of two into one as the merger of one will into another: "For in wedlock the man resembleth the reason and the woman the body. Now reason ought to rule and the body to obey if a man will live. Also St. Paul sayeth the head of the woman is the man."[14] Another author opined in 1563 that it promotes "concord very much when the wife is ready at hand at her husband's commandment, when she will apply herself to his will."[15] William Perkins, writing in

1609, gave a wife two duties: "to submit herself to her husband and to acknowledge and reverence him as her head in all things"; and "to be obedient unto her husband in all things . . . wholly to depend upon him both in judgment and will."[16] Clearly, the wife is to be the efficacy of her husband. But in Genesis and hence in *Paradise Lost,* love and will are not joined until after the Fall, when Eve is sentenced to obedience: "to thy Husband's will / Thine shall submit, hee over thee shall rule" (10.195–96).

Adam sees no distinction between himself and Eve because of their common substance and their love. The seventeenth-century reader would have known why Adam believed he and Eve were one soul: according to the "All-in-All" topos, his soul was in the rib that became Eve. Because Adam thinks he and Eve are one soul, one heart, and one mind, he expects Eve to be his efficacy, an expectation some readers have endorsed. Hunter, for instance, writes that

> true marriage is actual union of two individuals. . . . [In a true] union the superior nature joins with the inferior nature without the entire destruction of the latter: the two constitute a single entity in which something of each survives though the superior, in this case the man, is the determining factor, just as the divine dominates the human in the Incarnation. The relationship between Adam and Eve in *Paradise Lost* must be understood as deriving from this concept of union: they are not equal . . . but together make "one Flesh, one Heart, one Soul." . . . Adam falls not because of a romantic attachment for Eve but because their union is a true one.[17]

More recently, Diane Kelsey McColley relies on Hunter's explanation of subordinationism to suggest that "the relation of Adam and Eve, though human, vulnerable, and fraught with challenge, is potentially and increasingly the image of the Son's relation to the Father within the Godhead. For both Eve and the Son, obedience is a response to goodness inseparable from an unhampered creativity."[18]

But the human parents cannot reproduce the paradoxes and perfection of the three-personed God; nor can one person be "the determining factor" for another in spiritual matters. Eve cannot (and should not) duplicate the ability the Son has (springing from perfect love for the perfect object) of willing independently and obeying freely at once; Adam cannot match the Father's capacity (arising from perfect wisdom and goodness) simultaneously to govern and to set free.[19] Basic to Milton's theology is the premise that all the components of the universe, including the angels, are "parts of God from which God willingly removed his will."[20] Eve, we might say, is a part of Adam from whom God removed Adam's will. Not understanding this at first, Adam expects her to be the beautiful countenance on which his will is "without cloud / Made visible." Consequently, his attitude differs considerably from the Father's. The Father encourages the Son's separate personhood by creating him King and fosters the Son's separate efficacy by giving him "The Chariot of Paternal Deity" (6.750) to fight Satan:

> Go then thou Mightiest in thy Father's might,
> Ascend my Chariot, guide the rapid Wheels
> . . . bring forth all my War,
> My Bow and Thunder, my Almighty Arms.
>
> (710–13)

And the Son *is* a separate person; his main role in the universal drama, finally, is not to echo the Father's demand for justice, but to express and enable mercy. But Adam's confusion about the exact meaning and the limits of his and Eve's union causes him to behave quite differently. As book 9 demonstrates, he tries to restrain Eve's separate personhood and make her his efficacy. Adam argues from substance and ignores essence.

Adam's error is twofold. First, he assumes that Eve owes him the love that creatures owe their Creator, forgetting that while he is her parent, he is not her maker.[21] Second, Adam brings the romantic ideal of oneness into the spiritual domain. He loves his image, his "self before [him]," so dearly that he wonders whether the Creator "from my side subducting, took perhaps / More than enough" (8.536–37)—he wonders whether he is so enamored because Eve is too much himself.[22] Over and over, however, Raphael points to the differences between Eve and her father-husband: she is "Less excellent" (566) than Adam; less worthy of another's "subjection" (570); she is a fair "outside" (568), mere "shows" to Adam's "realities" (575); and more "adorn[ed]" than he so that he might the more delight in her (576). Though the romantic union Adam so prizes is the ideal of the love poets, it is incompatible with the moral freedom the Father requires as "proof . . . sincere / Of true allegiance, constant Faith or Love" (3.103–4). Obviously, Eve justifies tempting Adam with thoughts of love, and Adam eventually tries to justify his fall by appealing to the quasi-mystical union he feels with Eve:

> So forcible within my heart I feel
> The Bond of Nature draw me to my own,

> My own in thee, for what thou art is mine;
> Our State cannot be sever'd, we are one,
> One Flesh; to lose thee were to lose myself.
>
> (9.955–59)

As Regina Schwartz notes, "Adam invokes identity—the sharing of substance—as his reason for sinning. . . . Because Adam does not feel distinct from Eve, his will cannot be distinct from Eve's."[23] But the Creator underscores the moral undesirability of being, thinking, or acting as one. Rebuking the newly fallen Adam, the Son brushes aside the man's efforts at self-justification by emphasizing Eve's inferiority—her difference from Adam.

The oneness that Adam feels is of the kind celebrated by the love poets, but in the spiritual realm such an emotion is plainly dangerous. Significantly, Milton reserves complete union for the angels. Kerrigan and Braden remark that, though lover-poets for ages had been frustrated by the impossible dream of the merger of lovers' bodies and souls, "God has solved the problem Lucretius defined. Raphael reveals that when good angels copulate, they mingle all the way. . . . Love as the angels know it is a mixture of depths, a relief from solitude. The loving angels become each other with no trace, suggestively, of a dread of lost autonomy."[24] While total union may produce unimaginable ecstasy, it can also produce fear, as these authors point out. As Empson suggests, the angels' capacity to love by interpenetration appeals to them only within limits: "Though capable of re-uniting themselves with God the angels do not want to, especially because this capacity lets them enjoy occasional acts of love among themselves." The angels resist "dissolving themselves into God"—they do not desire yet the total and permanent union.[25]

We need not agree that the angels dread dissolution or reabsorption into God to agree that love can produce fear. When he sees the beautiful Eve in book 9, even the fierce Satan is shaken from his definitive evil:

> That space the Evil one abstracted stood
> From his own evil, and for the time remain'd
> Stupidly good, of enmity disarm'd.
>
> (463–65)

Quickly, however, he recollects himself, saying, "Shee [is] fair, divinely fair, fit Love for Gods, / Not terrible, though terror be in Love" (489–90). "The 'terror . . . in love' (490) he names . . . is the desire to serve and adore; love threatens to undermine autarchic selfhood when 'not approached by stronger hate.'"[26] The terror in love is a possible loss of autonomy and identity, a potential absorption (or reabsorption) into the Other that will destroy the essence, the individuality and difference of the lover. The experiences of Satan and Eve in *Paradise Lost* show that this fear transcends the differences between spiritual and romantic love.

IV

From the perspectives of Eve and Satan, the unity proposed or assumed by their superior Others seems to threaten the diminishment or obliteration of their identities. Given their histories and experiences, the merger of separate identities seems a real possibility. They know or have heard of states of undifferentiated oneness: the times before the Son was "begotten" by the Father, before Sin sprang from Satan, and before Eve was created from Adam. There are occasions, besides, when the boundaries between seemingly separate beings are said to be nonexistent, as when Sin claims that Satan is the doer of her deeds, and when Adam declares Eve to be his bone, his flesh, or his other half. In this universe of divisible and potentially reabsorptive creators, threats to a creature's individuation are credible.

Though the Father fosters the individuation of the Son, he decrees, as it seems to Satan, an undifferentiated unity for the angels under the Son: "your Head I him appoint" (5.606) he informs them,

> And by my Self have sworn to him shall bow
> All knees in Heav'n, and shall confess him Lord:
> Under his great Vice-gerent Reign abide
> United as one individual Soul
> For ever happy; him who disobeys
> Mee disobeys, breaks union, and that day
> Cast out from God and blessed vision, falls.

(607–13)

Sin is defined here as breaking union, as originating, or as persisting in, nonconformity or difference. The angels are to be one individual soul, "forming an indivisible entity" (*Oxford English Dictionary*). Not all the angels are willing to be subsumed into a larger soul, however happy. Satan rebels because he thinks the union robs him of the distinction of his exalted rank.[27] The unity proposed by the Father threatens, as Satan thinks, to absorb him

into the unindividuated body of his Creator (though he scoffs at
this characterization of the Son in Abdiel's speech in 5.835–38).
Union with the Son threatens his identity as one of the exalted
beings in Heaven.

To what Satan imagines as an undistinguished place as part of
the angelic body, he prefers his identity as one "of the first" (659)
Archangels, "great in Power, / In favor and preeminence" (660–61).
His fear regarding the Son is not wholly unfounded. Although Abdiel argues that the provident God is far from thinking "To make
us less, bent rather to exalt / Our happy state" (829–30), the Father
declares to the Son: "under thee as Head Supreme / Thrones,
Princedoms, Powers, Dominions I reduce" (3.319–20). A tangible
demonstration of the change wrought by the Exaltation occurs on
the last day of the War in Heaven when Michael surrenders the
leadership of his army to the Son (6.775–79).[28] Satan's appeal to
his peers assumes that they, too, would be loathe to surrender their
distinctive preeminence to the new king who will eclipse them all
(5.772–77).[29] We know that Satan's precious difference, his deliberate Otherness, will be preserved when "Hell, her numbers full, /
Thenceforth shall be for ever shut" (3.332–33).

Adam's romantic insistence on Eve's oneness with him sets the
context for Eve's insistence on her individuation in book 9. Once
again, "New Laws from him who reigns new minds may raise / In
[them] who serve" (5.680–81). For the first time, Adam tries to
restrict Eve's freedom of action when, for the first time, Eve conceives a course of independent action. In her dissension with
Adam, she shows conclusively that the "Union of Mind" her husband described to Raphael no longer exists. About working together and facing temptation, Eve is of a different mind from
Adam. The loving and protective "Head" appeals to his former
rib: "leave not the faithful side / That gave thee being" (9.265–66).
Though from the most loving of motives, Adam questions Eve's
completeness and autonomy. Were "we not endu'd / Single with
like defense, wherever met [?]" she asks (324–25). Were we "Left
so imperfet by the Maker wise / As not [to be] secure . . . single
or combin'd[?]" (338–39). Are we really the two halves of one
whole, she inquires; am I not entire and individuated? Against
Adam's unintended challenge, Eve asserts her ontological and
moral completeness.

To his credit (and with exquisite irony), Adam has said that he
would benefit by Eve's presence if he were tried—like a jousting
knight:

I from the influence of thy looks receive
Access in every Virtue . . .

. . . .

. . . while shame, thou looking on,
Shame to be overcome or over-reacht
Would utmost vigor raise, and rais'd unite.

(309–10, 312–14)

But it is never a question of Eve's protecting him or acting for him, as he proposes to do for her. Eventually, the fallen Adam admits that he could not have commanded Eve to remain by his side: "beyond [warning] had been force, / And force upon free Will hath here no place" (1173–74). Likemindedness or free obedience cannot be compelled; though Adam and Eve may be "one flesh" in love, they cannot be "one soul, one mind" in their moral lives.[30] It is not surprising that when Satan tempts Eve he appeals to her singularity: she is the "sole Wonder" of the world, the "Fairest resemblance of thy Maker fair," and it is "right [that she] should'st be obey'd" (533, 538, 570). Eve is receptive to acknowledgment of her individuation. Subsequently, when Adam berates the fallen Eve, she asks angrily: "Was I to have never parted from thy side? / As good have grown there still a lifeless Rib" (1153–54). Later, the repentant woman reassures her husband. So concerned at first to be acknowledged as entire and complete in herself, Eve recedes into Adam's side, declaring, "I never from thy side henceforth [intend] to stray" (11.176)—as, indeed, it is impossible for a rib to do. Finally, an even more subdued wife declares to her husband: "thou to me / Art all things under Heav'n, all places thou" (12.617–18). All things, all places: Adam has become Eve's temporal "All in All." Thus joined, they make an ambiguous and disturbing image of union.

V

A common substance unites three pairs of characters in *Paradise Lost*. The original "physical" oneness of these characters is reproduced in various modes: sexual union characterizes the oneness of Adam and Eve, Satan and Sin; one mind and one will unify both the Father and the Son, Satan and Sin; Adam and Eve are one in their love. The unions between these characters please or are useful to them, and the possibility is held out to two of these pairs of an even more total union in sexual or heavenly bliss. An idea whose several forms might seem exotic in the late twentieth century—of two become one, of the absorption of one into an Other, or of the other into the One—was familiar in the seventeenth century. But in the particular experiences of Satan and Eve, Milton dramatizes the human need for self-possession, for individuation. In the story of Adam and Eve, Milton deliberately gives prominence to the romantic ideal of oneness to expose it as error. Milton's God creates morally whole people—he cannot be loved or served by halves. The poet shows the conflict between the discourse and emotion of love and the necessity for spiritual self-determination.

Milton reminds his readers that Adam and Eve were created to love and obey God first of all. Significantly, in regard to *his* Maker, Adam assumes a spontaneous nexus of creation, love, and will when he asks Raphael,

> What meant that caution join'd, *if ye be found*
> *Obedient?* can we want obedience then
> To him, or possibly his love desert
> Who form'd us from the dust[?]
>
> (5.513–16; emphasis in the text)

Adam provides his own answer quite soon, but his question indicates the ideal relationship between the divine Creator and the human creature responsive to his love. All of God's creatures are to imitate the Son in loving obedience: "He that hath my commandments, and keepeth them, he it is that loveth me. . . . If a man love me, he will keep my words: and my Father will love him, and we will come unto him, and make our abode with him. He that loveth me not keepeth not my sayings" (John 14.21, 23–24). *Paradise Lost* is specific on this question several times, as when Raphael bids Adam farewell: "Be strong, live happy, and love, but first of all / Him whom to love is to obey" (8.633–34). Milton means to instruct the reader through Adam's errors in acting on the premises of romantic love rather than on the commandment of his Creator.

Of course, people can aspire to a total union with God in present or eternal bliss, as the earlier quotation from Browne suggests, and they can aspire also to a union of will with him. Several of George Herbert's poems provide examples, as does "Obedience":

> O let thy sacred will
> All thy delight in me fulfill!
> Let me not think an action mine own way,

> But as thy love shall sway,
> Resigning up the rudder to thy skill.
>
> (16–20)

Herbert's supposed description of *The Temple* to Nicholas Ferrar claims the attainment of such a state: in the poems, Ferrar would find "a picture of the many spiritual Conflicts that have past betwixt God and my Soul, before I could subject mine to the will of Jesus my Master, in whose service I have now found perfect freedom."[31] The state of having a will confluent with God's does not come easily, however, as is evident in Eve's and Adam's disobedience. Indeed, the difficulty of the ideal inspires John Donne's plea for extreme measures:

> Batter my heart, three person'd God; for, you
> As yet but knocke, breathe, shine, and seeke to mend;
> That I may rise, and stand, o'erthrow mee, and bend
> Your force, to breake, blowe, burn and make me new.
>
> (1–4)[32]

The Bible calls every believer to be the efficacy of God, and every daughter of Eve, the efficacy of her husband, but these are hard precepts.

Donne's desire to be subsumed, overwhelmed by an irresistible force, is unusual. A total union in love, with God or with another, is fearful. Sinners reluctant to love God for fear of losing the imperfect identities they value are not so different from the creatures in *Paradise Lost* who fear being swallowed up or reabsorbed into the seemingly divisible plenitude from which they were once created. Such an eventuality is not unreal in a universe where, in the beginning, the Son was in the Father, Sin in Satan, and Eve in Adam. I remarked earlier that the last image of Adam and Eve in *Paradise Lost* is ambiguous and disturbing, inasmuch as it suggests Eve's regression into riblike passivity. It evokes Milton's even more powerful and grotesque image of a multiple oneness, the great promise of love and heavenly bliss.

> A cry of Hell Hounds never ceasing bark'd
> · · · · · · · · · · · · · · · ·
> . . . yet, when they list, would creep,
> If aught disturb'd thir noise, into [Sin's] womb,
> And kennel there, yet there still bark'd and howl'd
> Within unseen.
>
> (2.654, 656–59)

Sin's unindividuated progeny vex her with "sorrow infinite" and "conscious terrors" (797, 801). This image of creatures permanently attached to the One that gave them being is the analogue of the conscious rib attached to its sheltering side, an evil analogue of the many in the One, of all the creatures in the All, their parent. The image can be read as an emblem of the pain produced by union with Sin. But it shocks by concretizing total and permanent union: Sin and her offspring represent the threat of holy or romantic bliss.

Notes

I acknowledge with gratitude the assistance I have had with this paper. At a very early stage, Gary Stringer helped me to articulate and flesh out some of the essay's main points. John T. Shawcross read an earlier version and made many valuable suggestions for improvement. At Murfreesboro and thereafter, Stuart Curran, Bill Hunter, Jane Hiles, Kristin Pruitt, Robert Entzminger, John Ulreich, Margaret Dean, and Judith Herz gave me the benefit of their insights and questions. Despite this impressive list, the errors remaining are mine.

1. John Milton, *Paradise Lost,* in *John Milton: Complete Poems and Major Prose,* ed. Merritt Y. Hughes (New York: Odyssey, 1957). All references to Milton's poetry are to this edition and are cited parenthetically in the text.

2. William Empson, *Milton's God,* rev. ed. (London: Chatto and Windus, 1965), 142. Sir Thomas Browne, *Hydriotaphia or Urne Buriall,* in *The Prose of Sir Thomas Browne,* ed. Norman J. Endicott (New York: Norton, 1972), 285. Some believers thought "All in All" also meant the final erasure of hell, the need for a separate domain obviated by God's salvation of all. According to Robert M. Myers ("'God Shall Be All in All': The Erasure of Hell in *Paradise Lost,*" *The Seventeenth Century* 5 [1990]: 50–51), in *Paradise Lost* Milton suggests the possibility of Hell's dissolution several times.

3. William Kerrigan and Gordon Braden, *The Idea of the Renaissance* (Baltimore: Johns Hopkins University Press, 1989), 194.

4. Raymond B. Waddington, "'All in All': Shakespeare, Milton, Donne, and the Soul-in-Body Topos," *ELR* 20 (1990): 40–68. For a brief but important discussion of "All in All" in *Paradise Lost,* see also John T. Shawcross, *John Milton: The Self and the World* (Lexington: University Press of Kentucky, 1993), 270–71.

5. All biblical references are to the King James Version and are cited parenthetically in the text.

6. Empson, *Milton's God,* 107.

7. Ibid.

8. Ibid., 106.

9. In *The Oxford Study Bible,* ed. M. Jack Suggs, Katharine Doob Sakenfeld, and James R. Mueller (New York: Oxford University Press, 1992), 13, a note on Gen. 2.24 explains that in the story of Eve's creation from Adam's rib and the subsequent statement that "the two become one," a "folk explanation is given for the origin of the sexual urge." On Adam and Eve's individuality and oneness, see Shawcross's discussion of the hand-in-hand image (*John Milton: The Self and the World,* 193–96).

10. Albert C. Labriola, "'Thy Humiliation Shall Exalt': The Christology of *Paradise Lost,*" *Milton Studies* 15 (1981): 32. See also John Peter Rumrich, *Matter*

of Glory: A New Preface to "Paradise Lost" (Pittsburgh: University of Pittsburgh Press, 1987), 162: "The begetting of the Son . . . does not mean that the being now entitled the Son never existed previously. He did, but he existed as the Word and was otherwise unapparent."

11. William B. Hunter, "Further Definitions: Milton's Theological Vocabulary," in *Bright Essence: Studies in Milton's Theology,* ed. W. B. Hunter, C. A. Patrides, and J. H. Adamson (Salt Lake City: University of Utah Press, 1973), 15, 16.

12. On the discussion between the Father and the Son in book 3, see Albert C. Labriola, "'God Speaks': Milton's Dialogue in Heaven and the Tradition of Divine Deliberation," *Cithara* 25 (May 1986): 5–30; and Michael Lieb, "The Dialogic Imagination," in *The Sinews of Ulysses: Form and Convention in Milton's Works* (Pittsburgh: Duquesne University Press, 1989, 76–97).

13. Empson, *Milton's God,* 106; Waddington, "'All in All,'" 47; Kerrigan and Braden, *The Idea,* 200.

14. Juan Luis Vives, *A Very Fruitful and Pleasant Book Called the Instruction of a Christian Woman* (1523), trans. Richard Hyrde (London [1529?]), in *Daughters, Wives and Widows. Writings by Men about Women and Marriage in England, 1500-1640,* ed. Joan Larsen Klein (Urbana: University of Illinois Press, 1992), 115.

15. "An Homily of the State of Matrimony" from *The Second Tome of Homilies* (London, 1563), in *Daughters, Wives,* ed. Klein, 17.

16. William Perkins, *Christian Economy: or, A Short Survey of the Right Manner of Erecting and Ordering a Family According to the Scriptures,* trans. Thomas Pickering (London, 1609), in *Daughters, Wives,* ed. Klein, 172, 173.

17. Hunter, "Milton on the Incarnation," in *Bright Essence,* ed. Hunter, Patrides, and Adamson, 141.

18. Diane Kelsey McColley, *Milton's Eve* (Urbana: University of Illinois Press, 1983), 51. See also Shawcross's discussion (*John Milton: The Self and the World,* 8–13). For Shawcross, Eve's subordination is finally unimportant, given the woman's role in salvation: "It is Eve who speaks last in the poem, a significant position, in lines that stress the protevangelium, yielding hope and putting the focus on woman's role in life" (13).

19. James Grantham Turner (*One Flesh: Paradisal Marriage and Sexual Relations in the Age of Milton* [Oxford: Oxford University Press, 1987], 112) quotes William Heale's *An Apologie for Women* (1609) about the mystery of one flesh in marriage: "In this Golden Age the marriage-partners were no more distinct than the persons of the Trinity, and there were 'no wordes of rigorous predomination, no thoughte of unkind preheminence.'" Obviously, Heale believed Adam and Eve together were like the one God, but how he then explained their falls is not clear.

20. Empson, *Milton's God,* 139.

21. Adam is Eve's "parent" in the same sense that Satan is Sin's. Adam conceives of Eve in *Paradise Lost,* 8:383–97, 415–26.

22. In a Seinfeld episode, Jerry meets a woman he considers the female version of himself. Two of his comments reminded me of Adam's colloquy with Raphael: "Now I know what I've been looking for all these years—myself. And now I've found me." Later, he says, "I've swept myself off my feet."

23. Regina M. Schwartz, "The Toad at Eve's Ear: From Identification to Identity," in *Literary Milton: Text, Pretext, Context,* ed. Diana Treviño Benet and Michael Lieb (Pittsburgh: Duquesne University Press, 1994), 8.

24. Kerrigan and Braden, *The Idea,* 200.

25. Empson, *Milton's God,* 139.

26. Kerrigan and Braden, *The Idea,* 206.

27. According to Rumrich, Satan also rebels because, having "in effect created a new rank, 'the head of the angels,'" Deity now demands a "doubled submission to the Father and 'to his image'" (*Matter of Glory,* 162).

28. Shawcross suggests that the return of the all into the One is "metaphorized" when Michael "leads back ('re-duces') the faithful angels to become body to the Head, who is God" (*John Milton: The Self and the World,* 271).

29. See Labriola, "'Thy Humiliation,'" 36.

30. See Diana Treviño Benet, "Abdiel and the Son in the Separation Scene," *Milton Studies* 18 (1983): 129–43 and for further discussion, "'No Outward Aid Require': A Note on Eve in Separation," *ANQ* 2 (1989): 90–94.

31. References to Herbert's poetry and prose are from *The Works of George Herbert,* ed. F. E. Hutchinson (Oxford: Clarendon, 1959), 104, xxxvii.

32. John Donne, "171 Holy Sonnet," in *The Complete Poetry of John Donne,* ed. John T. Shawcross (New York: Doubleday, 1967), 344.

"Argument Not Less But More Heroic": Eve as the Hero of *Paradise Lost*

JOHN C. ULREICH

Milton's attempt to "soar / Above th' Aonian Mount" (1.14–15)[1] by promulgating a new, distinctively Christian, idea of epic heroism has proven to be an extraordinarily fertile soil for germinating seeds of controversy—as he perhaps foresaw and would certainly have relished. For his deliberate effort to revitalize the epic by destroying it has also proven to be a sovereign remedy against the possibility that his "great Argument" (24) might be allowed by aftertimes to "sick'n into a muddy pool of conformity and tradition."[2] When he chose to juxtapose classical with Christian virtues, displacing (but *not* effacing) "the wrauth / Of stern Achilles" with "Patience" (9.14–15, 32) and "one mans firm obedience" (*Paradise Regained* 1.4), he grounded his epic in a "hateful siege / Of contraries" (*Paradise Lost* 9.121–22) that is at the same time a "Grateful vicissitude" (6.8) of self-renewing creative energy. And so, despite the best efforts of well-meaning critics to reduce his poem to orthodoxy, and even in the teeth of Milton's own heroic effort to justify God's ways by rendering ungrateful humanity "inexcusable" (The Argument, book 5), the poem insures the phoenixlike re-creation of its own imaginative life—precisely *because* it submits itself willingly to those energies that are always threatening to consume it, rousing itself "From under ashes into sudden flame . . . then vigorous most / When most unactive deem'd" (*Samson Agonistes* 1691, 1704–5).

This dialogic strategy[3] has a number of curious consequences, not the least piquant of which is that *Paradise Lost* seems to be a heroic poem without a hero.[4] Given that Milton invests so much energy in his conception of "one greater Man" (1.4), it is hard to account for the apparent absence of any character who might plausibly be said to embody the poet's idea. Dryden's objection to Milton's epic, that it is not "an heroic poem, properly so called," was roundly answered by Dr. Johnson: "the question . . . whether the poem can properly be termed *heroic* . . . [is] raised by such readers as draw their principles of judgment rather from books than from reason."[5] But Johnson's magisterial gesture serves rather to crystallize the problem than to resolve it: as Johnson himself observed, Milton is a notoriously bookish writer. And the corollary question, "Who is the hero?" is not so readily dismissed. Dryden's Satan and Addison's Messiah both have obvious claims, but neither these nor any of the other usual suspects—Adam? Man? the Bard?—has won universal assent.[6]

On this occasion, I propose to reopen the question by arguing that the hero of the poem is Eve. Two radically different, and perhaps incompatible, lines of argument lead to this conclusion. In the first place, I observe, Eve embodies more fully and perspicuously than any other character those qualities that Milton explicitly identifies as crucial to the new and greater heroism appropriate to a Christian epic that was intended to be "doctrinal and exemplary" (*Reason of Church Government* 1:815). At the same time, Eve's transgression initiates the properly human action of the poem by fulfilling God's intention that she and Adam should become "Authors to themselves" (*Paradise Lost* 3.122). My purpose in what follows is to sketch these two lines of argument and to account for their apparent incongruity.

I. Orthodoxy: Doctrinal and Exemplary

The new heroism that Milton celebrates in *Paradise Lost* and *Paradise Regained* is characterized, not by traditional masculine prowess—"plain Heroic magnitude of mind / And celestial vigour" (*Samson Agonistes* 1279–80)—but by the sort of virtue that is usually commended to females: by "the better fortitude / Of Patience" (*Paradise Lost* 9.31–32), by "suffering" (12.569), and by "long obedience" (7.159). Eve has clearly been created to embody these virtues, answering both Adam's need for an "other self" (8.450) and God's "great Idea" (7.557) of subordination.

Like Adam, Eve reflects "The image of thir glorious Maker," radiating "Truth, Wisdom, Sanctitude severe and pure, / Severe, but in true filial freedom plac't" (4.293–94). Eve's freedom is defined by a twofold submission to authority: "Hee for God only, shee for God in" Adam (299), her "Author and Disposer" (635). In her unquestioning obedience to both God and Adam, the "Daughter of God and Man" (9.291) fulfills her purpose and achieves *filial* freedom: "Unargu'd I obey; so God ordains, / God is thy Law,

thou mine: to know no more / Is womans happiest knowledge"
(4.636–38).

True filial submission manifests itself most completely in the
"better fortitude" (9.31) of self-sacrifice. The true form of "Heroic
Martyrdom" (32) is, of course, most conspicuously exemplified by
the Son of God, whose merit is demonstrated by his willingness
to offer his life in order to redeem soon-to-be-fallen humanity:

> Behold mee then, mee for him, life for life
> I offer, on mee let thine anger fall;
> Account mee man; I for his sake will [die].
>
> (3.236–38)

From this reasonably orthodox perspective, the defining moment
of Eve's heroism occurs when the "Daughter of God" offers her
life for Adam's in atonement for their sin, echoing the self-sacrifice
of God's Son:

> [I will] importune Heav'n, that all
> The sentence from thy head remov'd may light
> On me, sole cause to thee of all this woe,
> Mee mee onely just object of his ire.
>
> (10.933–36)

As William Shullenberger has observed, Milton's "representation
of true heroism [is] embodied in the gracious actions of Christ and
of Eve": after the Fall, "Eve breaks the grip of self-hatred and
mutual accusation by subordinating herself, by pleading for
Adam's forgiveness, and by offering her own life as a sacrifice out
of her love for Adam, even as the Son had offered his in the heavenly council scene (10.909–46; cf. 3.236–65)."[7]

As Adam rather ungenerously points out, her gesture is based
on a faulty premise, since she lacks the spiritual capital to appease
God's wrath. But Eve's "unwarie" (10.947) willingness to sacrifice
herself is *not* pointless, because it produces "Commiseration" in
Adam (940) and thus begins their regeneration. The long downward
slide into sin, death, and despair—"in the lowest deep a lower
deep / Still threatning to devour" (4.76–77) fallen humanity—is
mysteriously reversed by God's grace, manifested in Eve as charity and thus communicated to Adam, who enjoins her:

> But rise, let us no more contend, nor blame
> Each other, blam'd enough elsewhere, but strive

In offices of Love, how we may light'n
Each others burden in our share of woe.

(10.958–61)[8]

Eve's heroic offer to sacrifice herself for Adam's sake produces the transformation of evil into good that manifests "eternal Providence" (1.25): "O goodness infinite, goodness immense! / That all this good of evil shall produce" (12.469–70).

II. Heresy

Unfortunately, this happy image of Eve as Redeemer is marred by certain features that "interfere with the [heroic] interest" (as Shelley said of Satan).[9] The sin for which she must atone is "By [her] done and occasiond" (12.475). Instead of fulfilling the end of her creation by promoting "good works in her Husband" (9.234), Eve breaks faith and is thus "Defac't, deflowrd, and . . . to Death devote" (901).

Or so it would seem. Adam's lament and subsequent condemnation plainly accord with the judgment of the narrator, who seeks to "justifie the wayes of God to men" (1.26). But whether that is also Milton's judgment may at least be questioned. After all, unquestioning obedience to authority would hardly commend itself to Milton as an ideal of human behavior. For as he argues in *Areopagitica*, "when God gave [us] reason, he gave [us] freedom to choose, for reason is but choosing" (2:527). And until it is tested, freedom remains abstract, a potential to be realized rather than a fact of experience. Eve's "Unargu'd" obedience (*Paradise Lost* 4.636) is tantamount to an "implicit faith" (*Areopagitica* 2:543).

From this perspective, Eve's argument for a division of labor seems more reasonable—and decisively more Miltonic—than Adam's docile submission to divine authority. She too insists that "reason is but choosing." Her willingness to question authority suggests a desire to improve herself by "triall . . . by what is contrary" (*Areopagitica* 2:515). Her transgressive behavior contrasts sharply with Adam's unquestioned—indeed *implicit!*—obedience to God's authority: "O Woman, best are all things as the will / Of God ordain'd them" (*Paradise Lost* 9.343–44). In this context, Adam's authorized affirmation of freedom and right reason (344–56) seems faintly platitudinous, if only because he does not really desire Eve's freedom, or his own. At this crucial moment, Adam becomes Milton's prime example of "a heretick in the truth."[10]

From her discussion with Adam concerning their domestic economy, Eve learns to *choose* by rejecting a definition of herself as
"fugitive and cloister'd" (*Areopagitica* 2:515): "what is Faith,
Love, Vertue unassaid?" (*Paradise Lost* 9.335), she pointedly asks.
The voice is Eve's, but the guiding hand is Milton's:

> If every action which is good, or evill . . . were to be under pittance,
> and prescription, and compulsion, what were vertue but a name, what
> praise could be then due to well-doing? . . . We our selves esteem not
> of that obedience, or love, or gift, which is of force: God therefore left
> [her] free, set before [her] a provoking object, ever almost in [her] eyes;
> herein consisted [her] merit, herein the right of [her] reward, the praise
> of [her] abstinence. (*Areopagitica* 2:527)

More immediately, Eve is simply taking a hint from Raphael:
"how / Can hearts, not free, be tri'd whether they serve / Willing
or no[?]" (*Paradise Lost* 5.531–33). And Raphael is obviously taking his directions from God himself: "Not free, what proof could
they have giv'n sincere / Of true allegiance, constant Faith or
Love[?]" (3.103–4).
This more than rhetorical question defines the issue of Eve's
putative *sufficiency* (3.99): if it is to become virtuous, her innocence must be *tried*, and "trial is by what is contrary" (*Areopagitica* 2:515). When Eve goes to encounter her destiny, her quest is
sanctioned by the highest authority in Milton's universe—by the
poet himself, the maker of that Maker who ordains our freedom:

> Authors to themselves in all
> Both what they judge and what they choose; for so
> I formd them free, and free they must remain.
> (*Paradise Lost* 3.122–24)

Eve's encounter with the Serpent may seem unfortunate—at
least from the narrator's perspective, an "event perverse"
(9.405)—but her decision is not unambiguously wrong. Indeed, her
choice—or something like it—is plainly *necessary* to the fulfillment
of God's redemptive plan for humanity. And her aspiration to god-
hood is sanctioned, both morally, by the (typo)logical development
of the action, "From shadowie Types to Truth . . . from servil
fear / To filial" (12.303, 305–6), and spiritually, by the dynamic
architecture of Milton's universe, in which, "by gradual scale
sublim'd" (5.483), "Flesh" becomes "Spirit" (12.303) and "works
of Law" become "works of Faith" (306). Eve's satanically inspired

dream of transcendence (5.30–93) is promptly endorsed by Raphael:

> Your bodies may at last turn all to Spirit,
> . . . and wing'd ascend
> Ethereal, as wee.
>
> (497–99)

Unfortunately, Raphael fails to suggest any practical means to the accomplishment of this transformation. So far as man's *spiritual* development is concerned, the analogy of the self-subsuming plant is not very instructive, for while it provides a potent image of self-transcendence ("flowrs and thir fruit / Mans nourishment" [482–83]), it offers no clue about the mysterious process of sublimation (483) by which *their* bodies may turn to Spirit. And when Adam anxiously questions God's program—"What meant that caution joind, *if ye be found / Obedient?* (513–14; emphasis in the text)— Raphael's response is decidedly repressive:

> Attend: That thou art happie, owe to God;
> That thou continu'st such, owe to thy self
> That is, to thy obedience; therein stand.
>
> (520–22)

The affable Archangel has nothing further to say about any "Ethereal" ascent, and so Adam and Eve are left to figure out for themselves how to fulfill the purpose of their creation.

That is precisely the question that Eve confronts at the forbidden Tree: how shall the transformation of Man into God be accomplished, if not by acquiring "interdicted Knowledge" (52)? From this perspective, the defining moment of Eve's active heroism occurs when she *chooses*—even if mistakenly—"knowledge both of good and evil" (9.752) and becomes fully human. When Eve decides to eat the fruit, she is not seduced by Satan's flattery but won over by his argument; she makes a conscious, and conscientious, choice. Satan argues:

> will God incense his ire
> For such a petty Trespass, and not praise
> Rather your dauntless vertue . . . ?
> God therefore cannot hurt ye, and be just;
> Not just, not God; not feard then, nor obeyd:
> Your fear it self of Death removes the fear.
>
> (692–94, 700–702)

Upon reflection, Eve agrees:

> what forbids [God] but to know,
> Forbids us good, forbids us to be wise?
> Such prohibitions bind not.
>
> (758–60)[11]

In *choosing* to violate God's apparently senseless prohibition, she does what she believes to be right. And her action certainly suggests a "better fortitude" than Adam manifests by staunchly clinging to the status quo. Although Eve's fatal appetite for knowledge precipitates "all our woe" (1.3), it is also an expression, however flawed, of what may indeed be called "plain Heroic magnitude of mind." In God's eyes, Eve is no doubt inexcusable. From our fallen perspective, however, Eve's magnanimity seems genuinely heroic: by manifesting her "dauntless vertue," she becomes fully human.

III. Hateful/Grateful Contraries

The reference to Satan's malicious praise for Eve's "vertue" highlights the tragic irony of her choice: she gains freedom only by losing her life. At the same time, the subversive phrase draws attention to the problematic status of my defense of her action along decidedly unorthodox lines. The question is: How does it happen that Milton's representation of Eve appears sometimes to undermine his professed intention of justifying God's ways?

A variety of possible answers suggest themselves, all of them focusing more or less on the problematic notion that Eve's transgression is sanctioned by the logic of the poem.[12] Much recent criticism of Eve has been primarily directed either toward interrogating Milton's misogyny or reaffirming his humanism.[13] The latter enterprise has produced impressive results—sometimes, however, more remarkable for the fineness of the workmanship than for solidity of matter. Shullenberger's very suggestive idea of "relational identity" seems to me to be a case in point. He argues, plausibly, that "all human beings, men and women, discover freedom and authority through fidelity, filiality, the recognition of one's dependence on the ground of one's being." It may be true, as Shullenberger asserts, that "the assumption of a central, independent, experientially-based 'self' on which feminist readings are founded is exposed by the poet as, in the cases of Adam and Eve, naive, and in the case of Satan, demonic."[14] But it is also true that a *self*, properly so called, can be created only by plunging into the existential abyss that threatens always to devour us. And I do not believe that this supposedly "modernist" idea really differs from Milton's radical belief in Christian Liberty, which "FREES US FROM THE SLAVERY OF SIN AND THUS FROM THE RULE OF THE LAW AND OF MEN . . . SO THAT, BEING MADE SONS INSTEAD OF SERVANTS AND GROWN MEN IN-STEAD OF BOYS, WE MAY SERVE GOD IN CHARITY THROUGH THE GUIDANCE OF THE SPIRIT OF TRUTH" (*Christian Doctrine*, 6:537).

The basic premise underlying apologetic efforts like Shullen-berger's, which attempt to save misogynistic appearances by hy-pothesizing some transcendent image of "common humanity," has been powerfully deconstructed by Janet Halley. She asks, "Is au-tonomous female subjectivity possible?" and answers that, "in practice, [a wife's] wisdom and power—indeed, her subjectivity—originate in [her husband's]."[15] The consequence is a fundamental "asymmetry of male and female will in heterosexual harmony." Shullenberger tacitly acknowledges this when he notices Milton's "explicit assertion of gender differences—masculine rationality and attention to principle, feminine attention to natural process and the sustenance of relation-ship."[16] From a feminist perspective, such "gender differences" have tended historically to "incorpo-rat[e] the female voice and the female will only by subsuming them in male intention."[17] Between them, the feminist critique and the humanist apologetic define the polarity of my own attempt to an-swer Halley's provocative question about the possibility of fe-male autonomy.

By focusing my argument on the issue of Eve's autonomy, I have tried to circumvent some of the problems arising out of Shullen-berger's historical perspective. The result is an attempt, by "an-swering" Halley's critique, to construct a possible model of au-tonomous selfhood along Miltonic lines. The basis for this radical reconstruction is Milton's own insistence that human beings choose to become "Authors to themselves." From this perspective, Eve is the first human creature to become her own author—not because she usurps authority, nor yet because Adam abdicates, but because she discovers the authority that is properly hers by experiencing its limits. The limiting experience is, of course, death. Even the Son of God must rise by falling, fortunately; he estab-lishes his authority, "Merit [rather] then Birthright" (3.309), by "dying to redeem" even himself (299). Perhaps the defining paradox of Milton's "great Argument" is that one becomes a self only by an act of self-annihilation.

Given Eve's problematic selfhood, and the tragic self-loss from which it *necessarily* issues, the question finally becomes: In what sense can a "good God" be imagined to will the self-destruction of his creatures? Any plausible answer to such a question must, I think, remain provisional: "still searching what we know not, by what we know, still closing up truth to truth as we find it" (*Areopagitica* 2:551). Both the historical practice of Milton criticism and my own procedure are illuminated by the metaphor that he deploys in *Areopagitica* to represent the Temple of Truth: "when every stone is laid artfully together, it cannot be united into a continuity, it can but be contiguous in this world. . . . the perfection consists in this, that out of many moderat varieties and brotherly dissimilitudes . . . arises the goodly and the gracefull symmetry that commends the whole pile and structure" (2:555).[18] The present essay is, so to speak, just one more stone added to the pile: at best, perhaps, a contiguous dissimilitude—though not, I hope, a stumbling block. I do think the frequently apologetic tendency of Milton scholarship needs sometimes to be resisted, if only to reencounter the intractability of the poem itself. But I have not chosen to promulgate a subversive image of Eve solely for that reason. On the contrary, I believe that such an image is an indispensable *part* of the truth.

At the same time, my own commitment to the hermeneutic enterprise obliges me to suggest how this particular stone is to be fitted into the general architecture. How are we to account for the presence of such apparently destructive energies in a poem ostensibly committed to rationalizing evil? A general answer to this question, it seems to me, will most profitably pick up where Joan Webber left off: "The God that [Milton] justifies is a God in process, whose very justification lies in his capacity to encourage change."[19] Creation is a dialectical process: change necessarily implies evil as well as good, a destruction of the old as well as a creation of the new, so it is finally "creation . . . [the] sheer love of becoming, despite all the pain and frustration intrinsic to the process, that justifies the ways of God to men."

The question of theodicy becomes slightly more manageable when we shift the interpretive focus from theology to psychology, from God's putative goodness to Eve's problematic autonomy: how does *Paradise Lost* sustain an equivocal juxtaposition of radically contradictory heroic ideals—passive and/or active, submissive and/or assertive, obedient and/or transgressive? The very

terms in which the question is formulated suggest the need for a
kind of double vision that struggles to keep *both* images in focus
simultaneously. When I attempt to do so, I discover that the bi-
nocular resolution of these images can be defined by a structural
paradox: "whosoever will save his life, shall lose it: and whosoever
will lose his life for my sake shall find it" (Matt. 16.25).

IV. Graceful Symmetry

Eve's encounter with the Serpent confronts her with the mystery
of her own identity. Created in a double likeness, in God's image
once removed, she is caught between her own "watry" image
(4.461) and the "less [amiable]" (479) but more substantial figure
of Adam, of whom she is only an image.[20] She lacks "Substantial
Life" (485)—as the voice of Milton's God makes painfully clear:
"What thou seest, / What there thou seest fair Creature is thy self
. . . [a] shadow" (467–68, 470). What choice does Eve have except
to merge once again with the original from which she was sub-
tracted? "[F]ollow me" (469), the voice urges,

> And I will bring thee where no shadow staies
> Thy coming, and thy soft imbraces, hee
> Whose image thou art.
>
> (470–72)

Although she flirts briefly with a return to herself, Eve yields to the
overwhelming power of patriarchal authority—for the time being.
But "submissive" (498) Eve is also meant to be her own
Author—for so God has ordained: she and Adam are

> Authors to themselves in all
> Both what they judge and what they choose; for so
> I formd them.

Since Eve is plainly not created as a self, we may not unreasonably
suppose that she has been created to become one. And so we are
not surprised when she goes to discover the rudiments of that self
in Nature, among the flowers which are her image, "Her self . . .
[the] fairest . . . Flowr" (9.432). What the Serpent seems to show
her is precisely the self that she has been instructed to become: a
"Goddess humane" (732). But in order to become that divinity of
which she is only a likeness, she must lose her human self—as

Satan acknowledges: "So ye shall die perhaps, by putting off / Human, to put on Gods" (713–14). In Milton's revision of Genesis, alienation and the loss of Eden are not so much the result of God's jealousy—"And now, lest he . . . take also of the tree of life, and eat, and live for ever" (Gen. 3.22)—as they are the necessary consequence of becoming a fully human soul. Eve's original creation was an attenuation—a partial separation from the source of her likeness. To reunite with that source, she must first complete the separation and become truly the "Author" of herself.

Another term for this paradoxical self-authority is freedom: "I formd them free, and free they *must* remain, / Till they enthrall themselves" (3.124–25; emphasis mine). In Milton's Christian humanist terms, spiritual freedom is always a paradox: perfect freedom consists in filial submission to the divine will, enthrallment to God, the "Author" of one's being. The alternative to obedience is satanic enslavement to one's own will, self-chosen but finally self-destructive. What we call "autonomy" is really a delusion, an enslavement of the authentic self to the insatiable appetite for power, the "empty dream" (7.39) of self-sufficiency.

Autonomy is, however, a *necessary* delusion, for there can be no surrender without a self to be yielded up. Only a soul that has been formed, by negation and disobedience, can be transformed by the rediscovery of obedience. Eve responds to this necessity, as Adam does not. When he urges upon her "a fugitive and cloistered vertue"—"leave not the faithful side / That . . . shades thee and protects" (9.265–66)—she "sallies out and sees her adversary" (*Areopagitica* 2:515). Eve understands, by intuition, that we are purified by being tried, that *voluntary* obedience (as opposed to spontaneous impulse) consists, not in unquestioning submission to authority, but in the *re*affirmation of a virtue that has been tested.

Such freedom as Adam and Eve enjoy in Paradise is therefore defined by "the Tree / Of prohibition" (*Paradise Lost* 9.644–45), the "Sole pledge of [their] obedience" (3.95). As Milton explains in the *Christian Doctrine:*

> It was necessary that one thing at least should be either forbidden or commanded, and above all something which was in itself neither good nor evil, so that man's obedience might in this way be made evident. For man was by nature good and holy, and was naturally disposed to do right, so . . . he would not have shown obedience at all by performing good works, since he was in fact drawn to these by his own natural impulses, without being commanded.
>
> (6:351–52)

Spontaneity is not freedom, which must be *chosen*. Without that active choice, our obedience, and every human value derived from it "were . . . but a name" (*Areopagitica* 2:527). As Eve well knows, "Faith, Love, Vertue unassaid" are meaningless until they have been *tried* "by what is contrary."

Unfortunately, however, freedom can be experienced only by losing it, or by losing that spontaneity that is the image of freedom. Untested freedom is no freedom at all. But the process of testing is radically antithetical to the existence of spontaneous innocence. In order to be actualized as freedom, natural impulse must be disciplined. That is, it must be sacrificed to choice: spontaneity must be willed.

From the perspective of Christian Liberty, therefore, in which alone true filial freedom consists, Eve's fall is no fall at all. Or rather, to shift the terms of the paradox, her fall is a necessary— and fortunate[21]—step in humanity's evolution toward full, creative freedom, the discovery and acceptance of our mortality: "Except a corn of wheat fall into the ground and die, it abideth alone: but if it die, it bringeth forth much fruit" (John 12.24). For as St. Paul has said, "that which thou sowest is not quickened, except it die" (I Cor. 15.36).

When Satan tells Eve that she "shall not Die" (9.685), he is, of course, lying. But when he suggests that she will be "putting off / Human" in order "to put on Gods," his lie conceals a truth deeper than any that he can grasp. As Webber has shown, Milton's "epic implicitly or explicitly holds to two basic and essentially unsupportable assumptions. The first is that the hero's primary task is the acceptance of his [or her] own mortality; the second, partly following from the first, is that life and creativity are somehow worth the pain."[22]

When Eve chooses death over spurious and self-limiting immortality, she unconsciously imitates her Creator, the Word who is both her origin and her end, who is "Made flesh, when time shall be, of Virgin seed" (3.284) in order to fulfill the purpose of his Creation by "Giving to death, and dying to redeem . . . Mans Nature" (299, 304). So too does Eve, the "Mother of Mankind" (5.388), fulfill the purpose of her creation: "though all by mee is lost . . . By mee the Promis'd Seed shall all restore" (12.621, 623).[23]

Notes

1. John Milton, *Paradise Lost*, in *The Complete Poetry of John Milton*, ed. John T. Shawcross, rev. ed. (New York: Doubleday, 1971). All references to Milton's poetry are to this edition and are cited parenthetically in the text.

2. John Milton, *Areopagitica,* in *Complete Prose Works of John Milton,* 8 vols., ed. Don M. Wolfe et al. (New Haven: Yale University Press, 1953–82), 2:543. Unless otherwise noted, all references to Milton's prose are to this edition and are cited parenthetically in the text.

3. The word "dialogic" invokes Mikhail Bakhtin, especially *The Dialogic Imagination: Four Essays,* trans. Caryl Emerson and Michael Holquist (Austin: University of Texas Press, 1981), 426: "Everything means, is understood, as part of a greater whole—there is a constant interaction between meanings, all of which have the potential of conditioning others." This seems an apt description of the state of affairs both within *Paradise Lost* itself and in the critical dialectic that it engenders. As it happens, however, my present interest is more sharply focused, on the idea of *dialogue* as a speaking between *two* voices: a *polarity.* And my understanding of this radical term owes less to Bakhtin than it does to Owen Barfield, especially in *What Coleridge Thought* (Middletown, Conn.: Wesleyan University Press, 1971).

4. I allude, of course, to Thackeray's subtitle for *Vanity Fair: A Novel Without a Hero* (1847).

5. John Dryden, in *John Milton: The Critical Heritage,* ed. John T. Shawcross (New York: Barnes and Noble, 1970), 101; Samuel Johnson, *Lives of the English Poets,* vol. 1, *Cowley to Prior* (New York: Doubleday, 1957), 132. Dryden, who objected that Milton's "event is not prosperous like that of all other epic works," inaugurated the "Romantic" notion that Satan is the hero of the poem: "*Paradise Lost* would have been properly heroic, he suggested, if the devil had not been his hero, instead of Adam" (*Critical Heritage,* ed. Shawcross, 23.) John Dennis agreed with Dryden: "the Devil is properly [Milton's] Hero" (*Critical Heritage,* ed. Shawcross, 129). Addison rebutted this idea: "he that looks for an Hero in [the poem], searches for that which Milton never intended" (*Critical Heritage,* ed. Shawcross, 166). Johnson suggested that Adam is, indeed, a proper hero, since "there is no reason why the hero should not be unfortunate, except established practice" (*Lives,* 132). All of these arguments—including Addison's assertion that, if there must be "an Hero in it . . . 'tis certainly the Messiah" (*Critical Heritage,* ed. Shawcross, 166)—presuppose a classical idea of heroism.

6. Satan has always been the favorite candidate, of course, and not only with professional neo-Romantics like Harold Bloom. For example, Wallace Stegner, in *Crossing to Safety* (New York: Random House, 1987), 216, writes: "We had all read *Paradise Lost.* Had any of us read *Paradise Regained?* . . . The wicked and unhappy always [steal] the show because sin and suffering [are] the most universal human experiences. Technically, Christ was the hero of *Paradise Lost;* actually, Satan was. Fallen grandeur was always more instructive than pallid perfection." My own apology for Eve has obvious affinities with humanist arguments for Satan, inasmuch as I praise her "dauntless vertue" (9.694) for "ventring" (690) "to transgress / The strict forbiddance" (902–3). But the case for Eve must be developed along somewhat different, *Christian* humanist lines. And I rather fancy that Eve's subversive heroism is, in Shelley's words (apropos Prometheus), "more poetical" than Satan's because she is "susceptible of being described as exempt from the taints of ambition, envy, revenge, and a desire for personal aggrandisement" ("Preface to *Prometheus Unbound,*" in *Selected Poetry and Prose,* ed. Carlos Baker [New York: Modern Library, 1951], 443).

7. William Shullenberger, "Wrestling with the Angel: *Paradise Lost* and Feminist Criticism," *Milton Quarterly* 20 (1986): 71, 76. Eve's self-abnegation transforms Adam's egotistical lament: "On mee, mee onely, as the source and spring /

Of all corruption, all the blame lights due / . . . from deep to deeper plung'd!" (10.832–33, 844). Whereas her healing words descend from the Word himself, Adam's self-torment reflects the Satanic predicament: "Me miserable! . . . / . . . my self am Hell; / And in the lowest deep a lower deep / Still threatning to devour me opens wide" (4.73, 75–77).

8. Adam echoes St. Paul's definition of practical charity: "all the law is fulfilled in one word, even in this: Thou shalt love thy neighbour as thyself. . . . Bear ye one another's burdens, and so fulfil the law of Christ" (Gal. 5.14, 6.2). All biblical references are to the King James Version and are cited parenthetically in the text.

9. Shelley, "Preface," 443.

10. As Milton has famously argued:

Well knows he who uses to consider, that our faith and knowledge thrives by exercise. . . . Truth is compar'd in Scripture to a streaming fountain; if her waters flow not in a perpetu-all progression, they sick'n into a muddy pool of conformity and tradition. A man may be a heretick in the truth; and if he beleeve things only because his Pastor sayes so, or the Assembly so determins, without knowing other reason, though his belief be true, yet the very truth he holds, becomes his heresie.

(*Areopagitica* 2:543)

11. As William Empson (*Milton's God,* rev. ed. [London: Chatto and Windus, 1965], 160) observed,

This means that you ought not to obey a God if your conscience tells you that his orders are wrong; and . . . if your God then sends you to Hell for disobeying him, you were still right to have obeyed your conscience. . . . If God is good, that is, if he is *the kind of teacher who wants to produce an independent-minded student,* then he will love [Eve] for eating the apple. . . . But if he didn't mean that, then . . . it doesn't appear that he deserves to be obeyed. (Emphasis mine)

12. Among the "variety of possible answers," the most useful hypotheses attribute any endorsement of Eve's action to Milton's political intention, whether unconscious or deliberate. According to the hypothesis of what E. M. W. Tillyard, in *Studies in Milton* (London: Chatto and Windus, 1955), called "unconscious meaning," Milton was (in Blake's words) "a true Poet and of the Devil's party without knowing it" (William Blake, *The Marriage of Heaven and Hell,* in *Selected Poetry and Prose,* ed. Northrop Frye [New York: Modern Library, 1953], 124). This argument seems less plausible for Eve than for Satan, however, because the evidence supporting a subversive (as opposed to submissive) heroism in Eve is both abundant and overt. Meanings so close to the surface of the poem are likely to be in some sense deliberate. That is basically William Empson's argument: Eve "feels . . . that God wants her to eat the apple, since what he is really testing is not her obedience but her courage" (Empson, *Milton's God,* 159). A third hypothesis, promulgated by Stanley Fish, discerns in Milton's representation of Eve a polemical intention that is pedagogical rather than political. Fish imputes any sympathy for Eve to the unregenerate imagination of the reader. According to this neo-Calvinist hypothesis, faith must be affirmed "independently of reason": "Believing in experience, in reason, in things seen . . . is believing in oneself" (*Surprised by Sin: The Reader in Paradise Lost* [Berkeley: University of California Press, 1971], 243, 252).

13. Until as recently as twenty-five years ago, most apologists for Milton's epic gave relatively little thought to Eve's role, and what thought they did give was seldom generous in assessing her capabilities. If not created to fall, she was

certainly Adam's "inferiour, in the mind / And inward Faculties" (8.541–42), and thus vulnerable to temptation. Although she never seemed responsible for her actions in quite the way that Adam did, she was very much to blame. Thus, for example, Northrop Frye ("The Revelation to Eve," in *"Paradise Lost": A Tercentenary Tribute,* ed. Balachandra Rajan [Toronto: University of Toronto Press, 1967], 18–47) argues that human nature is polarized between Adam's rationality and Eve's sensuality, so that they represent two conflicting myth systems: the "rational" father-god myth with intrinsic moral principles and a mother-goddess myth of (at best) ambiguous morality grounded in "appetite." Questions about Milton's "Turkish contempt for females" (Johnson, *Lives,* 122) are not likely to be resolved any time soon, but Diane McColley (*Milton's Eve* [Urbana: University of Illinois Press, 1983], 3) has radically redefined the terms of the debate by showing that the figure of Eve imagined by much previous scholarship was not Milton's creation but an artifact of "a reductive critical tradition." McColley's saving the appearance of Eve for the Christian humanist hypothesis is a triumph of Miltonic hermeneutics. My own, neo-humanist essay begins, in a sense, where hers leaves off, with a recuperated image of Eve as one who is both "sufficient to stand and able to grow" (McColley, *Milton's Eve,* 4).

14. Shullenberger, "Wrestling," 76, 79.

15. Janet E. Halley, "Female Autonomy in Milton's Sexual Poetics," in *Milton and the Idea of Woman,* ed. Julia M. Walker (Urbana: University of Illinois Press, 1988), 231, 244.

16. Shullenberger, "Wrestling," 75.

17. Halley, "Female Autonomy," 247.

18. Milton's architectural metaphor is explicated by Stevie Davies' idea of "holistic interpretation": "a listening art which detects many—often irreconcilable—voices in the one poem, the total meaning not being understood as a resolution of those antiphonic voices which sing so intensely against one another but as the complexity of their vital contradiction" (*Harvester New Readings: Milton* [New York: Harvester Wheatsheaf, 1991], 7, 10). What Davies calls "a holistic reading practice" commends itself to me especially as the practice of *re*reading—continually reviewing and revising one's assumptions in the light of new observations and using those observations to construct new hypotheses.

19. Joan Webber, "Milton's God," *ELH* 40 (1973): 519, 526.

20. The construction of Eve as Adam's likeness is Miltonic rather than biblical. According to Genesis, the male and the female are made equally in the likeness of Elohim: "God said, Let us make man in our image, after our likeness. . . . So God created man in his own image . . . male and female created he them" (Gen. 1.26, 27). Later on, however, YaHWeH Elohim rejects human aspirations to god-likeness: "the LORD God said, Behold, the man is become as one of us, to know good and evil. . . . Therefore the LORD God sent him forth from the garden of Eden" (3.22–23). The paradox is both sharpened and occluded (or explained away) by modern biblical scholarship, which understands the contradictory valuations of divine similitude as a consequence of multiple (in this case dual) authorship. The idea that humanity is made in God's likeness belongs to a Priestly (P) tradition, dating from the fifth (or perhaps as early as the eighth) century B.C.E. The radically contrary idea, that humanity is cast out of Paradise for its attempt to become like gods, belongs to the Yahwist (J) narrative tradition, probably written as early as the tenth century B.C.E. Milton did not require the perspective of modern scholarship to notice the paradox that he makes the logical crux of his

poem: how can God be justified in punishing us for trying to become more like the One in whose image and likeness we have been created—by him?

21. Invoking the paradox of the Fortunate Fall is obviously problematic. See, for example, A. O. Lovejoy, "Milton and the Paradox of the Fortunate Fall," in *Essays in the History of Ideas* (Baltimore: Johns Hopkins University Press, 1948) The word "necessary" is especially troublesome; see, for example, John C. Ulreich, Jr., "A Paradise Within: The Fortunate Fall in *Paradise Lost*," *Journal of the History of Ideas* 32 (1971): 351–66. As Dennis Danielson and other apologists for Milton's "Good God" have pointed out, the hypothesis of a fortunate fall can easily seem to reduce Milton's theodicy to idiocy, or worse: "If God *needed* the Fall in order to reveal what Lovejoy calls 'the plenitude of the divine goodness and power' (164), then Milton's careful avoidance of absolute predestination, his assertion of free will and its reflection of the divine image . . . virtually his whole justification of the ways of God—all turn out to be little more than a useless facade over the nightmare abyss of 'divine' intentions" (Dennis Danielson, *Milton's Good God: A Study in Literary Theodicy* [London: Cambridge University Press, 1982], 202). Nonetheless, I would now argue, the alchemy of Milton's epic does transform evil into good by sublimating the source of "all our woe" into the fountainhead of "Joy and eternal Bliss" (12.551): the "loss of Eden" (1.4) makes possible the *re*creation of "A Paradise within . . . happier farr" (12.587), "more wonderful / Then that which by creation first brought forth / Light out of darkness!" (471–73). I am, however, less concerned with the issue of theodicy than I am with Milton's exploration of free will and necessity as they bear on his representation of Eve. In these terms, the *felix culpa* is not so much a theological mystery as a spiritual paradox: moral freedom is necessarily created by the loss of spontaneous innocence.

22. Webber, "Milton's God," 516–17.

23. This is Eve's version of the *felix culpa*, at once prophetic and Johannine. It is perhaps also Milton's (rather cryptic) gloss on a (pseudo) Pauline enigma in 1 Timothy: "the woman being deceived was in the transgression: Notwithstanding she shall be saved in childbearing" (2.14–15).

Milton's Eve as Closed Corpus, Open Book, and Apocryphal Text

ELIZABETH MAZZOLA

Nothing was forever buried in Milton's imagination: outworn symbols become useful as typologies, fallen angels become divine agents, lost paradises become epic poems. One of his most strained images—which surfaces first in the divorce tracts—not only explains why Miltonic memory is so roomy, but also suggests the tremendous agony of its accommodations, especially when two figures or symbols are made to share the same status or carry the same weight. In this case, however, Milton is describing the tensions produced by a failed marriage: "instead of beeing one flesh," husband and wife "will be rather two carkasses chain'd unnaturally together; or as it may happ'n, a living soule bound to a dead corps."[1] This analogy becomes increasingly powerful in Milton's poetics, which often strain to yoke together two different ontologies, as when Milton combines Christian and pagan traditions. But Milton's Eve offers another solution to these tensions. Appearing and disappearing repeatedly in *Paradise Lost,* she assumes a large part of the burden of memory herself.

I

Other critics have viewed *Paradise Lost* as an ideal container for obsolete items. Isabel MacCaffrey argues that "The uniqueness of *Paradise Lost* is in a sense its perfect victory over uniqueness; the very thoroughness with which Milton has assimilated the themes."[2] Part of the poem's unique success, MacCaffrey implies, has to do with the obsolescence of its subject matter: "when the myth . . . became irrelevant to the world's convictions, the poetic manner created to embody it became obsolete or, vainly applied to non-mythical subjects, extraneous and dead."[3] In other words, Milton's poem actively produces relics. Composed more than a thousand years after the sealing of the biblical canon, *Paradise Lost* is itself an apocryphal text: a less authentic, even spurious, third testament, a narrative restricted to cabalistic circles, of dubious importance and questionable authority.

To be sure, many poems might fall under such a label. This is because "apocrypha" usually designate a collection of biblical narratives authored not by scribes but by scholars, written in Greek rather than in Hebrew, or simply written too late. In any case, they describe material conceived of as literature—meant to repair institutional structures and canonical texts—rather than traditional oral stories (the literal word of God) accidentally preserved. But within *Paradise Lost* are buried other apocryphal stories: banned or hidden information to which we no longer have access, like Eden itself, now barricaded from view, or simply the experience of Adam quietly laboring in the Garden by himself while Eve converses with the snake. This is the other meaning of "apocrypha," signifying books set aside for the wise, but suggesting too a form of cultural detritus specifically excluded from providential schemes.

There are still other imaginative relics that continue to haunt the perimeter of Eden. Neither wholly inside nor outside its borders, they include repudiated texts or shadowy figures like Milton's Hebrew sources or even Eve herself, which belong to sacred memory and at the same time interrupt it. Perhaps the categories of "sacred" and "secular" are inadequate to the complexities of Milton's narrative, as Mark Wollaeger argues, because *Paradise Lost* provides its readers with a chance to watch these sacred memories recede from view.[4]

II

Some of Shakespeare's relics work as antecedents for the images Milton withdraws. Just as Eve makes it possible for Adam to understand himself (perhaps she is such a good listener because she mirrors him so well), Desdemona, shunted between father and husband, provides a similar service for Othello. In the same way that Eve manifests Adam's heart's desire, Desdemona reports that "I saw Othello's visage in his mind" (1.3.252).[5]Anticipating Milton's emphasis on "rational burning" above carnal satisfaction, Othello requests his new bride's company on their wedding night

not

To please the palate of my appetite,

Nor to comply with heat, the young affects
In me defunct, and proper satisfaction,
But to be free and bounteous of her mind.

(1.3.261–65)[6]

Moreover, Milton's and Shakespeare's narratives are both constructed to place female characters outside cognitive limits, even though, ironically, both characters are prized for their attentiveness. Maybe the frequent connection noted between Iago and Milton's Satan is explained in contrast by the latitude each is given by the narrative. But Desdemona and Eve are quickly repudiated and made obsolete by the stories that surround them.[7] It might be Desdemona's pliancy that finally proves her undoing, her genealogy that "unmoors" her; as Othello angrily promises Lodovico, "she can turn, and turn, and yet go on" (4.1.249). Still, if Milton seems to come to the same conclusion about Eve in *Paradise Lost,* he ultimately reserves judgment. Much of the poem is organized instead around what to do with Eve, how and where to locate her; it is more obsessed with the power to evoke her and to put her to sleep again.

In fact, throughout *Paradise Lost,* Eve is continually recalled, never superseded. Like Othello's missing handkerchief, she consistently provides "ocular proof" (3.3.366), usefully testifying to many conflicting readings. Wollaeger reminds us that narratives continually generate their own secrets or "new opacities," but we should be alert both to the "temporal ironies" at play here and to a vastly expanding network of epistemological ironies as well.[8] This ironic network is different from the one produced by Spenser's discarded images and exposed optical illusions—like the Bower of Bliss or false Florimell, the abandoned hermaphrodite and even the absent body of Gloriana—that litter *The Faerie Queene,* so that something is always rotting in the state of fairyland. Instead, Milton's divorce tracts, like his epic, contain and even cultivate his ambivalence about marriage. In the rest of this essay, I examine how Renaissance culture frequently disowned cognitive stances, epistemological frameworks, and ideological positions in order to shape a rhetorical construct we would call history. But in *Paradise Lost,* Milton calls this construct Eve.

III

The same tensions Milton deals with in *Paradise Lost,* where he negotiates the awkward gap between the moral status of the past and its chronological positioning, are behind Brian Walton's *Biblio Sacra Polyglotta* (1654–57).[9] Walton's text arranged columns of Scripture in nine languages, including Aramaic, Hebrew, Syriac, Chaldee, and Greek, alongside the Vulgate, so that the polyglot Bible is not organized by typology but by discontinuity.[10] Yet like the ledger book it resembles, this version of the Bible presupposes a balanced set of accounts. Moreover, while Luther had argued that Scripture provides its own interpretation, the polyglot Bible puts this premise into operation. Interpretation could truly "begin all over again" when grammatical errors and false idioms were finally collected.[11] But the result was that, now comprehensible in any language, biblical history no longer carried any weight. Taken out from behind the veil of sacred history, Reformation Scriptures were thus exhibited like the tabernacle's secret contents and "recontextualized within a history of historical documents as fragments from a lost world impinging on the present [like] so many museum pieces."[12] Jason Rosenblatt argues that Milton's "recontextualizations" have different results, however, because they continue to sanction authority. "Milton sees himself as a moral archaeologist," Rosenblatt claims, "picking up shards of truth banned for years in custom and error."[13] Similar results were produced through the efforts of John Selden, whose antiquarian interests included extensive researches into Hebraic legal codes, culminating in the *Uxor Hebraica* (1646), a massive compendium of ancient nuptial rites and marriage customs. Like Milton's divorce tracts, this work is occupied with the conditions under which a man could repudiate his wife.[14] What is particularly intriguing is the way these antiquarian pursuits were undertaken with the intention of dislodging contemporary materials. There are other important connections between Milton's and Selden's work. Unlike the polyglot Bible, which confidently sidesteps—or straddles— such issues, Milton's and Selden's "moral archaeology" exposes Renaissance ambivalence about history by implicitly raising the following questions: In what ways does the past antedate the present? How does the present point to the past? On what grounds can we even compare the two? And what holds the two constructs, like the columns exhibited in Walton's polyglot Bible, together?[15]

IV

Let me return to my initial example, not for an answer but for a rationale. Unlike Shakespeare's Othello, who forces Desdemona out of his story altogether, Milton allows Eve to "go on," perhaps because the wife who abandoned him eventually returned. "Long choosing, and beginning late" (9.26),[16] Milton's plans for *Paradise Lost* are sidetracked when his marital bliss is shattered and his first wife Mary Powell, whom he married in June 1642, leaves him a few months later to return to her father's house. A year after her departure, a tract entitled *The Doctrine and Discipline of Divorce* (1643) appears, followed by a second edition a year later. In close succession appear three more tracts: *The Judgement of Martin Bucer* (1644), *Tetrachordon* (1645), and *Colasterion* (1645). Mary Powell then returns and the arguments for divorce subside.

Many readers have wrestled with this history to pinpoint strains in the divorce tracts between Milton's incipient feminism and chronic misogyny or between a newfangled egalitarianism and old-fashioned hierarchism.[17] Other readers have consulted this history to untangle the close-knit threads of sacred ambitions and profane accidents in *Paradise Lost*.[18] James Grantham Turner, for instance, concludes that "The divorce issue, exploding with the Civil War, forced [Milton] to treat a personal episode as a national crisis, and it plunged him into a total engagement with the story of Genesis, which he was half inclined to dismiss as 'remote' or to convert into a Platonic myth. Without the divorce tracts, Milton might have produced a turgid Arthuriad or Cromwelliad instead of *Paradise Lost*."[19]

I would argue that the "divorce issue" forces Eve—rather than Arthur—to become the idol Milton smashes. With this in mind, we might explore Eve's literary function and obsolescence, and re-trace her poetic rebirths and disappearances, in terms of specifically historiographical pressures. The "divorce issue" provides Milton with a potent metaphor and rich literary method. Etymologically meaning to turn away, the term "divorce" does not specify a direction or signal a final goal (*Oxford English Dictionary*). For Milton, it serves at once as a means to reclaim old positions and a method of revision, a way both to review the past and reconstitute the present.

Created after the rest of Eden is finished, Eve is produced as supplement and obstacle, buried prize and secondhand fiction. Like Mary Powell, Eve jointly functions as source and result, cause and effect, since another contest being waged whenever Eve resurfaces in the poem is between past and present. We see this when, even after Eve arrives on the scene, Adam introduces her as a vision, something he has dreamed of (8.460–77, 482). Moreover, when Eve recounts her genealogy in book 4 (449–76), it is the story of her being educated about her origins (482–86) so that she might "invisibly [be] thus led" (476).[20]

Eve's abject status continually locates her in *Paradise Lost*, and Milton's poem dutifully catalogs her displacements. Her birth is really an awakening from sleep that "reposes" her (4.449–52), and she continues to recede from view in the rest of *Paradise Lost*, so that her presence is never required in Paradise. In books 8 and 11, she is absent from the angelic narrations. After eating the apple, Eve worries that "I shall be no more, / And Adam wedded to another Eve" (9.827–28). When Adam relates his own birth narrative, he recounts the creation of an unnamed helpmeet who then disappears. The first image we have of Eve from her husband is as a fugitive, more a figure for the apocryphal Lilith who shadows the walls of Eden than the "present object" Eve ultimately calls herself in book 10 (996).[21] Milton's treatment of Eve reflects Renaissance religious and political anxieties, which Shakespeare also explored, about which texts were authoritative or which conversations counted. But Eve's problematic status points to anxieties experienced at an even deeper level, over just which cultural memories ought to be repressed.

V

After the recovery of Hebrew materials including Midrash, the Talmud, and other rabbinical commentaries in order to shape a more authoritative Scripture, many Protestants were forced to confront apocryphal texts. Some reformers, by simply claiming the Gospels existed prior to the biblical canon, evaded the problem of the Apocrypha entirely.[22] At least Luther is more openly ambivalent. "I so hate Esther and II Maccabees," he claims, "that I wish they did not exist. There is too much Judaism in them and not a little heathenism."[23] Typically the historical solution to this problem had been to suppress apocryphal materials yet again. As Frank Kermode explains, after the closing of the biblical canon in 100 C.E., those books that had been hidden away for the wise now "acquired dyslogistic overtones, and the apocryphal came to mean the false or inauthentic."[24]

Miltonists like Wollaeger and Virginia R. Mollenkott have been able to recover the influence of apocryphal texts in Milton's poetry.[25] In fact, Wollaeger maintains, "the neglected category of apocryphal texts operates as a third term between the poetic and the sacred."[26] He goes on to argue that its liminal status is exploited by Milton when the apocryphal Raphael, guarding the gate of Hell during creation, later asks Adam to recount his story in book 8.[27] More recently, Rosenblatt has concluded that "the Hebraic factor in the Edenic books does not annul Milton's radically Pauline theology, nor does Milton's Paulinism cancel his Hebraism. The Hebrew Bible and the Pauline epistles are the principal matrices of Milton's poetry."[28]

The presence of both traditions accounts for the discrepancies Turner detects in the divorce tracts. He argues that "The text of 'lost Paradise' is thus both 'vanisht' and ever-present. Moses's legislation, and Milton's heroic endeavors to restore it, rest on a central contradiction: they will lead us back to the Paradisal happiness by pushing to its logical conclusion the fact that it is beyond our strength ever to return there."[29] Stephen Fallon has examined this "radical instability" on a stylistic level, and comments that "Rhetorical practice mirrors theme in the divorce tracts. Dichotomies proliferate: body/soul, fault/blamelessness, necessity/freedom, grunting Barrow/gentle spirit, and so on"; "[w]riting about marriage and divorce," he adds, "Milton relies upon union and separation." But Fallon also notes that "[there is a] surplus of divorcive energy in Milton's endeavors to 'fadge together' in his tracts antipathetic arguments that, like individuals separated by 'natural antipathies,' refuse to be married."[30] While Fallon's conclusion is that Milton is basically addressing two different audiences—dualists, who need sex, and monists, who could do without—[31] I would suggest that Milton is instead wrestling with two different but equally lively and ongoing traditions in the Renaissance, Christianity and Judaism.[32]

The tension between patristic thinking and rabbinical argument in Milton's divorce tracts duplicates the frustrating conflicts he chronicles there between husband and wife. Taking up Mosaic law, which recognized incompatibility as a grounds for divorce, Milton proposes:

Thence this wise and pious Law of dismission now defended took beginning: He therfore who lacking of his due in the most native and humane end of mariage, thinks it better to part then to live sadly and injuriously to that cherfull covnant (for not to be belov'd & yet retain'd, is the greatest injury to a gentle spirit) he I say who therfore seeks to part, is one who highly honours the maried life, and would not stain it: and the reasons which now move him to divorce, are equall to the best of those that could first warrant him to marry. (*The Doctrine and Discipline of Divorce* 2:253)

This text is troubled by the sad history it recounts. Bitter reflections disturb its surface, and buried narratives unravel its forward-looking aims. The real question that poses itself, as Annabel Patterson acutely observes, is "Who . . . is doing the divorcing, and at what moment does it occur?" Just who is it who is "retained, but not to be beloved?"[33] A similar confusion about whether the mistreated object is an unloved husband or unread text arises when Milton describes his rescue of the long-neglected Mosaic Scriptures in his preface to the 1644 edition: "Bringing in my hands an ancient and most necessary, most charitable, and yet most injur'd Statute of Moses: not repeald ever by him who only had the authority, but thrown aside with much inconsiderate neglect, under the rubbish of Canonicall ignorance: as once the whole law was by some such like conveyance in Josiahs time" (2:224).[34]

This contest over biblical sources and allegiances—and its solution, as well—is recast in *Paradise Lost,* because the past is now separate and frozen in Eve: a construct that, if easily awakened, is just as easily dismissed. As a result, we first meet Eve as a memory or, rather, something already repressed.[35] Only after he has angrily dismissed Desdemona does Othello maintain he can still recall his wife (4.1.249). But Eve's birth narrative itself begins with her turning away. After awakening, she reports:

> I thither went
> With unexperienc't thought, and laid me down
> On the green bank, to look into the clear
> Smooth Lake, that to me seem'd another Sky.
> As I bent down to look, just opposite,
> A Shape within the watr'y gleam appear'd
> Bending down to look on me, I started back,
> It started back, but pleas'd I soon return'd,
> Pleas'd it returned as soon with answering looks
> Of sympathy and love.
>
> (4.456–65)

Caught in a circuit of narcissism and myopia, her ambivalence ultimately finds more suitable lodging in Adam, whose first words upon seeing his mate are "Return fair Eve" (4.481).[36] The way Eve continues to slide in and out of narrative view in the poem seems to mirror Milton's own ambivalence about his Hebrew sources. Perhaps, like the divorce tracts, these sources serve both as a point of departure and as a longed-for goal in *Paradise Lost.* Or maybe the historical ideal is simply to be able to move back and forth between them. This is a precedent, of course, with which our first parents unsuccessfully experimented. Because of the many "looks [that] intervene and smiles" (9.222) between Adam and Eve, she wants to divide their labors in book 9 and proposes to Adam that they temporarily separate (214).

VI

Of all the suppressed narratives and ruins collected in Milton's poem, the chronology of Eve is the most obscured and the most contested. She remains as well the most troublesome element in his apocryphal text: at once sacred afterthought, spurious hearsay, occult figure, and floating signifier. If analyzing Milton's treatment of Eve is a way to gauge his complex relationship to apocryphal material, it also discloses his contradictory ambitions for *Paradise Lost* as sacred text. Joseph Wittreich, for instance, claims that "Interpretive commonplaces are not explained, but explained away, by a poem that is itself (in the version we all read) a second edition and that in its last books portrays Eve as herself a second edition."[37] Surely, though, Milton's presentation of Eve indicates a troubled relationship to his own past as well, since the figure whose birth and absence are repeatedly recounted in *Paradise Lost* haunts the divorce tracts too, in the specter of the wife repudiated in favor of a more paradisal marriage.

The same Reformation debates surrounding Apocrypha over how to establish their sacred standing or determine exactly what they illustrate encircle Eve. In both cases, the problem is repudiating something that might, if only secondarily, be one of God's creations. There are other questions we might ask, however. By what principle is Eve displaced and reclaimed again and again in the poem? What is being synthesized in Milton's dialectics of repudiation?[38] I think that drawing on apocryphal materials—which not only describe angels and devils, but offer reasons for divorce besides adultery—provides Milton with a method for experimenting with ontological categories of past and present, vision and reality, memory and actuality. These alternatives are repeatedly introduced in *Paradise Lost*. For one thing, the bodies of Adam and Eve may eventually disappear if all goes well (5.496–97). Conversely, as Raphael warns, Adam might sink to the status of a beast in stooping to worship Eve (8.579–82).

These possibilities were not restricted in the seventeenth century to Milton's Paradise. Closely allied with reformist imperatives, colonial agendas, and archaeological impulses, Renaissance historiography becomes more and more adept at producing ruins. Church and state offices at this time are busily deposing a king, mutilating icons, disposing of Arthur, and inventing divorce (tricks that, in *Othello,* still required a handkerchief).[39] At the same time, early modern travel lore and anthropology get more precise at delimiting the nonexistent or nonessential. But the long-devalued and now-recovered Apocrypha permit Milton a wider range of epic possibilities and casualties. They provide him with an endless stream of faulty originals and discarded alternatives and furnish a bottomless site for the production of knowledge and history.

As H. F. Fletcher suggests, Milton was probably familiar with Hebrew scholar Johann Buxtorf's rabbinical commentary, in which Lilith figures largely.[40] But some of these ontological possibilities have already been taken up before Milton fashions Eve out of a rib: Hamlet finally assumes the place of a ghost; Spenser's Florimell is doubled by a snowman; his knight Guyon is really an elf; and Prince Arthur spends his youth hibernating in fairyland. Spenser's fairy queen herself, who visits Arthur in a dream, evokes the "night fairy" Lilith's seductions.[41] Henry VIII's researches into divorce, annulment, excommunication, and papal fallibility comprise a similar set of forays into those shadowy regions. In each of these cases, the past collides with the present because each is construed from an entirely different set of materials.

One could even argue that seventeenth-century history is organized by the endless stream of originals in the pool that so absorb Eve. They are doubled at this same time by the cabalistic invention of the golem, an artificial anthropoid created by Jewish mystics to challenge Christian humanistic learning. This plot backfires, however, when the golem reveals their project to be bankrupt, arriving on the scene only to announce that "God is dead."[42] The fulfillment of cabalistic history here coincides with sacred obsolescence. Another painful lesson in ontology is provided by the false prophet Sabbatai Sevi, whose pronouncements shook Palestine and all of Europe in 1665 when he announced that he was the Messiah, only to apostatize to Islam a year later.[43]

Herself a comparable piece of apocryphal history, Eve can likewise absorb doctrinal disturbances. But there are still other apocryphal analogies. R. W. Southern explains why Islam, whose "contradictions" had been intolerable to the medieval imagination, no longer represented a threat to early modern Europe. Previously, Southern writes, Islam's ontology not only challenged Christian doctrine but subverted itself:

> what was to be made of a doctrine that denied the divinity of Christ and the fact of his crucifixion, but acknowledged his virgin birth and

his special privilege as a prophet of God; that treated Old and New Testaments as the word of God, but gave sole authority to a volume which intermingled confusingly the teachings of both Testaments; that accepted the philosophically respectable doctrine of future rewards and punishments, but affronted philosophy by suggesting that sexual enjoyment would form the chief delight of Paradise?[44]

These challenges are weakened, however, in the "vastly extended world picture of the seventeenth and eighteenth centuries," when Europe subsumes America and so conducts its own history westward, rewriting the East in the process.[45] Like New World exploits, *Paradise Lost* suggests how the establishment of traditional (or national or theological) boundaries coincides with their transgression.[46]

VII

Perhaps Islam was no longer a threat to the seventeenth-century imagination because, like *Paradise Lost,* it now could both expose and contain cultural images normally repressed. More frequently such dreams to abolish memory collapse into literature, which increasingly becomes a vehicle for experiences we cannot have or possibilities we have deliberately excised. In *Civilization and Its Discontents* (1930), Freud describes such imaginative collapse as sublimation. But less than a decade later, he proposes in *Moses and Monotheism* (1939) to recover what is lost in the process and explores Moses in some of the same ways I have been reading Eve, as false prophet, renounced choice, and finally buried alternative. Here Freud also theorizes how biblical narratives like Exodus actively push aside their founders:

> The distortion of a text is not unlike a murder. The difficulty lies not in the execution of the deed but in the doing away with the traces. One could wish to give the word "distortion" the double meaning to which it has a right, although it is no longer used in this sense. It should mean not only "to change the appearance of," but also "to wrench apart," "to put in another place."[47]

Freud claims the text of *Moses and Monotheism* was written twice over since he had tried to put it away, "but it haunted [him] like an unlaid ghost."[48] One reason Freud may have wanted to bury the story was that the "unlaid ghost" of Moses, who puts a face on forgetting, simultaneously serves as a mnemonic device (like the golem) that dislodges Hebrew culture. In the same way, Milton's classical allusions in *Paradise Lost* repeatedly point to literary tradition as bankrupt.

It is a commonplace that history must wait for its subjects to be dead. Less commonly recognized is history's obsession with failures and its appetite for relics. Like Milton, other Hebraists such as Luther and Selden were consumed by the divorce debate because, when personal histories were temporarily caught in this narrative loop, at least such stories, "turning back on [themselves,]" would create their own feedback.[49] We might see *Paradise Lost* as a vast holding ground for such extraneous cultural materials or Renaissance fallout uneasily accommodated by providential schemes. Like Eve, such a construct proves that culture is working, since through it the past is continually displaced.[50] Moreover, history can prevent catastrophic confusion about its sources and narratives, like that which rocked Europe in the wake of Sabbatai's apostasy, precisely by shifting epistemological focus onto these kinds of mistakes. Even Sabbatai's followers ultimately decide that the Messiah must go unrecognized.[51]

"[T]he more abject the failure," Lacan explains, "the better the subject remembers it."[52] Milton's history in *Paradise Lost* fastens on Eve as hermeneutical catastrophe and in this way is able, repeatedly, to let her go. In contrast, Othello learns about anachronism too late, turning Turk at the end of the play after murdering Desdemona and tragically reinventing himself as a threat long-since forgotten about (5.2.253–57). Possibly learning from Othello's mistake, Milton, in his divorce tracts, more successfully accommodates personal failure and rescues apocryphal meanings. Inside them are contained the ruins of an abandoned marriage, shortly recovered when his wife returns home, but finally sanctified more than twenty years later in *Paradise Lost*.

It is not only *Paradise Lost* that Milton retrieves. Cleanth Brooks argues that Milton's Eve "anticipate[s] Freud's observations on the comparative difficulty the female has in the transition to adult heterosexuality."[53] In *Moses and Monotheism*, Freud slightly adjusts those observations, however. In describing the latency period, Freud comments that "man is derived from a species of animal that was sexually mature at five years, and [this] arouses the suspicion that the postponement, and the beginning twice over, of sexual life has much to do with the transition to humanity."[54] If history as a catalog of failures and relics eases this transition, perhaps Eve's interrupted genealogy—much like Mary Powell's

"sweet reluctant amorous delay" (*Paradise Lost* 4.311)—provides
Milton with a necessary, even "charitable" lag.

Notes

Ernest B. Gilman, Jeanne Roberts, Barbara Fisher, and Philip Beitchman have
helped me clarify my ideas. I am also grateful to Charles Durham and Kristin
Pruitt, organizers of the 1995 Conference on John Milton at Middle Tennessee
State University. Some early hypotheses were shared at the New York University
Seminar on the Renaissance and at a Folger Shakespeare Library Evening
Colloquium.

1. John Milton, *The Doctrine and Discipline of Divorce*, in *Complete Prose
Works of John Milton*, 8 vols., ed. Don M. Wolfe et al. (New Haven: Yale University Press, 1953–82), 2:326. All references to Milton's divorce tracts are to this
edition and are cited parenthetically in the text.

2. Isabel Gamble MacCaffrey, *"Paradise Lost" as "Myth"* (Cambridge: Harvard University Press, 1959), 2.

3. Ibid., 4.

4. See Mark A. Wollaeger, "Apocryphal Narration: Milton, Raphael, and the
Book of Tobit," *Milton Studies* 21 (1985): 148.

5. William Shakespeare, *Othello*, ed. M. R. Ridley (New York: Routledge,
1993). All references to *Othello* are to this edition and are cited parenthetically
in the text.

6. While these connections have not been previously noted, a number of critics have linked the two works in other ways. James Grantham Turner (*One Flesh:
Paradisal Marriage and Sexual Relations in the Age of Milton* [Oxford:
Clarendon, 1993], 288) suggests the following analogy between *Othello* and *Paradise Lost*: "[Like Othello and Desdemona] Adam and Eve are at the same time
young lovers, tragically snatched away after a few nights of love, and a mature
couple." Stanley Cavell (*Pursuits of Happiness: The Hollywood Comedy of Re-
marriage* [Cambridge: Harvard University Press, 1981]) brings together Shake-
spearean romances and Hollywood talkies to provide a model of conversation in
Hollywood films of the 1930s and 1940s and to explain the relative success of
second marriages in these films. Milton's divorce tracts and Freud find their way
into Cavell's extremely rich discussion. The allusions may be more extensive
than even Cavell implies, however. He points out that in *The Philadelphia Story*,
Tracy Lord (Katherine Hepburn) is told by her father that she "lacks an understanding heart" (137); in *The Doctrine and Discipline of Divorce* (2:12), Milton
evokes Solomon's "understanding heart" (1 Kings 3.12). See Merritt Hughes's
notes in *John Milton: Complete Poems and Major Prose* (New York: Odyssey,
1957), 703 n. 44.

7. Even at the outset, both brides are prized for a modesty that almost renders
them unfit for marriage. Absorbed by her image in the pool, Eve is initially reluctant to yield to Adam's more solid image. Similarly, Desdemona is "So still and
quiet, that her motion / Blush'd at her self," and upon learning of the nuptials,
Brabantio is skeptical that his daughter, "Against all rules of nature," could "fall
in love with what she fear'd to look on" (1.3.95–98).

8. Wollaeger, "Apocryphal Narration," 137, 142.

9. Brianus Waltonus, *Biblio Sacra Polyglotta* (London, 1657). Denis Saurat
(*Milton: Man and Thinker* [1925; reprint, New York: Haskell House, 1970], 252)

claims that Milton knew Walton personally and had the polyglot Bible at his disposal.

10. Focusing on Renaissance New Testament scholarship that was written in Latin, Debora K. Shuger does not examine polyglot bibles at length, but she does suggest seeing their columns of text as "stratified divisions" (*The Renaissance Bible: Scholarship, Sacrifice, and Subjectivity* [Berkeley: University of California Press, 1994], 23).

11. Gerald L. Bruns, *Hermeneutics Ancient and Modern* (New Haven: Yale University Press, 1992), 140.

12. Ibid., 149.

13. Jason Rosenblatt, *Torah and Law in "Paradise Lost"* (Princeton: Princeton University Press, 1994), 98.

14. Rosenblatt claims that Milton and Selden had met by 1643 or 1644 (*Torah*, 87). See also Eivion Owen, "Milton and Selden on Divorce," *Studies in Philology* 43 (1946): 233–57.

15. A similar set of questions is posed by contemporary rabbinical scholars like Daniel Boyarin, who seek to redress Pauline claims about how the "spirit" of the Gospels replaces the "dead letter" of the Torah. Instead, Boyarin argues, a Christian confusion over the meaning of history is at work in such claims. See "The Subversion of the Jews: Moses's Veil and the Hermeneutics of Supersession," *Diacritics* 23 (summer 1993): 16–35.

16. John Milton, *Paradise Lost*, in *John Milton: Complete Poems and Major Prose*, ed. Merritt Y. Hughes (New York: Odyssey, 1957). All references to *Paradise Lost* are to this edition and are cited parenthetically in the text.

17. See Stephen Fallon, "The Metaphysics of Milton's Divorce Tracts," in *Politics, Poetics, and Hermeneutics in Milton's Prose*, ed. David Loewenstein and James Grantham Turner (New York: Cambridge University Press, 1992), 87; and Mary Nyquist, "The Genesis of Gendered Subjectivity in the Divorce Tracts and in *Paradise Lost*," in *Re-membering Milton: Essays on the Texts and Tradition*, ed. Mary Nyquist and Margaret W. Ferguson (New York: Methuen, 1988), 99–127.

18. See Annabel Patterson, "No Mere Amatorious Novel?" in *Politics*, ed. Loewenstein and Turner, 85–101.

19. James Grantham Turner, "The Intelligible Flame," in *John Milton*, ed. Annabel Patterson (New York: Longman, 1992), 75. John Halkett (*Milton and the Idea of Matrimony: A Study of the Divorce Tracts and "Paradise Lost"* [New Haven: Yale University Press, 1970], 93) pursues a similar reading, commenting that in the divorce tracts Milton descends the Platonic ladder since his depiction of unhappy marriages repeatedly shows men converted into beasts. See also Ernest Sirluck's introduction to the divorce tracts in *Complete Prose Works*, 2:137–58.

20. Nyquist explores this issue in detail, explicitly raising the question: "Why does Milton have Eve tell her story of her earliest experiences first, in Book 4? Why, if Adam was formed first, does Adam tell *his* story to Raphael *last*, in Book 8?" ("The Genesis," 115). She argues that the "narrative distribution" of their experiences is "ideologically motivated" and claims that following the natural order would have made Eve seem like a necessary supplement (115, 119).

21. The term "present object" was also applied to Hamlet's father's ghost (1.1.161). See William Shakespeare, *Hamlet*, ed. Harold Jenkins (London: Routledge, 1993).

In the cabala, Lilith was Adam's first wife whom God introduced when Adam was seen coupling with animals. But Lilith quickly abandons Adam after they fight over lovemaking positions. Obliquely mentioned only once in the Torah (Isa.

34.14), Lilith is described by Harold Bloom as a "column left alone of a temple once complete" (*Figures of Capable Imagination* [New York: Seabury, 1976], 265). According to cabalistic legend, Lilith is a hag or succubus (etymologically, one who lies under) who nightly haunts Paradise seducing the sons of men. The etymology also suggests a "screech owl" or "lamia" (Vulgate). Interestingly, in Jewish tradition she is exorcised using formal divorce imagery.

There are oblique references to Lilith in *Paradise Lost,* too. She might be one of the "millions" of creatures Adam describes to Eve who nightly walk the Earth (4.677–78). Eve herself may allude to Lilith in acknowledging her own limitations:

> I chiefly who enjoy
> So far the happier Lot, enjoying thee
> Preeminent by so much odds, while thou
> Like consort to thyself canst nowhere find.

> (4.445–49)

Milton would also have recognized the Lilith figure who haunts Spenser's *Epithalamion* as the "shriech Oule" (*The Yale Edition of the Shorter Poems of Edmund Spenser,* ed. William Oram et al. [New Haven: Yale University Press, 1989], 345) who troubles the newly married couple's evening consummation. Connections between Spenser's *Epithalamion* and Keats's *Lamia* are explored by Elizabeth Mazzola, "Marrying Medusa: Spenser's *Epithalamion* and Renaissance Reconstructions of Female Privacy," *Genre* 25 (1992): 193–210.

22. See John Cosin, *A Scholastical History of the Canon of the Holy Scripture of the Certain and Indubitate Books thereof as they are Received in the Church of England* (London, 1657); and William Whitaker, *A Disputation on Holy Scripture, against the Papists, especially Bellarmine and Stapleton* (1558), translated and edited for the Parker Society, vol. 45 (London, 1849).

23. Martin Luther, as cited in S. L. Greenslade, *The Cambridge History of the Bible: The West from the Reformation to the Present Day* (New York: Cambridge University Press, 1963), 6–7.

24. Frank Kermode, "The Canon," in *The Literary Guide to the Bible,* ed. Robert Alter and Frank Kermode (New York: Cambridge University Press, 1987), 601.

25. Virginia R. Mollenkott, "The Pervasive Influence of the Apocrypha in Milton's Thought and Art," in *Milton and the Art of Sacred Song,* ed. J. Max Patrick and Roger H. Sundell (Madison: University of Wisconsin Press, 1979), 23–43. Two of the most important early readings of Milton's Hebraism were proposed by H. F. Fletcher in *Milton's Semitic Studies, and Some Manifestations of Them in His Poetry* (Chicago: University of Chicago Press, 1926), and *Milton's Rabbinical Readings* (Urbana: University of Illinois Press, 1930). Fletcher has his critics, however; that Milton's rabbinical Hebrew was quite poor is suggested by Samuel S. Stollman in "Milton's Rabbinical Readings and Fletcher," *Milton Studies* 4 (1972): 195–215.

26. Wollaeger, "Apocryphal Narration," 151.

27. Wollaeger notes: "In the Cambridge manuscript none of the four drafts of a projected tragedy on the theme of *Paradise Lost* refers to Raphael. The first draft includes Michael; neither the second nor the third names any unfallen angel; and in the fourth it is Gabriel who descends to the earth to describe Paradise" ("Apocryphal Narration," 155 n. 23).

28. Rosenblatt, *Torah,* 11. Golda Werman focuses on rabbinical commentaries known as Midrash—rather than on the Apocrypha—as Milton's crucial source.

In *Milton and Midrash* (Washington, D.C.: Catholic University Press, 1995), 1, she reads Milton himself as a Midrashist who offers a "poetic commentary." Werman expertly treats the confusion surrounding Milton's numerous Hebrew sources, including rabbinical commentaries, Selden's translations, and cabalistic texts; she also forcefully argues that Milton had no firsthand knowledge of Jewish Midrashist materials and worked instead from a 1644 Latin translation of a late Palestinian Midrash.

29. Turner, *One Flesh*, 193–94.

30. Fallon, "The Metaphysics," 69–70.

31. Ibid., 71.

32. Joseph Wittreich ("'Inspir'd with Contradiction': Mapping Gender Discourses in *Paradise Lost*," in *Literary Milton: Text, Pretext, Context*, ed. Diana Treviño Benet and Michael Lieb [Pittsburgh: Duquesne University Press, 1994], 135) makes a similar point, explaining that "*Paradise Lost* . . . emerges from a controversy over privilege and priority in interpretation (Genesis 1 versus Genesis 2, the Old versus the New Testament, the Hebrew versus the Christian Bible) and issues its own statement concerning that debate." Moreover, Wittreich claims, the poem successfully accommodates "a variety of authoritative traditions (Hebrew and Christian) and different interpretive voices (patristic as well as rabbinical, Catholic as well as Protestant, humanist as well as Puritan)," 156.

33. Patterson, "Amatorious Novel," 93.

34. There may be unintended irony here, for the "rubbish" to which Milton alludes is the rubble of the Temple of Jerusalem, undergoing repair when the Torah is discovered buried inside. See Bruns's account of the story (*Hermeneutics*, 67).

35. In a narrative designed to catalog firsts and outline providential history, Milton must alter chronology in order to represent Eve: history has to be unwritten because Eve really has no place in it. See Nyquist's account of the tensions between the two versions of Genesis in "The Genesis."

36. And after the Fall, Adam chastises Eve:

> Would thou hadst heark'n'd to my words, and stay'd
> With me, as I besought thee, when that strange
> Desire of wand'ring this unhappy Morn,
> I know not whence possess'd thee; we had then
> Remain'd still happy, not as now, despoil'd
> Of all our good, sham'd, naked, miserable.
>
> (9.1134–39)

In other words, simply leaving Adam was a "divorcive act."

37. Wittreich, "'Inspir'd,'" 155–56. I would argue that Eve is both revised and unwritten, because at times she is removed from a sacred context altogether.

38. Olga Lucia Valbuena supplies one answer, suggesting that for Milton divorce was a more potent political metaphor than marriage ("Milton's 'Divorcive' Interpretation and the Gendered Reader," *Milton Studies* 27 [1991]: 118). Halkett likewise notes that divorce in *Paradise Lost* is a creative act (*Milton and the Idea of Matrimony*, 2). And Patterson ("Amatorious Novel," 89) suggests that in *The Doctrine and Discipline of Divorce* Milton "introduces the 'scanning of error' as a narrative principle."

39. David Loewenstein describes iconoclasm as "an essential means of effecting historical change," in *Milton and the Drama of History: Historical Vision,*

Iconoclasm, and the Literary Imagination (Ithaca: Cornell University Press, 1990), 5.

40. Some of the implications (and problems) of Fletcher's book-length argument in *Milton's Rabbinical Readings* are cited by Rosenblatt, *Torah*, 84, 97.

41. Kenneth Gross, *Spenserian Poetics: Idolatry, Iconoclasm, and Magic* (Ithaca: Cornell University Press, 1986), 50.

42. See Moshe Idel, *Golem: Jewish Magical and Mystical Traditions on the Artificial Anthropoid* (New York: State University of New York Press, 1990); and Gershom Scholem, *The Messianic Idea in Judaism and Other Essays* (New York: Schocken, 1971).

43. This disaster is recounted by Gershom Scholem, *Sabbatai Sevi: The Mystical Messiah 1626–1676* (Princeton: Princeton University Press, 1973); also of relevance are Philip Beitchman, "Milton and Cabala, Reconsidered" (unpublished essay), and Elizabeth Mazzola, "Apocryphal Texts and Epic Amnesia: The Ends of History in Spenser's *Faerie Queene*," *Soundings* 78 (spring 1995): 131–42.

44. R. W. Southern, *Western Views of Islam in the Middle Ages* (Cambridge: Harvard University Press, 1962), 6.

45. Ibid., 12.

46. See Jacqueline Kaye, "Islamic Imperialism and the Creation of Some Ideas of 'Europe,'" in *Europe and its Others: Proceedings of the Essex Conference on the Sociology of Literature, July 1984,* ed. Francis Barker et al. (Colchester, England, 1985), 66.

47. Sigmund Freud, *Moses and Monotheism*, trans. Katherine Jones (1939; reprint, New York: Vintage Books, 1967), 52. Yosef Hayim Yerushalmi, *Freud's Moses: Judaism Terminable and Interminable* (New Haven: Yale University Press, 1991), 34, carries this reading a step further:

> As a historical essay, *Moses and Monotheism* offers a singular version of history as essentially a story of remembering and forgetting. To be sure, this is analogous to Freud's conception of the life history of the individual. What has been overlooked is how strangely analogous it is also to the biblical conception of history, where the continual oscillation of memory and forgetting is a major theme through all the narratives of historical events.

48. Freud, *Moses and Monotheism*, 131–32.

49. See Jacques Lacan, "The Circuit," in *The Seminar of Jacques Lacan. Book II*, ed. Jacques-Alain Miller, trans. Sylvana Tomaselli (New York: Norton, 1991), 88.

50. The importance of conversation in Miltonic marriage is equalled by the emphasis Freudian analysis places upon it. David Bakan writes, for example, that the psychoanalyst "must receive the training (orally) in the training analysis. As the modern practicing psychoanalyst is quick to tell anyone, psychoanalysis is not to be learned from books" (*Sigmund Freud and the Jewish Mystical Tradition* [Princeton: D. Van Nostrand Company, 1958], 35–36).

51. Bakan (*Sigmund Freud*, viii, 25, 132) sees Sabbatai's revolutionary movement (and its repression) as paradigmatic for Freud. Bakan (247) also makes an interesting case for linking Freud's patient, Dora—as a collection of hermeneutical possibilities and errors—with "Torah."

52. Lacan, "The Circuit," 85–86.

53. Cleanth Brooks, cited in Nyquist, "The Genesis," 122.

54. Freud, *Moses and Monotheism*, 94. Patterson ("Amatorious Novel," 98) makes a similar point: "If writing is, as some think, the art of *not* saying what one means, the most profound avoidance, some of Milton's finest writing occurs in the effort to conceal from his readers and probably from himself the precise effect on his psyche of the long-delayed induction into heterosexual experience."

"Eves Apologie": Agrippa, Lanyer, and Milton

KARI BOYD McBRIDE and JOHN C. ULREICH

Our understandings of early modern England have been enriched by attention to "nonliterary" writings of the period that had previously gone unnoticed or that had, at best, been seen as tangential to literary studies. Particularly enlightening has been the relatively recent interest in the well-recorded debate on the woman question in studies and anthologies published over the past few decades.[1] The resources unearthed by such studies have enlarged and complicated our readings of early modern writers, particularly, one might argue, major authors like John Milton, who have often been cast as monumental figures transcending their eras, and also, paradoxically, such marginalized authors as Aemilia Lanyer, who have been rediscovered so recently as to seem sometimes unconnected to literary, material, or political histories. Because Lanyer and Milton in particular share an interest in theorizing womankind through biblically based poetic narrative rather than through polemic and because the issues the two find crucial to such theory seem uncannily similar, we thought it might prove fruitful to read Lanyer and Milton in relationship to each other and to the larger debate about women. Here we have limited our study to the history of one biblical text central to the *querelle des femmes* as it was articulated in sixteenth- and seventeenth-century England. The resulting contextualization and intertextualization of Lanyer's and Milton's arguments, we believe, illuminate the strategies and perspectives of each author in ways that suggest new readings of their work and of their place in literary history.

Of course, the terms of the *querelle*, its proof texts and exempla, were determined long before either Lanyer or Milton entered the debate. And while certain scriptural sites were commonly evoked to support arguments for women's equality or authority (the faithfulness of Judith, the obedience of the Virgin Mary, Mary Magdalene's witness to the Resurrection), the central texts that could not

100

be ignored were ones that suggested women's inferiority or even inherent sinfulness. In that long litany of misogyny, the biblical text most frequently cited to authorize the silencing and subjection of women was from the first Epistle to Timothy: "Let the woman learn in silence with all subjection. But I suffer not a woman to teach, nor to usurp authority over the man, but to be in silence" (2.11–12).[2] The Paulinist writer[3] goes on to justify this commandment by reference to Gen. 2–3: "For Adam was first formed, then Eve. And Adam was not deceived, but the woman being deceived was in the transgression" (1 Tim. 2.13–14). The New International Version crystallizes the problematic identification of sin with deception: "Adam was not the one deceived: it was the woman who was deceived and became a sinner."[4] In other words, it is the condition of being deceived that defines sin.

The logic of the biblical assertion is singularly unimpressive, even by the rather relaxed standards of misogynist discourse; not even Augustine can make it work:

> [Satan] first tried his deceit upon the woman . . . the weaker part of that human alliance . . . not supposing that the man would . . . be deceived [decipi], but that he might yield to the error [errori] of the woman. . . . We cannot believe that Adam was deceived [seductum] . . . and therefore transgressed [transgrediendam] God's law, but that he by the drawings of kindred yielded to the woman, the husband to the wife. . . . For not without significance did the apostle say, "And Adam was not deceived [seductus], but the woman was deceived [seducta]."[5]

Augustine attempts to mitigate the absurdity of Adam's not being "in the transgression" by separating the act of sin from the condition of being deceived: "The apostle does not say, 'He did not sin,' but 'He was not deceived.'" But the essential link between the woman's weakness and humankind's sin remains nonetheless firmly rooted in Eve's being deceived (seducta).

The crucial term derives from Gen. 3.13: "The Serpent beguiled me, and I did eat." The Hebrew verb, נשא (nasha), has meanings ranging from "beguile" through "seduce" and "deceive" to "greatly deceive." The Vulgate translates the word as decepit but uses forms of seducere in the Pauline texts. So, for instance, the Vulgate 1 Tim. 2.14 reads, "et Adam non est seductus; mulier autem seducta in praevaricatione fuit." The Septuagint has ἠπατήσ in Genesis, and the Greek New Testament has forms of απατάω or εξαπατάω; the prefix, εκ, normally carries a sense of thoroughness or completeness. Thus an exact translation of the 1 Timothy passage might be: "Adam was not deceived, but the woman, being utterly deceived, was in the transgression."[6]

It should be noted that the relative meanings of *decipere* and *seducere*, as well as their English equivalents, "deceive" and "seduce," do not carry the same connotations that they do in modern English. *Decipere* has associations with hunting (to seize an animal while running) and so means to catch, ensnare, entrap, beguile, elude, deceive, or even cheat. *Seducere* has less violent associations, but not necessarily sexual connotations, and means to lead aside or apart, to lead away, or to carry off.[7] When the words come into English, "deceive" retains the sense of entrapment: to catch by guile, to overcome by trickery, to mislead, or to beguile or betray into mischief or sin. "Seduce" still has a primarily nonsexual connotation in early modern usage, while its primary meaning (of which sexual seduction is a species) is "to persuade (a vassal, servant, soldier, etc.) to desert his allegiance or service."[8] Thus Eve's deception implies Satan's trickery, while her seduction implies a sin of disloyalty, suggesting that she is traitor more than adulteress. Both terms, however, tended to be used interchangeably in Latin and English translations of the original text; both could express the Greek text's greater condemnation of Eve's sin in the service of the argument for women's subjection to men, particularly in marriage.

The Augustinian reading of this passage remained the standard interpretation through the Reformation, as the glosses to the 1 Timothy text in the 1560 Geneva Bible make clear: "The woman was first deceived, & so became the instrument of Satan to deceive the man: and thogh therefore God punisheth them with subiection and paine in their trauel, yet if they be faithful and godlie in their vocation they [s]hal be saued."[9] The glosses in the 1602 edition emphasize the gender hierarchy that such a history of sin implies, holding that "it is not lawfull for women to teach in the Congregation, because by this meanes, they should be placed aboue men, for they should be their master: which is against Gods ordinance," and stating that "the woman is subject to man . . . because . . . God enjoyned the woman this punishment, for that man was deceiued by her."[10]

It is not surprising to discover John Milton adding himself to the roll of those who rely on this text to enforce—as it were, in passing—the silencing of women. According to his *Christian Doctrine,* and in keeping with apostolic tradition, "each believer in turn should be authorized to speak . . . according to his gifts. . . . Women, however, are enjoined to keep silence in the church."[11]

And Milton is even more emphatic about Eve's greater guilt when he retranslates verse 14 in the *Christian Doctrine:* "Adam was not deceived, but the woman, having been deceived, was the cause of the transgression."[12] Again, it is perhaps not surprising that Aemilia Lanyer would refer to the same passage in the "Salve Deus Rex Judaeorum," given the fixed nature of the *querelle* and its concomitant proof texts by the early seventeenth century. Lanyer, however, reverses the logic of the biblical text, altering the value of deception in the attribution of sin so that, in "Eves Apologie," the material of the 1 Timothy text serves to extenuate Eve's trespass. Here deception excuses rather than incriminates: Eve in "undiscerning Ignorance" (769) "was deceived" (773). Adam, on the other hand, "can not be excusde" (777) because "he knew" (788) what he was doing: "Her fault though great, yet hee was most too blame" (778).[13] Remarkably, Milton deploys the same subversive strategy in *Paradise Lost.* When Adam falls "Against his better knowledge, not deceav'd" (9.998), he becomes *more* culpable than Eve precisely because he is not seduced or deceived.[14] Milton's Adam, like Lanyer's, is thus "Render[ed] . . . inexcusable" (The Argument, book 5), for, as Philip Gallagher has observed, "the seriousness of a sin is directly proportional to the knowledge with which it is willfully committed."[15]

Ordinarily, an intertextual conjunction of this kind establishes its own context, the originary word—whether "deceived" or "seduced"—engendering, in the work of Lanyer and Milton, a new species of meaning. But in this case, the lineage of authorship is more complex: the context for Lanyer's and Milton's analyses is not merely the 1 Timothy use of "deceived" but also the myriad invocations and interpretations of both the 1 Timothy passage and Gen. 2–3 in the misogynist and protofeminist polemic of the sixteenth and seventeenth centuries. As Susanne Woods (citing Linda Woodbridge) has suggested, "Eve's lesser knowledge and Adam's knowing acceptance of disobedience were key points for those Renaissance writers who sought to defend women against the common charge that they were responsible for the fall of humankind."[16] Thus both Lanyer and Milton read the 1 Timothy text in its biblical context—in Milton's case, in several languages—and, again, through the lens of contemporary discussion of the passage, all within the larger debate on the woman question.

Thus Woods's summary of the situation only begins to hint at the complexity of the argumentative lineage of this text in the *querelle des femmes.* While Woodbridge's discussion of Renaissance feminist tracts does not deal with Lanyer's poem, she does make it clear that, for most participants in the debate, the primary locus for the argument that Eve was less culpable than Adam was not the text of 1 Timothy itself but rather the way that text was used in Henricus Cornelius Agrippa's *De nobilitate et praecellentia foeminei sexus* and its numerous English translations.[17] James Grantham Turner shows Lanyer's extensive reliance on Agrippa's argument generally, and in particular on "the idea of the lesser culpability of Eve."[18]

Turner's argument also implicitly links Lanyer's feminist apologetic with Milton's representation of paradisal marriage, but without any attempt to draw an explicit connection. Indeed, according to the meager evidence available, Milton is not known to have read Lanyer or the feminist tracts. But such a connection can be suggested, we believe, by a close examination of Agrippa and several of his English translators. Although the evidence is (as yet) far from conclusive, a close comparison of the "Salve Deus" with translations that preceded and followed it establishes at least the possibility that Lanyer's revision of Agrippa's argument influenced subsequent translations and may, therefore, also have influenced— even prompted, in part—Milton's argument regarding Eve's culpability.

In Agrippa's version of 1 Timothy, Eve does not exactly sin in eating the forbidden fruit but rather errs in opening the door to Adam's sin: "Moreover, God did not rebuke the woman because she ate, but because she gave occasion of evil to the man, and did so unwittingly [*imprudens*], because she was tempted to it by the devil. Accordingly, the man sinned out of certain knowledge [*ex certa scientia*]; the woman erred unknowingly [*ignorans*], and [was] deceived."[19] This argument appears to be a parodic inversion of Augustine's: there Eve's being deceived evinces her sin; here, it excuses her. While Augustine shows Eve as weak, and thus the preferred target of the serpent's deceit, Agrippa elides that point in emphasizing Adam's sinfulness.

The earliest English translation of Agrippa, David Clapam's 1542 *Of the Nobilitie of Women*, follows Agrippa very closely in his revision of both the biblical and Augustinian texts, but deletes reference to "knowledge" (*scientia*) altogether, substituting a verbal locution ("knew well") for the noun. Clapam also reverses the final clauses, making Eve's "being deceyued" dependent upon her ignorance. These small changes have the effect of further diminishing Eve's culpability: "Furthermore, God rebuked not the woman, for that she had eaten, but because she gaue occasion of yvelle vnto the man, and that dyd she unwarely, intyced thereto by the dyuell. The man knew well he dyd amisse: but the woman being deceyued, erred ignorantly."[20]

Both Agrippa's and Clapam's revision of the argument of 1 Timothy may also imply the possibility of an Eve who is different from—and perhaps even superior to—Adam, a point significant (in differing ways) to Lanyer's and Milton's portrayals of Eve as well as to many of the voices in the wider debate about women. So, for instance, Jane Anger (1589) argues that man was "formed *In principio* of drosse and filthy clay" while woman was made "of mans fleshe, that she might bee purer than he"; thus women "are more excellent then men."[21]

This playful Agrippan trope is seriously deployed by two of Lanyer's contemporaries. Ester Sowernam (1617) says, "Adam was not so absolutely perfect but that in the sight of God he wanted an Helper. Whereupon God created the woman, his last work, as to supply and make absolute that imperfect building which was unperfected in man."[22] Constantia Munda (1617) calls woman "the second edition of the Epitome of the whole world, the second Tome of that goodly volume compiled by the great God of heaven and earth."[23] (Second editions, one presumes, correct the errors of first editions.) All these arguments allow for the possibility that woman formed a distinct species unto herself. Both Lanyer and Milton respond to these argumentative possibilities.

Lanyer's defense of Eve rehearses and elaborates the Agrippan arguments.[24] But what appear as excuses for Eve's behavior in Agrippa become positive attributes in the "Salve Deus." So Eve's "undiscerning Ignorance" is a kind of purity that "perceav'd / No guile, or craft" (769–70):

> For had she knowne, of what we were bereav'd
> To [the serpent's] request she had not condiscended.
> But she (poore soule) by cunning was deceav'd,
> No hurt therein her harmelesse Heart intended.
>
> (771–74)

Here Eve's being "deceav'd" is not her sin, but a sin against her goodness. Further, her lesser sin in offering the fruit to Adam is elided by reference to his greater sin:

> But surely Adam can not be excusde,
> Her fault though great, yet hee was most too blame;
> What Weaknesse offerd, Strength might have refusde,
> Being Lord of all, the greater was his shame.
>
> (777–80)

Thus Adam's not having been deceived makes him the greater sinner, and Eve's sin "appear[s]" proportionately "much lesse" (762). It is therefore an injustice that women, in the "Salve Deus" personified as Patience in contrast to Adam in his "[in]discretion," have borne the greater blame:

> And then to lay the fault on Patience backe,
> That we (poore women) must endure it all;
> We know right well he did discretion lacke,
> Beeing not perswaded thereunto at all.
>
> (793–96)

Perhaps most striking is the way that "knowledge," though part of Adam's greater sinfulness here as in Agrippa, is simultaneously transferred to Eve as a sign of her superiority to Adam:

> If Eve did erre, it was for knowledge sake,
> The fruit beeing faire perswaded him to fall:
> No subtill Serpents falshood did betray him.
>
> (797–99)

Lanyer's reworking of this proof text, which turns Agrippa's excusing of Eve into the means for exalting her above Adam, may have influenced later translators of Agrippa. Hugh Crompton's verse translation of 1652, *The Glory of Women*, may echo Lanyer's comparison of Eve's sin with Adam's greater evil:

> Not that the crime by woman was began,
> But as she gave occasion to the man:
> She first was snared in the Devils wile,
> And thus deceiv'd strove others to beguile:
> Poor Adam to his knowledge did transgress,
> So did not Eve, which makes her sin the less.[25]

At the same time, Crompton has transferred the epithet "poor" to Adam, excusing him through emotional, if not logical, appeal. And, unlike Lanyer (though perhaps in response to her argument), Crompton here stresses Adam's knowledge, not Eve's desire for the same.[26]

Henry Care's translation of 1670, *Female Pre-eminence*, restores Lanyer's "poor soule" to Eve: "When Woman sin'd, she did it, poor Soul, unwitingly, being deluded by the insinuating Serpent: so that it appears the Man sinned against perfect knowledge, and the positive Command of his Maker: the Woman out of ignorance, seduced by the crafty wiles of the *Tempter*."[27] Likewise, Care's "positive Command" may echo the "strait command" that Lanyer's Adam received "from Gods mouth."

These similarities are tantalizing, but they do not allow us finally to locate Lanyer in this lineage of argument. While it is almost certain that she knew Agrippa's contribution to the *querelle*, we cannot be sure that other disputants knew of her work. For very different reasons, it is difficult to know how and where to place Milton in this debate. First, his affinities are generally Augustinian rather than Agrippan. So, for example, Milton endorses the subjugation of women, even in contexts (such as the divorce tracts) where he argues for marriage as a mutual relation.[28] And there is no evidence that he knew of either Agrippa or Lanyer. However, certain features of Milton's argument in *Paradise Lost* suggest that he may be answering contentions about the nature of woman that were current in the larger debates of the *querelle*. More significantly for our purpose, he seems to be responding to those very argumentative points about the relative culpability of Adam and Eve that are unique to Lanyer, showing him to be finally closer to Lanyer than to Agrippa and others.

Like Lanyer, Milton does not argue that Eve differs fundamentally or essentially from Adam. He does, however, occasionally seem to be responding to other voices in the *querelle* that did argue for Eve's essential superiority, especially in the scene where Adam receives instruction from the angel. Adam suggests Eve's superiority—she seems "in her self compleat" (8.548), "Seems wisest, vertuousest, discreetest, best" (550)—and repeats the very argument used by some defenders of women:

> Authority and Reason on her wait,
> As one intended first, not after made
> Occasionally; and to consummate all. . . .
>
> (8.554–56)

Raphael responds by rebuking Adam, reaffirming Eve's subjection to the more reasonable Adam. This theme is taken up again when Eve, having tasted the fruit, considers the possibility of becoming "more equal, and perhaps, / A thing not undesirable, sometime / Superior" (9.823–25). And when Adam calls Eve "last and best / Of all Gods works" (9.896–97) in the speech wherein he decides to eat the fruit, his fatal misjudgment of her nature precipitates his sinful action. Milton was clearly familiar with the Agrippan argument of the *querelle* on this point and determined to show its error.

At the same time, Milton accepts, in varying degrees, three of the alterations of or additions to Agrippa common among pro-women apologists, including Lanyer. So Milton argues for Eve's *relative* weakness, a quality that extenuates but does not exculpate her sin. Milton also argues that Eve's love for Adam played a part in her sharing the fruit with him. Here, especially, one is tempted to think that Milton is answering Lanyer's ultimately implausible contention that Eve's "fault was only too much love" ("Salve Deus" 801). In his rendering of the scene in book 9, Eve's "love" is predominantly self-love, and her decision to share the fruit mostly ensures that Adam will never be "wedded to another Eve" (828). Finally, Milton, like Lanyer, shows that Eve trespassed for love of knowledge, though Eve's rationalization of her decision in Milton (745–779), again, complicates an issue that is more straightforward in Lanyer.

But the most striking affinity between the two accounts is in their correction of the mischievous Agrippan distinction between Eve's "error" and Adam's "sin." That is, Agrippa, Lanyer, and Milton all extenuate Eve's trespass by distinguishing between Eve's deceivable ignorance and Adam's "better knowledge." Agrippa and his two earliest translators, Clapam and Barker, exculpate Eve by distinguishing her mere *error* from Adam's much graver *sin*. But later translators, that is, those who follow Lanyer (Crompton, Fleetwood, and Care), agree with Lanyer in rejecting this distinction, and so does Milton: in their arguments, Eve's guilt is less than Adam's, but both sin, so Eve remains culpable—and responsible. These confluences of argument suggest that Milton may be answering Lanyer's reading of 1 Timothy in particular and the Eden narrative in general. Whether or not such a direct link can ever be established, it is clear that both Lanyer's and Milton's representations of Eve participate in, and perhaps inflect, early modern discourse about women.

We would suggest, therefore, that acknowledgment of the similarity of their arguments invokes new kinds of readings for both authors' works. The possibility that Milton read Lanyer's "Salve Deus," a work whose distinctly Protestant and prophetic qualities would have appealed to him, suggests that her little book could very well have had an impact beyond what the extant records of the period indicate. In any case, Lanyer's "apologie in defence of Women" must continue to be read in the context of protofeminist polemic, to which she makes a significant, and radical, contribution. Further, Milton's Eve also requires to be read, even more extensively than heretofore (as by Gallagher, McColley,[29] Nyquist, and Turner) in the light of early modern treatises on the nature of women and the entire history of the *querelle des femmes*. While the apparent purpose of both authors may be to "justifie the wayes of God" (*Paradise Lost* 1.26) and while their chosen genres may not fit easily in the categories common to the *querelle*, their works develop some of its most interesting arguments and demand to be counted in that debate.

Notes

1. See especially Diane Bornstein, ed., *The Feminist Controversy of the Renaissance: Facsimile Reproductions* (Delmar, N.Y.: Scholar's Facsimiles and Reprints, 1980); Coryl Crandall, *Swetnam the Woman-Hater: The Controversy and the Play* (Lafayette, Ind.: Purdue University Press, 1969); Moira Ferguson, ed., *First Feminists: British Women Writers 1578–1799* (Old Westbury, N.Y.: Feminist Press, 1985); Katherine Usher Henderson and Barbara F. McManus, eds., *Half Humankind: Contexts and Texts of the Controversy About Women In England, 1540–1640* (Urbana: University of Illinois Press, 1985); Simon Shepherd, ed., *The Woman's Sharp Revenge: Five Women's Pamphlets from the Renaissance 1580–1640* (New York: St. Martin's, 1985); Betty Travitsky, ed., *The Paradise of Women: Writings By Englishwomen of the Renaissance* (Old Westbury, Conn.: Greenwood, 1981); and Linda Woodbridge, *Women and the English Renaissance: Literature and the Nature of Womankind* (Urbana: University of Illinois Press, 1985).

2. Unless otherwise noted, all biblical quotations are from the King James Version and are cited parenthetically in the text.

3. 1 Timothy, along with 2 Timothy and Titus, is one of the pseudo-Pauline "pastoral letters" thought to have been written in the first quarter of the second century.

4. *The NIV Study Bible: New International Version,* ed. Kenneth Barker (Grand Rapids: Zondervan, 1985).

5. Augustine, *The City of God,* trans. Marcus Dods (New York: Modern Library, 1950), 14.11.458–59. The Latin text (*De civitate dei: Patrologiae latinae cursus completus,* vol. 41, ed. J. P. Migne [Paris, 1864], 419) reads,

feminae, a parte scilicet inferiore illius humanae copulae . . . non existimans virum facile credulum nec errando posse decipi, sed dum alieno cedit errori. . . . Ita credendum est illum virum . . . ad Dei legem transgrediendam non tamquam verum loquenti credidisse seductum, sed sociali necessitudine paruisse. Non enim frustra dixit apostolus: *Et Adam non est seductus, mulier autem seducta est* (emphasis in the text).

6. In 2 Cor. 11.3, however, the King James Version translates ἐξηπάτησεν as "beguiled."

7. E. A. Andrews, ed., *A Latin Dictionary,* s.v. *decipio* and *seduco.*

8. *Oxford English Dictionary Online,* s.v. "deceive" and "seduce."

9. *Geneva Bible: Facsimile of the 1560 Edition,* ed. Lloyd E. Berry (Madison: University of Wisconsin Press, 1969).

10. The final gloss adds the comforting words that "their subiection hindereth not but that women may be saued as well as men, if they behaue themselves in

those burdens of mariage holily and modestly, with faith and charitie" (*The Geneva Bible: The Annotated New Testament,* 1602 edition, ed. Gerald T. Sheppard [New York: Pilgrim, 1989]).

11. "Of Church Discipline," *Christian Doctrine,* trans. Charles R. Sumner, in *The Works of John Milton,* 18 vols., ed. Frank Allen Patterson et al. (New York: Columbia University Press, 1931–38), 16:325, 327. Subsequent references to this edition are cited as Columbia Milton. Milton also quotes here (16:327) the even more familiar text from 1 Cor. 14.34 (which is cross-referenced to the 1 Timothy text in many Bibles, including the Geneva): "'let your women keep silence in the churches, for it is not permitted unto them to speak, but they are commanded to be under obedience, as saith the law (Gen. iii.16).'"

12. The Latin text in Columbia Milton reads: "Adamus non fuit seductus, sed mulier seducta causa transgressionis fuit."

According to *De Doctrina Christiana:* "De gubernatione speciali hominis ante lapsum: ubi etiam de sabbatho et coniugio" (Columbia Milton, 15:112); and again: "De lapsu primorum parentum et de peccato" (15.178). The translation is our own. Sumner (misleadingly) quotes the King James Version. John Carey's translation (*Complete Prose Works of John Milton,* 8 vols., ed. Don M. Wolfe et al. [New Haven: Yale University Press, 1953–82], 6:355, 382) is more accurate, but it does not reflect Milton's syntax, which reproduces the structure of the Greek while simultaneously glossing the problematic ξγπαραδασει

Unless otherwise indicated, all references to Milton's prose are to this edition and are cited parenthetically in the text.

13. Aemilia Lanyer, *The Poems of Aemilia Lanyer: "Salve Deus Rex Judaeorum,"* ed. Susanne Woods (Oxford: Oxford University Press, 1994). All references to Lanyer's poem are to this edition and are cited parenthetically in the text.

14. John Milton, *Paradise Lost,* in *The Complete Poetry of John Milton,* ed. John T. Shawcross, rev. ed. (New York: Doubleday, 1971). All references to *Paradise Lost* are to this edition and are cited parenthetically in the text.

15. Philip Gallagher, *Milton, the Bible, and Misogyny,* ed. Eugene R. Cunnar and Gail L. Mortimer (Columbia: University of Missouri Press, 1990), 101.

16. Susanne Woods, Introduction to *The Poems of Aemilia Lanyer,* xxxvi.

17. Agrippa's English translators were David Clapam (1542), William Barker or Bercher (1559), Edward Fleetwood (1652), Hugh Crompton (1652), and Henry Care (1670). James Grantham Turner (*One Flesh: Paradisal Marriage and Sexual Relations in the Age of Milton* [Oxford: Clarendon, 1987], 110 n. 26) inaccurately states that Clapam's translation was "reissued as *The Commendation of Matrimony* (1545)," but the 1545 volume is, in fact, a translation by Clapam of an entirely different work by Agrippa.

18. Turner, *One Flesh,* 111. He concludes that, for Agrippa, the arguments may have been an exercise in rhetorical game playing, but "For Lanier . . . the Agrippan revision" of traditional misogynist arguments "is a matter of serious and uncompromising concern" (113).

19. Neque praeterea increpavit Deus mulierem, quia comederat, sed quia mali occasionem dedisset viro atque id quidem imprudens, eo quod per diabolum tentaretur. Vir itaque ex certa scientia peccavit, mulier erravit ignorans, et decepta (Henricus Cornelius Agrippa, *De nobilitate et praecellentia foeminei sexus* [1532], ed. R. Antonioli [Geneva: Librairie Droz, 1990], 66). The English translation in the text is ours.

20. David Clapam, *A Treatise of the Nobilitie and Excellencie of Womankynde* (London: Thomas Bertholeti, 1542), sig. C5v–C6r.

21. Jane Anger, cited in *Half Humankind*, ed. Henderson and McManus, 180–81. See also *First Feminists*, ed. Ferguson, 65.

22. Ester Sowernam, cited in *Half Humankind*, ed. Henderson and McManus, 223–24.

23. Constantia Munda, cited in *Half Humankind*, ed. Henderson and McManus, 248.

24. It is impossible to know whether Lanyer read Latin well enough to have referred to the original Agrippan text. Her poems suggest strongly that she knew the works of classical and contemporary poets, and she may well have had some knowledge of Latin, though women were commonly restricted from studying the classical languages. The Latin title of her book, *pace* some critics' contentions, does not prove competence in the language but merely familiarity with common scriptural tags. In fact, the line *Salve deus rex judaeorum* does not appear in exactly that form in any Vulgate text. Lanyer's scriptural references are often exact quotations, taken either from the Geneva Bible or from biblical excerpts in the Book of Common Prayer.

25. Hugh Crompton, *The Glory of Women, or a Looking-Glasse for Ladies . . . Now Turned into Heroicall Verse* (London, Robert Ibbison, 1652), quoted in Gallagher, *Milton, the Bible*, 100.

26. A translation of the same year by Edward Fleetwood (*The Glory of Women or a Treatise Declaring the Excellency and Preheminence of Women above Men . . .* [London: Robert Ibbison, 1652]) makes neither of these gestures, providing instead a straightforward and very precise translation of Agrippa.

27. Henry Care, *Female Pre-eminence, or the Dignity and Excellency of that Sex, above the Male* (1670), in *The Feminist Controversy*, ed. Bornstein, 31.

28. On this point, we particularly like Mary Nyquist's study that reads Milton's supposed liberatory stance on women in the light of contemporary arguments about women and marriage, showing the range of possibilities open to Milton and arguing that he maintained a relatively conservative position on woman's nature ("The Genesis of Gendered Subjectivity in the Divorce Tracts and in *Paradise Lost*," in *Re-membering Milton: Essays on the Texts and Traditions*, ed. Mary Nyquist and Margaret W. Ferguson [New York: Methuen, 1988], 99–127). Also of relevance is Angela J. Balla's "Voluptuous Vessels and Fit Conversing Souls: 'The Indefinite Likenesse of Womanhood' in Milton's Divorce Tracts" (unpublished paper, University of Arizona, 1995), which examines Milton's oft-cited argument in *The Doctrine and Discipline of Divorce* for divorce by "mutuall consent" (2:242) in light of his more numerous and predominant claims that limit women's agency in marriage vis-à-vis men's.

29. Diane Kelsey McColley, *Milton's Eve* (Urbana: University of Illinois Press, 1983).

Differance and the *Deus Absconditus:* The Satanic Predicament in *Paradise Lost*

CLAUDE N. STULTING, JR.

During the past two hundred years or so, critics of *Paradise Lost* have often argued that Satan's punishment involves the imposition of constraints upon his freedom.[1] The common view suggests that, after his rebellion against God, Satan is cast into the vast confines of Hell, where he lies shackled, "Chained on the burning lake" (1.210).[2] Satan then directs his energy toward breaking out of his chains so that he might frustrate the will of God, "To do," as he says, "aught good never" (1.159). Satan's punishment consists of his containment in Hell, and it is only natural that he would endeavor to escape this imprisonment where God has bound him. Of course, Satan successfully escapes his exile in Hell, and he achieves much that he intends to do. But this in no way alters the essential character of his punishment as restraint. Indeed, Satan's heroic energy, his "eruption" beyond his prescribed boundaries, is fueled precisely by restraint.

So goes a widely held view of the nature of Satan's punishment.[3] Such a view, however, is inadequate to account for Satan's circumstance, for it fails to realize that God never intends to restrain Satan in the first place.[4] Indeed, containment is not a part of Satan's fate; rather, it is a radical *lack* of containment that constitutes his fallen condition. In what other terms, then, might we better understand the punishment that Satan suffers? I want to propose that Jacques Derrida's description of language as a field of *differance* and free play, which I discuss below, provides an illuminating and novel angle of vision through which we can more adequately comprehend Satan's predicament. In turn, Satan's condition can serve as a useful heuristic device to illuminate the theological ramifications of the Derridean project and cast that illumination back on Derrida himself.

I

One of Jacques Derrida's most fundamental and most frequently iterated claims is that there is no self-subsistent or independent meaning.[5] Such is the upshot of his critique of the metaphysics of presence (logocentrism), the "determination of being in general as *presence*."[6] In whatever guise presence may assume ("presence of the thing to the sight as *eidos*, presence as substance/essence/ existence, temporal presence as point of the now or of the moment, the self-presence of the cogito, consciousness, subjectivity, the co-presence of the other and the self, intersubjectivity as the inten-tional phenomenon of the ego"),[7] it amounts to the positing of an absolute truth or signified that serves as the external ground of a signifier or a signifying system of meaning. Logocentrism, ac-cording to Derrida, claims that there is a determinate truth that resides antecedently to a signifier, at the end of a series of signifi-ers, or in any way without the signifier, in such a way as to guaran-tee, certify, and limit the operation of signifiers and the meanings they convey. To this logocentric claim, which he sees as the ines-capable metaphysical outlook of the entire Western ontotheologi-cal tradition, Derrida responds with his deconstructive "claim" that there can be no such transcendent signifieds. Once a tran-scendent signified becomes a part of discourse, a part of linguistic signifiers, that signified necessarily comes to inhabit the very signi-fying system of which it presumes to be the external foundation. And it follows then that what has heretofore been understood as a transcendent signified assumes the character of any ordinary immanent signifier.

Derrida utilizes Ferdinand de Saussure's insight that signifiers bear no positive meaning in and of themselves; since the relation-ship between a signifier and its signified is completely arbitrary, de Saussure says, the meaning-bearing capability of signifiers is only differentially determined. One signifier can mean, refer to *this* sig-nified, only because another signifier refers to *that* signified. But Derrida takes de Saussure's point one step further. Because of the differential character of signifiers, Derrida doubts our ability to embrace the full presence of a signified. When we refer or point to a signified, all we have recourse to is other signifiers, and so we never reach the referent of the signified because of the ongoing substitution of signifiers. This is the supplementary character of language, and it illustrates for Derrida how signifiers indefinitely defer the signified so that we are left only with an unending chain of signifiers.[8] The differential character of signifiers and the endless deferral of the signified among signifiers constitute what Derrida calls *differance*, a neologism incorporating the double sense of "differing" and "deferring."[9] And it is as *differance* that any presumed transcendent signified, by virtue of its being a signifier, must be understood. It loses its transcendental, privileged character as a signified and becomes subject to the infinite free play of signifiers wherein constant deferral never allows the revelation of a full presence or truth. The production of meaning is perhaps similar to the wandering of Theseus in the palace of Cnossos, only that the infinite play of signifiers affords us no determinate thread, as it were, with which we may find a way out to some signified destination. There is no signified or entity that means something by itself.[10]

It follows from Derrida's deconstruction of the metaphysics of presence, i.e., of transcendent and independent signification, that any and all meaning is simply an effect of language. Since meaning can no longer be determinately grounded in a signified or an external referent that stands outside the operation of signifiers, meaning becomes an intramural affair; it can arise only within the indefinitely deferred bounds of signifying systems. The corollary is that objects themselves no longer have meanings that are "proper" or fully present in them; the meaning of objects is forever contingent. We can no longer experience meaning in the full presence of an object apart from the play of differential systems.[11] Derrida therefore insists that "signifying, the producing of meaning in language, is a function of the language and not some outside object-world."[12] To illustrate the object-free character of language, Derrida gives the example, "The circle is square." This sentence, he points out, obeys the rules of grammaticalness, but though it may be a *contrasens*, it is not nonsense. The proof for this claim is that one can indeed say that the sentence is not true, that no such object exists. And since the sentence is grammatically sound, the sentence means something, i.e., it signifies, despite the absence of an object. "That means," Derrida writes, "that the power of meaning of language is, to a point, independent of the possibility of its object." Whatever Derrida might "mean" with the qualifier "to a point," his fundamental claim is clear enough: the condition of an act of language amounts to being able to say, "I am dead."[13] All discourse, including the discourses of philosophy and science that might seem to have as their *telos* some external object, or signified referent, and whose intelligibility would appear to depend on their independent status, is in fact only an effect produced by language itself.[14]

For Derrida, finally, *il n'y a pas d'hors-texte*.[15] It is this that gives us entry into an understanding of the real nature of Satan's condition.

II

What for Derrida constitutes language's *differance* finds resonance, first, in the highly indeterminate way in which Milton describes Hell in *Paradise Lost*. On the one hand, Hell is a place clearly contained and circumscribed. It has "foundations" that are "fast . . . bound" (6.870) and which, "Yawning . . . on them [the demons] closed" (875). On the other hand, however, Hell is a "hollow" and "unbottomed infinite abyss" (2.518, 405), a place of "darkness visible" and a "boundless deep" (1.63, 177). Hell is a "spacious gap" (6.861), a "wasteful deep" (862), a "bottomless pit" (866) that has been "cast too deep" (869). And the description of Hell when Satan recovers from his fall suggests a place of liminality, a place "betwixt and between": Satan soars up off the burning lake until "on dry land / He lights, if it were land that ever burned / With solid . . . fire" (1.227–29).

Hell, therefore, is a place that, though it seems to be decisively enclosed, remains indefinitely extended. Indeed, it appears at times that Satan's habitation is not Hell but Chaos,[16] that

> hoary deep, a dark
> Illimitable ocean without bound,
> Without dimension, where length, breadth, and highth,
> And time and place are lost.
>
> (2.891–94)

Indeed, Hell is disturbingly indeterminate. Unlike the "bounds" (6.859) and "crystal wall" (860) of Heaven out of which Satan is cast, Hell has no such clearly established geographical boundaries and no determinate or centered presence to situate such boundaries.

If for Derrida the relation of signifiers to signifieds is endlessly deferred and the boundaries of meaning constantly recede before an endless stream of *differance,* then, for Satan, in precisely the same manner, the boundaries of Hell constantly recede before him; Satan, too, is doomed to an endless deferral within the "boundaries" of Hell: "in the lowest deep a lower deep / Still threatening to devour me opens wide" (4.76–77). The fuller context of his speech here allows us to understand how Satan experiences Hell's lack of a limiting, logocentric presence:

> Me miserable! Which way shall I fly
> Infinite wrath, and infinite despair?
> Which way I fly is hell; my self am hell;
> And in the lowest deep a lower deep
> Still threatening to devour me opens wide,
> To which the hell I suffer seems a heaven.
>
> (4.73–78)[17]

But Hell is not only an outer physical reality but also an inner psychic condition. Since Satan metaphorically identifies himself with Hell, it is situated wherever he happens to be. Satan *is* Hell; yet, paradoxically, the boundaries of Hell continue to recede before him; beyond the "lowest deep" lies a "lower deep" still. Again, in the same way that for Derrida language is "constituted" by *differance,* so also is Satan's Hell, both physically and psychically, constituted by infinite deferral; Hell, too, is a place of *differance.* There is in neither a ground of presence, a center, which with precise boundaries secures the territory, be it linguistic in the one case or geographic and psychic in the other.

Within the vast recesses of his indeterminate Hell, Satan can only wander. The verb "wander" is important in *Paradise Lost,*[18] and it clearly suggests what Derrida means by "free play." Milton frequently describes Satan's journey to the newly created Earth as a "wandering" (2.404, 830; 3.499, 631, 667). And Satan himself, in a striking oxymoron, declares to Chaos and Night that he has arrived at their "nethermost abyss . . . by constraint / Wandering this darksome desert" (2.969, 972–73). That Satan is a "wanderer" (and not a prisoner) is also recognized by Daniel Defoe, who, in *The History of the Devil: Ancient and Modern,* writes that

> Satan, being thus confined to a vagabond, wandering, unsettled condition, is without any certain abode; for though he has, in consequence of his angelic nature, a kind of empire in the liquid waste of air, yet this is certainly part of his punishment, that he is . . . without any fixed place, or space, allowed him to rest the sole of his foot upon. In short, the true account of the Devil's circumstance, since his fall from heaven, is much more likely to be this: that he is more of a vagrant than a prisoner, that he is a wanderer in the wild unbounded waste.[19]

Like Theseus in the labyrinth and Derrida in the maze of language, Satan is doomed to an endless free play within the abyss. As language wanders freely without a centering and transcendent signified that would establish through limits the meaning-bearing capacity of signifiers, Satan languishes indefinitely as a decentered being, i.e., without an ontological home that would secure his identity through limitation.

Wandering, however, is but one affliction that Satan suffers. Another, though related, torment is his "endless self-extension,"[20] which also echoes Derridean free play. In books 1 and 2, Milton compares Satan to a ship at sea and some ominous sea creature. When, for example, Satan, after his journey through Chaos, arrives within sight of "This pendant world" (2.1052), he

> Wafts on the calmer wave by dubious light
> And like a weather-beaten vessel holds
> Gladly the port, though shrouds and tackle torn.
>
> (1042–44)

The simile here suggests that Satan's identity is threatened by the turmoil of chaos—as a ship in a stormy sea—and that he is relieved to find shelter from that chaos.

A more interesting figure, however, is found immediately after he learns from Chaos and Night that he is near his destination; Satan is "glad that now his sea should find a shore" (2.1011). Here Satan is not a vessel at sea but the sea itself. This image makes clear, it seems, that Satan is glad not so much in finding refuge from external chaos but in finding a means of self-containment. His anxiety concerns not personal annihilation within the watery abyss; rather, his anxiety is over the prospect that his identity will be extended indefinitely, as a shoreless sea, to the point where he will suffer, as Derrida would put it, deconstruction. Indeed, the epic makes clear that it is not the presence of limits or constraints that threatens Satan on his journey to Earth; it is precisely the *absence* of such limits that endangers him:

> He spreads for flight, and in the surging smoke
> Uplifted spurns the ground, thence many a league
> As in a cloudy chair ascending rides
> Audacious, but that seat soon failing, meets
> A vast vacuity: all unawares
> Fluttering his pennons vain plumb down he drops
> Ten thousand fathom deep, and to this hour
> Down had been falling, had not by ill chance
> The strong rebuff of some tumultuous cloud
> Instinct with fire and nitre hurried him
> As many miles aloft.
>
> (2.928–38)

In the same way that for Derrida language is subject to the infinite "free play" of signifiers, Satan's endless wandering and self-extension constitute a "free play." As in Hell, Satan can find in Chaos no determinate boundary that would contain—and hence define—him; he is beaten about helplessly in the abyss, and it is only by virtue of the chaotic and fortuitous that he once again stands firmly on the shore. So Satan's condition turns out to be, as I have indicated, a radical *lack* of containment. Whether in Hell, in Paradise, or in Chaos, Satan enters into a "vast vacuity" that is too capacious for him to occupy.

Satan's larger predicament emerges clearly. Although he suffers anxiety at the absence of limits, Satan resists secure boundaries (a shore), because that would define, and hence, contain him. To seek out constraint would be for him to compromise the radical and unrestricted freedom he insists upon. Therefore, he must try to fill up that infinite space (a shoreless sea) that is available to him. However, to avoid all constraint in such an endless self-extension is, as we have seen, to risk eventual dissipation, an abyss of personal dissolution. To put it in Derridean terms, since Satan rejects stable presence, centered meaning, and self-limitation, he is condemned to free play, indeterminacy, and, eventually, deconstruction.

III

Satan's refusal of presence is tantamount to his rejection of form, an important feature in the structure of Milton's universe in *Paradise Lost*. Miltonic form can, I think, be construed as a manifestation of the metaphysics of presence, which for Derrida serves, albeit only apparently, to center, to guarantee, to limit, to circumscribe the meaning of language—to render language determinate and stable. In an analogous way, form, an inherent feature of the created order in Milton's universe, functions to define persons and objects with a clearly circumscribed and determinate identity. It is divinely endowed form that securely grounds and centers the identity not only of Adam and Eve but also of the entire hierarchy of creation, from the mushroom to the angel.[21]

But Satan cannot abide the boundaries that a form would impose; he takes form to be a constraint. In this he is mistaken. Heidegger reminds us of what the Greeks recognized, that a boundary is "not that at which something stops"; rather, a boundary is "that from which something begins its presencing."[22] A boundary is not, as Satan thinks, that which constricts one's freedom and thereby limits the presence of one's identity; on the contrary, a boundary is precisely that which endows one with the freedom to sustain an ongoing identity in the first place. But Satan shuns the boundaries of form that would endow him with an identity he could sustain over time, because he presumes that any such form would compromise the absolute freedom to which he persistently aspires.

If Satan refuses all stable boundaries, however, then he cannot be effectively present. At best, he is present only as absence, as trace, as *differance*. He can never possess any form, any identity, because he lacks containment. Satan's uncontained self-extension affords him no possibility for a determinate identity that is grounded in any "other" that stands over and against him.[23] God has withdrawn all limits around Satan. Indeed, God absents himself; God withdraws his presence. God is, in other words, the *deus absconditus,* the hidden God who prophetically renders judgment on Satan's pretensions to ontological autonomy.[24] God does not so much deconstruct Satan; rather, as the *deus absconditus,* God opens up a limitless space within which Satan deconstructs and disseminates himself. For Satan, then, *il n'y a pas d'hors-enfer.*[25]

IV

Milton's Satan, in fact, can help us understand the predicament of language in Derrida's writings. It is significant and telling that throughout his writings Derrida constantly employs an "absolutist" vocabulary. In *Of Grammatology,* Derrida's discussion of logocentrism consistently characterizes presence as "absolute," "full," or "fully present."[26] And in discussing phonocentrism, the claim that oral discourse is prior to written discourse in its disclosure of presence, speech is "full," intelligibility is "pure," and the *logos* is "absolute."[27] Elsewhere, in the essay "Signature Event Context," for example, Derrida calls into question whether the word "communication" corresponds with a concept that is "unique, univocal, rigorously controllable, and transmittable."[28] He wonders whether "communication" really has a "determinate content, and identifiable meaning, or a describable value."[29] Derrida remarks that the whole enterprise of communication can be controlled and limited through what is called "context," but then he asks whether the conditions of a context can really be "absolutely determinable," "certain or saturated" as has heretofore been assumed.[30] For Derrida, all terms such as "intention," "meaning," and "context" must be founded upon an absolute presence and, as Abrams puts it, "certified by criteria of what he calls 'ideal purity' and 'ultimate rigor'" if they are to have any identifiable meaning. Signs, intentions, contexts, and meanings must be univocal, unique, noniterable, singular, and rigorously controllable.[31] But Derrida's "all-or-none principle" leaves us with no alternative: if language cannot yield determinate meaning in its failure to satisfy *absolutely* rigorous criteria, then all utterances, whether written or spoken, are susceptible to deconstruction into semantic indeterminacy.[32] The *only* alternative, therefore, is the infinite play of self-referential linguistic signifiers.

But the irony is that even though he deconstructs the traditional absolutes of logocentrism, Derrida remains "committed to absolutes, for," as M. H. Abrams so cogently points out, "he shares the presupposition of the views he deconstructs that to be determinately understandable, language requires an *absolute* foundation, and that since there is no such ground, there is no stop to the play of undecidable meanings."[33] Although Derrida deconstructs logocentrism's absolutist requirements for determinate meaning, he nevertheless continues to acknowledge implicitly that such absolutes are indeed the ground for any determinate meaning. Derrida never denies, for example, that independent, absolute, and transcendent signifieds are the ground for a rigorously controllable meaning; he only claims that such a ground does not exist.

This absolutist vocabulary that Derrida employs can be accounted for on the basis of his own reading of the history of Western metaphysics. The logocentric notion of presence, Derrida claims, "has necessarily dominated the history of the world during an entire epoch."[34] The whole history of metaphysics is, for Derrida, constituted by the determination of being as present in its multifarious expressions.[35] He writes: "There is no sense in doing without the concepts of metaphysics in order to attack metaphysics. We have no language—no syntax and no lexicon—which is alien to this history; we cannot utter a single destructive proposition which has not already slipped into the form, the logic, and the implicit postulations of precisely what it seeks to contest."[36] The deconstructive task is a parasitic one; it cannot proceed without that cancerous logocentrism that for Derrida characterizes the whole history of Western metaphysics. Deconstruction requires something to deconstruct, and that something is precisely logocentrism.[37] What Derrida understands to be the history of all Western metaphysics, indeed, the *necessary* history of Western metaphysics, i.e., the metaphysics of presence, is the host animal upon which is engendered the Derridean (deconstructive) parasite, the "formless, mute, infant, and terrifying form of monstrosity."[38]

The obvious, yet important, question would then seem to be whether Derrida's interpretation of the Western metaphysical tradition is in fact an accurate reading. This is a curious question to pose vis-à-vis Derrida, because it assumes a notion of meaning, or interpretation, as closure, the very thing Derrida deconstructs. His very deconstructive enterprise, however, relies not merely upon the metaphysics of presence but also upon his *own interpretation* of the history of metaphysics *as* a metaphysics of presence. Derrida *must* argue that it is true in the traditional sense, or else his project will founder at this point as well. His reading of Western metaphysics *itself* postulates a final closure of meaning upon which deconstruction depends. Deconstruction may give birth to the infinite openness of meaning, but Derrida's *account* of Western metaphysics must itself stand as an instance of the closure of meaning. Ironically, this makes Derrida, to use Richard Rorty's term, a kind of "metaphysical prig," a devotee of what Derrida himself would call the metaphysics of presence: "You can still find the odd philosophy professor who will solemnly tell you that he is seeking what real philosophers have always sought—the *truth*, not merely a story or a consensus, but an honest-to-God accurate representation of the way the world is in itself."[39] If we were to alter the word "world" to "history of philosophy," then the whole statement would apply equally well to Derrida's account of the history of philosophy. Herein lies the real irony of Derrida's writings. So if it can be shown that Derrida's own reading of Western metaphysics is not subject to closure, i.e., if we can offer a different interpretation of the history of philosophy, then deconstruction will no longer have its parasitic raison d'être.[40]

Rorty holds that, although he may persuasively narrate his metaphysical drama, in the end Derrida constructs a false history of philosophy, that he gets the genre wrong. For example, Derrida believes that John Austin (among others) was aiming at some pure and rigorous concept of meaning in the manner of Descartes.[41] Rorty argues this is simply not true.[42] Again, in *Margins of Philosophy*, Derrida writes that "one cannot find, in the entire history of philosophy, a single . . . analysis that essentially contradicts Condillac's theory of meaning."[43] Rorty finds this to be a mistaken claim, one which he does not find substantiated in Derrida's work. And in Rorty's view, it has certainly become increasingly difficult to find a "real live metaphysical prig."[44] Whether or not one accepts Rorty's brand of pragmatism, it certainly renders an alternative narrative to Derrida's "absolutist" understanding of the history of philosophy, an understanding that necessarily has to make pretensions to semantic closure, for upon it depends his entire deconstructive edifice.

The inadequacy of Derrida's account of the history of philosophy applies equally to his understanding of God, who represents for Derrida one of the paradigmatic instances of absolute presence in the history of Western thought. But this is a flagrant misreading of God. In the biblical tradition at least, God, in whatever way he may be present to and for his people, is never present in the fully determinable way that Derrida thinks the tradition claims he is.[45] That God is never present in any direct manner can be seen in a number of ways: the danger of God as present to touch suggested by the frequent imagery of God as fire, i.e., an ungraspable reality that defies our attempts to possess—lest we die (Exod. 3.2ff.); the danger of God as present to sight suggested in Jacob's wrestling with God (Gen. 32.24–32) and Moses' request to see God (Exod. 33.17–23); the danger of God as present to voice suggested by the Jewish proscription against pronouncing the personal name of God, Yahweh; and, indeed, the very meaning of the name Yahweh, which does not satisfy Moses' request for an easily identifiable presence (Exod. 3.13–15).[46] Such is the divine hiddenness and inaccessibility by which God refuses his "normal" dealings with Israel.

But then there is also the biblical idea of God as the *deus absconditus*, which renders God's presence even more remote. What is it that provokes God to become a "hidden God"? When we presume to render God wholly and completely determinate, to make him a clear and visualizable prospect, to fully define him, to control and manipulate him, to fathom the depths of his mystery, to enclose and entrap him; *that* is when God withdraws his presence and becomes a hidden God, one who shows only his backside. "I will show them my back, not my face, in the day of their calamity," God declares.[47] This is a withdrawal that hurls us into an ecstasy of despair and threatens us with the kind of dissemination and dissolution that Milton's Satan suffers. God's presence becomes an absence in order to remind us that we cannot presume to make him fully present. It is precisely God's absence—God as *deus absconditus*—that throws us up against the impenetrable mystery of his presence.[48] So Derrida is wrong about God; in no way is the divine presence fully immanent.

Derrida does to the Western ontotheological tradition in general and to the biblical idea of God in particular what Satan does to Milton's God—he misreads. In the same way that Satan misreads the nature of God (and his own punishment) as an absolute presence that contains him, as Blake's Prolific misreads the Devourer, Derrida misreads the venture of Western thought as a search for an absolute presence that could contain meaning. But his misreading leads him to accept (albeit implicitly) the very assumptions that he wishes to deconstruct, i.e., that for meaning to be stable (i.e., contained), language must be grounded in some fully and absolutely determined presence. This is hybris directed not at God but at language. The upshot is that Derrida emerges as a satanic figure; without an absolute presence to contain him, he can only roam Satan-like in the maze and indeterminacy of a linguistic universe that cannot satisfy his own tacit assumptions. For Derrida, *il n'y a pas d'hors-texte* means that he wanders endlessly in a linguistic hell of his own making, keeping good company with the endless *differance* of Satan's spatial Hell.

Notes

1. Jules David Law, "Eruption and Containment: The Satanic Predicament in *Paradise Lost," Milton Studies* 16 (1982): 36.

2. John Milton, *Paradise Lost,* ed. Alastair Fowler (London: Longman, 1971). All references to *Paradise Lost* are to this edition and are cited parenthetically in the text.

3. See, for example, E. M. W. Tillyard, *Milton* (London: Longman, 1930), 276; C. S. Lewis, *A Preface to "Paradise Lost"* (Oxford: Oxford University Press, 1942), 97–98; A. J. A. Waldock, *"Paradise Lost" and Its Critics* (Cambridge: Cambridge University Press, 1947), 78; Isabel G. MacCaffrey, *"Paradise Lost" as "Myth"* (Cambridge: Harvard University Press, 1959), 180; Harold E. Toliver, "The Splinter Coalition," in *New Essays on "Paradise Lost,"* ed. Thomas Kranidas (Berkeley: University of California Press, 1969), 56.

Law argues that this "containment theory" of Satan's predicament finds its genesis in William Blake's *The Marriage of Heaven and Hell* (Law, "Eruption," 36–37). For Blake (or the Devil, whose voice we hear), it is "Energy," issuing from the body, that constitutes genuine life, "Eternal Delight"; opposed to this is "Reason," which is the "outward circumference" (i.e., the restraining limit) of energy. But in being restrained, energy, or desire, so the Devil thinks, gradually recedes until it "becomes passive, till it is only the shadow of desire. . . . The history of this," the Devil goes on to say, "is written in Paradise Lost, & the Governor or Reason is call'd Messiah." The Devil then concludes his argument with the following: "The reason Milton wrote in fetters when he wrote of Angels & God, and at liberty when of Devils & Hell, is because he was a true Poet and of the Devil's party without knowing it" (William Blake, *The Marriage of Heaven and Hell,* in *The Complete Writings of William Blake,* ed. Geoffrey Keynes [New York: Oxford University Press, 1972], 149–50; all references to Blake's *Marriage* are to this edition and are noted parenthetically in the text). But what is even more interesting is found in a subsequent passage of *The Marriage of Heaven and Hell*, a passage whose voice is no longer the Devil's. The setting is a printing house in Hell; Blake writes in this "Memorable Fancy":

> The Giants who formed this world into its sensual existence, and now seem to live in it in chains, are in truth the causes of its life & the sources of all activity; but the chains are the cunning of weak and tame minds which have power to resist energy; according to the proverb, the weak in courage is strong in cunning. Thus one portion of being is the Prolific; the other the Devouring: to the Devourer it seems as if the producer was in his chains; but it is not so, he only takes portions of existence and fancies that the whole. But the Prolific would cease to be Prolific unless the Devourer, as a sea, received the excess of his delights. (155)

Blake is here adumbrating the dialectical relationship between energy (the Prolific) and containment (the Devourer); this relationship, however, is misread by both. The Devourer fancies that the Prolific is bound by his chains, while the Prolific believes that any such constraint results in passivity, in its becoming only a "shadow of desire." Neither perceives that in fact they stand in a mutually dependent relationship; this is especially true with respect to the Prolific, for it is "the very restraining pressure of the Devourer that defines and sustains the Prolific" (Law, "Eruption," 37). The Prolific, in other words, can maintain its identity only when there is an occasion for it to break through the force of containment; only then does energy or desire avoid dissipation into nothingness and attain heroic stature. Indeed, as Blake remarks elsewhere in *The Marriage of Heaven and Hell*, "Without Contraries [e.g., Energy and Reason] is no progression" (149). Thus it is containment that fuels Satan's heroic energy. Law ("Eruption," 57–58) cites R. J. Zwi Werblowsky: "until Blake's *Marriage of Heaven and Hell* (about 1790) nobody ever appears to have been seduced by Satan's Promethean charms" (Werblowsky, *Lucifer and Prometheus: A Study of Milton's Satan* [London: Routledge, 1952], 3).

It seems, however, that in the epic itself the angels (both fallen and unfallen) and Satan himself understand God's punishment of Satan as constraint. See Gabriel (4.794–95, 904–11); Abdiel and Raphael (6.186, 8.235–36); Belial (2.129ff.); Beelzebub (2.320–23); Sin (10.365–69); Satan (1.650–58; 9.163–65).

4. God's "permissive will" (3.685) in no way ever devises to contain Satan. This becomes clear as early as book 1, when Satan lies chained on the fiery lake:

> So stretched out huge in length the arch-fiend lay
> Chain'd on the burning lake, nor ever thence
> Had risen or heaved his head, but that the will
> And high permission of all-ruling heaven
> Left him at large. . . .
> Forthwith upright he rears from off the pool
> His mighty stature.
>
> (1.209–13, 221–22)

Despite his chains, then, Satan is given free range to move about as he wishes. Later, his successful temptation of Adam and Eve in Paradise is known immediately to God,

> for what can scape the eye
> Of God all-seeing, or deceive his heart
> Omniscient, who in all things wise and just,

Hindered not Satan to attempt the mind
Of man, with strength entire, and free will armed.

(10.5–9)

One of the most telling indications of the nature of Satan's future punishment comes from Abdiel, who, just prior to the War in Heaven, tells Satan, "henceforth / No more be troubled how to quit the yoke / Of God's Messiah" (5.881–83).

The upshot is that Satan quite freely accomplishes all that he sets out to do. He escapes from Hell, crosses over Chaos, evades the guardian angels and leaps into Paradise, tempts Eve, and returns to Hell. All of this Satan does, of course, with the intent of frustrating God's will. As Satan puts it to Beelzebub early on,

> To do aught good never will be our task,
> But ever to do ill our sole delight,
> As being the contrary to his high will
> Whom we resist.

(1.159–62)

This statement clearly bears out both Satan's intentions and his freedom; the irony, however, is that, despite this freedom and the success of his mission, Satan never acts contrary to God's will, simply because God never intends to contain Satan in the first place.

5. Jacques Derrida: *Of Grammatology,* trans. Gayatri Spivak (Baltimore: Johns Hopkins University Press, 1976); "Structure, Sign, and Play in the Discourse of the Human Sciences," in *The Structuralist Controversy,* ed. Richard Macksey and Eugenio Donato (Baltimore: Johns Hopkins University Press, 1972), 247–65; "Signature Event Context," *Glyph* 1 (1977): 172–97.

6. Derrida, *Of Grammatology,* 12.

7. Ibid.

8. Derrida, "Structure, Sign, and Play," 260.

9. Derrida, *Of Grammatology,* 23.

10. Herbert N. Schneidau, "Word against the Word: Derrida on Textuality," in *Semeia 23: Derrida and Biblical Studies,* ed. Robert Detweiler (Missoula, Mont.: Scholars Press, 1982), 5–29.

11. Ibid., 5.

12. Ibid., 11.

13. From the Barthes-Todorov discussion in *The Languages of Criticism and the Sciences of Man,* ed. Richard Macksey and Eugenio Donato (Baltimore: Johns Hopkins University Press, 1970), 156.

14. Ann Jefferson, "Structuralism and Post-Structuralism," in *Modern Literary Theory: a Comparative Introduction,* ed. Ann Jefferson and David Robey (Totowa, N.J.: Barnes and Noble, 1982), 109.

15. "There is nothing outside the text."

16. Law, "Eruption," 45.

17. The absence of a limiting presence also causes among the demons an inner anxiety that is articulated by Beelzebub, as the devils consider their course of action:

> Who shall tempt with wandering feet
> The dark unbottomed infinite abyss
> And through the palpable obscure find out
> His uncouth way.

(2.404–7)

The impulse toward penetration, to break through and locate the "happy isle" (410), or Paradise, is mixed with a dread of reversing Chaos, an unchartered abyss, without markers, coordinates, or demarcation. See Law, "Eruption," 45.

18. When the "Stygian council" (2.506) disbands, the demons go off "wandering, each his several way / Pursues" (2.523–24). Later the fallen angels must endure, as one of their punishments, being sent forth "wandering o'er the earth" (1.364). In his edition of *Paradise Lost,* Alastair Fowler comments on the word "wander" (96 n. ii146–51).

19. Daniel Defoe, *The History of the Devil: Ancient and Modern, in Two Parts* (East Ardsley, England: E.P. Publishing, 1972), 94–95.

20. Law, "Eruption," 48–49.

21. For an account of the place of form in Milton's poetics, see John Peter Rumrich, *Matter of Glory: A New Preface to "Paradise Lost"* (Pittsburgh: University of Pittsburgh Press, 1987), 65–66; and Claude N. Stulting, Jr., "'Earth's Great Altar': Greek Patristic Theology and the Sacrament of Nature in Milton's *Paradise Lost*" (Ph.D. diss., University of Virginia, 1993), 165–203.

22. Martin Heidegger, *Poetry, Language, and Thought,* trans. Albert Hofstadter (New York: Harper, 1971), 154.

23. As Blake might put it in *The Marriage of Heaven and Hell,* Satan lives as the Prolific who has no Devourer, i.e., God, who would limit and thus sustain whatever identity he might have.

24. Sartre's notion of human identity is also founded upon the utterly autonomous and gratuitous positing of one's own self apart from any constraint or any "other." Such a self, in Sartre's view, is never guaranteed beyond the present; one must always be repositing one's identity time and time again. So there is never any stable or abiding self over time. See, for example, the character Antoine in Sartre's novel *Nausea.*

25. "There is nothing outside Hell."

26. Derrida, *Of Grammatology,* 8, 16.

27. Ibid., 8, 13.

28. Derrida, "Signature Event Context," 172.

29. Ibid.

30. Ibid., 174.

31. M. H. Abrams, "How to Do Things with Texts," *Partisan Review* 46 (1979): 571.

32. Ibid.

33. Ibid., 570 (emphasis mine).

34. Derrida, *Of Grammatology,* 7–8.

35. Derrida, "Structure, Sign, and Play," 249.

36. Ibid., 250.

37. But one cannot help but wonder, as Richard Rorty does ("Deconstruction and Circumvention" [unpublished essay, 1993], 4), "what will happen . . . when deconstructionists run out of patriarchal metaphysicians?"

38. Derrida, "Structure, Sign, and Play," 265. See also *Of Grammatology,* 5.

39. Rorty, "Deconstruction," 2–3.

40. Ibid., 4–15.

41. Derrida, "Signature Event Context," 180.

42. Richard Rorty, "The Meaning of the Text," notes taken from lecture given at University of Virginia, fall 1983.

43. Quoted in Rorty, "Deconstruction," 2.

44. Rorty, "Deconstruction," 2.

45. As a Sephardic Jew, Derrida should know better.

46. Mention should also be made of the strong emphasis given to the apophatic method in the theology of the Eastern Orthodox tradition. The apophatic approach stresses the *via negativa,* the unknowability and transcendence of God, what he is *not.*

47. Jer. 18.17, New Revised Standard Version.

48. So it is, too, in Satan's experience of Milton's God.

Romancing the Pope: Tasso's Narrative Theory and Milton's Demonization of a Genre

Attitudes toward Italy in early modern England frequently reveal mixed, if not self-contradictory, emotions. In *The Schoolmaster* Roger Ascham's famous denunciation of the Englishman Italianate exemplifies, in its purer form, a national rivalry exacerbated by the cultural politics of the English Reformation. When Ascham deplores "the enchantments of Circe, brought out of Italy, to mar men's manners in England," he especially laments the influence of "fond books, of late translated out of Italian into English, sold in every shop in London" (106–7).[1] But when he turns to a similarly lamentable native tradition, chivalric romance, it is the stigma of "papistry" that serves to qualify the *Morte Arthur* for condemnation as the product of "idle monks and wanton canons." For Ascham, Malory's Arthurian cycle may be "good stuff for wise men to laugh at, or honest men to take pleasure at; yet [he knows] when God's Bible was banished the court and *Morte Arthur* received into the prince's chamber" (107). Like the Italian provenance of a popular book, the memory of a Roman Catholic queen (or of Henry VIII before his break from the Church of Rome) prompts the moral alarm of this Protestant guardian of English faith and conduct. Moreover, to discredit Italian culture even further, he discriminates more finely among his adversaries. "More papists," he claims, "[may] be made by your merry books of Italy than by your earnest books of Louvain" (107).

For such early Elizabethans the charms of Italian culture give it a Circean allure, yet the assimilation of its accomplishments into later Tudor literature poses a more complex challenge than the terms of Ascham's warning suggest. The portrait of Italy that Thomas Nashe limns in *The Unfortunate Traveler* of 1594 leaves little doubt about the moral corruption that land threatens to bring

128

upon hapless English drifters within its borders. If Jack Wilton shows any prospect of reform, it appears notably in his departure from Italy at the conclusion of Nashe's tale. But poets, like Edmund Spenser and John Harington, who both published romances in the Elizabethan nineties, display a far more complex, and indeed curious, entanglement in the work of their chief Italian precursor in that genre, Lodovico Ariosto. For example, if we recall Ascham's denunciation of Arthurian romance, we may savor even more fully the amusing ironies of Spenser's representation of the prophet Merlin in *The Faerie Queene* via an Ariostan pre-text. In proclaiming his intention to "sing of Knights and Ladies gentle deeds" (1.proem.1.5),[2] Spenser announces his Ariostan ambitions at the poem's very outset; but any secure sense of national identity and distinction in Spenser's celebration of his queen's lineage seems extremely complicated, if not simply undone, when he models Merlin's prophecy of Britomart's dynastic fortunes upon Ariosto's representation of Bradamante's parallel experience at Merlin's tomb. Who—or, rather, whose—is this Welsh prophet of the Tudor monarchy repatriated from an Italian romance to announce the line that will lead to Queen Elizabeth, whom our English poet here aims to celebrate by imitating his Italian precursor?

Likewise John Harington, whose "Englishing" of *Orlando furioso* is virtually contemporary with Spenser's *Faerie Queene*, relates in his letters from Ireland a similarly intricate exchange between cultures. In 1599 Harington accompanied Robert Devereux, the second Earl of Essex, on his expedition to Ireland to put down the rebellion that had driven Edmund Spenser, among others, from that land. In recounting his experiences, Harington relates what we may cautiously term an example of the early modern Irish reception of *Orlando furioso,* which he read in his translation to various audiences in the Emerald Isle. Indeed, when he was entertained at the court of the arch-rebel Hugh O'Neill, the Earl of Tyrone, such a reading of canto 45 was prompted by the poet's gift of his translation to the Irish lord's sons, whose tutors, it seems, planned to teach them English from it.[3] Imagine how the author of *The Schoolmaster* would have responded to such a curriculum! The Italian poem was still found at once scandalous and seductive in England, as we can deduce from Elizabeth's fabled punishment of her godson for circulating his version of canto 28 among her courtiers: she required him to translate the remaining forty-five cantos as penance. Yet, in Harington's letters, his *Orlando furioso* becomes a kind of representation of English language and culture in Ireland.[4]

In theorizing about heroic poetry and in composing his own masterwork of that kind, Torquato Tasso's efforts to accommodate both the genre of romance and the legacy of Ariosto to his own ambitions do not entail the sharp differences of religion and national identity that complicate English imitations of such Italian precursors. Nonetheless, reckoning with the complex challenges of *Orlando furioso* posed perhaps the major problems for Tasso as a theorist and poet who sought to make a place for himself in the tradition he aimed to share with Ariosto; and Tasso's attempts to resolve these problems inspired his chief English inheritor, John Milton, in ways that reflect further complexities of the transmission of Italian culture in Protestant England during the early modern period. Moreover, since Spenser stands in a relation to Milton not unlike that of Ariosto to Tasso, especially when we view these poets from the perspective of genre, Spenser's importance in the exchange between the premier epic poets of their respective cultures, Tasso and Milton, warrants serious consideration, if we wish to appreciate that transaction in any detail.

From the very outset of *The Faerie Queene,* the religious antagonism between Christianity and Islam central to narrative poetry of the Italian Renaissance undergoes a striking transformation, as the Saracen infidel becomes the Roman heretic. Further, since this intrafaith enmity more immediately reflects internal divisions within the English church, it is inherently less stable than its Italian counterpart because it is less supported by corresponding differences of national, ethnic, or racial identity. When Spenser allegorizes the genre of romance in *The Faerie Queene*'s opening encounter in the wood of Errour, precisely what—or, rather, whose—heresies the dragon lady of that name represents readily remains open to question. The most striking image of that symbolic narrative occurs when, in her death throes, the serpentine female regurgitates a gush of texts. But this horrifying representation of religious controversy's sickening profusion in late Tudor England lacks denominational specificity. These books have no titles that decisively mark their Catholic provenance, despite interpreters' inclinations to read them in those terms. The indeterminacy of Spenser's allegorical intent at this juncture haunts this episode with shadows of the very doubts it is ostensibly designed to dispel, and thus it uncannily prefigures the sort of religious polemics that the Marprelate pamphlets and Milton's own antiprelatical tracts exemplify. Controversies within the Church of England from Elizabeth's final decade until the Restoration make what Milton calls "apish Romanizing" in *Areopagitica* a frequent accusation that English Christians hurl at one another (725).[5]

This Spenserian episode tellingly mediates between Tasso and Milton in a variety of ways: first, it focuses upon generic codes that preoccupied Tasso as a theorist and a practitioner of narrative poetry; second, Milton pointedly borrows from it in representing the romance of Satan, the tale of whose solitary voyage earthward becomes the vehicle for Milton's accommodation of errant heroism in *Paradise Lost*. Further, in this demonic romance Milton decisively employs the language of anti-Catholicism in ways that bespeak as much his own polemic against the established Church of England as his condemnation of the Church of Rome. Let me address these points and some of their corollaries as a means of developing my overall topic—Tasso's narrative theory and Milton's demonization of the genre of romance—within some of the manifold contexts of relevant traditions that these two poets inherit and seek to transform.

First of all, Spenser's wood of Errour pointedly alludes to the forest of Saron near Jerusalem, which figures so prominently in Tasso's allegory of his poem, *Gerusalemme liberata*. Indeed, Ismeno's enchantment of this site associates it explicitly with false beliefs and the errors of opinion in the words of Tasso's allegory, which could apply equally as well to the spiritual sense with which Spenser has so patently invested his wood. But, of course, Spenser's name for his wood in its literal or, rather, etymological, sense also invokes the structural feature that distinguishes the genre of romance, a poetic kind that interweaves the *errori,* or wanderings, of the heroes of such narratives. The discontinuities and interruptions of *Orlando furioso*'s multiple plotlines signal Ariosto's persistent play with this quality of romance; but Tasso, as a young theorist, memorably expressed his alarm at this aspect of romance, which threatened to run out of control unless disciplined by an overall unity of plot.[6] Variety within unity was young Tasso's most sanguine and eloquent formulation of this poetic ideal; but in arriving at this harmonization of rival principles of narration, he entertained a memorably troubled vision of the negative potential for chaos inherent even in this structural compromise. Just as Spenser's dragon lady vomits a spate of texts whose end comes as a great relief but whose possible endlessness remains a shadowy presence within his poem thereafter, so Tasso's vision of an interminable romance lingers on, despite his apparent quelling of such a threat by a higher ideal of order.[7]

In outlining his poem's plot for Orazio Capponi, Tasso noted about canto 4 not only its main events—"Consiglio de' demoni. Venuta d'Armida"—but also its structural function as a generator of *errori*—"Da questo canto, quasi da fonte, derivano quasi tutti gli episodi."[8] Milton's debt to Tasso for the demonic drama that opens *Paradise Lost* has long been acknowledged; and his deployment of classical topoi, in this context, to associate pagan motifs with satanic heroism, also follows Tasso's practice in the demonic council of canto 4.[9] But there is also a kind of generic theology of sin that decisively accommodates the dangerous unruliness of romance to Milton's religious convictions in a way that dispels the threat of chaos that haunts both Tasso's anxious theorizing about multiple plots and the potential recidivism of Spenser's dragon lady. By demonizing romance as a vehicle for satanic heroism, Milton transforms the dangerous multiplicity of that genre into a sign of human sinfulness, which will persist *saecula saeculorum*, or "world without end," once the adversary of humankind has induced Adam and Eve to disobey God's single prohibition. Only the apocalyptic Last Judgment and the reunion of God with his saints at that time enable Milton to keep the end in sight, as he unfolds his story of otherwise interminable error.

Employing allegory of the Spenserian sort, where embodied abstractions take part in the narrative action, Milton creates the figure of Sin by borrowing her serpentine tail and cannibalistic offspring from the representation of Errour in *The Faerie Queene*. Though other figures, such as the mythological Skylla, also lie behind Milton's creation, the echoes of Spenser's lines here sound a clearly discernible note. But Satan, in the course of his flight, makes his initial landing in a most Ariostan locale, the Limbo of Vanities or Paradise of Fools. Passing through the gates of Hell where his daughter, Sin, and Death, their incestuously conceived son, stand guard, Satan proceeds through the realm of Chaos and old Night and finally alights "upon the firm opacous Globe / Of this round World" (3.418–19). Distinctly reminiscent of the valley of lost things whence Astolfo retrieves the wits of mad Orlando, this way station on Satan's earthbound journey serves Milton as an occasion for anti-Catholic satire. He specifies such items among the airborne exempla of human vanity as

> Eremites and Friars
> White, Black and Grey, with all thir trumpery.
> Here Pilgrims roam, that stray'd so far to seek
> In Golgotha him dead, who lives in Heav'n;

And they who to be sure of Paradise
Dying put on the weeds of Dominic,
Or in Franciscan think to pass disguis'd.

(3.474–80)

The winds of vanity blow aimlessly hereabout and waft such tokens
of human folly about in their powerful gusts, for which Milton
punningly suggests a nearly scatological origin when he refers to
"the backside of the World" (494) to indicate the direction from
whence these draughts emerge. Lest the inspiration of this setting
from canto 35 of *Orlando furioso* should go overlooked, Milton
insists upon the function of this place as a receptacle of "All th'
unaccomplisht works of Nature's hand," which, he declares with
explicitly anti-Ariostan defiance, do *not* end up "in the neighboring
Moon, as some have dream'd" (455, 459).[10]

When young Tasso recorded his dread at the potentially endless
proliferation of plots in a romance of the Ariostan kind, he initially
proposed the *discordia concors* of variety in unity as a resolution
of this potential problem.[11] He later returned to this issue in the
revised and expanded version of the second of his *Discorsi
dell'arte poetica*, which becomes the third of his *Discorsi del
poema eroico*. Introducing that discourse and the crucial matter
of poetics that it will engage, Tasso has recourse to a quintessential
topos of cinquecento romance, the voyage of discovery.[12] In a passage reminiscent of his own account of *la nave della fortuna* in
Gerusalemme liberata, Tasso imagines the literary explorer as the
adventurer who passes through the straits of Hercules and on into
another hemisphere, where he must be guided by other stars (*altre
stelle*) if he is to make his way successfully.[13] The resemblance of
this imagery to the voyage of Carlo and Ubaldo to rescue Rinaldo
is hard to overlook in this context, where Tasso theorizes what
Milton will later call "advent'rous Song" (*Paradise Lost* 1.13) in a
phrase that makes poetic creation itself an heroic exploit.

But the figure in *Paradise Lost* who most obviously undertakes
such an exploratory mission to an unknown world is none other
than Satan, who thus transforms the daring entailed in a voyage of
discovery into sinful defiance of the divine will. While parallels
with Rinaldo's errancy and the voyage to Armida's isle by those
who rescue him clearly obtain with respect to the romance of Satan, this demonic adventurer is irredeemable. Further, he sets the
course by which Sin and Death initially make their way to Earth
after the primal offense of our first parents. Thereafter, until Arma-
geddon, that route will become a main-traveled road for both Sin

and Death, as well as their minions; and Milton explicitly associates this soon-to-be well-worn path with the Church of Rome via
a series of etymological puns whose intent is unmistakable. In order to solidify the bridge over Chaos from Hell to "This pendant
world" (2.1052), Death wields "his Mace petrific" (10.294), and "by
wondrous Art / Pontifical" (312–13), Sin and he complete "this new
wondrous Pontifice" (348), which follows "the track / Of Satan"
(314–15) and extends precisely to that most Ariostan spot,

> the selfsame place where hee
> First lighted from his Wing, and landed safe
> From out of Chaos to the outside bare
> Of this round World.
>
> (315–18)

The very "wondrousness" of this construction, which Milton emphasizes by repetition, clearly associates it, like the voyage whose
path it follows, with the genre of romance, one of whose definitive
features are the *meraviglie* that Tasso, in his early *Discorsi*, insists
upon accommodating to the terms of Christian religion.[14]

Of course, this demonization of romance does not in any way
isolate sinfulness from human agency, nor does it preclude the
features of this genre from deployment in representing both the
actions of Adam and Eve and the larger human story that origi-
nates with them. Rather, signs of this literary kind frequently beto-
ken notable lapses in conduct or, at least, the potential for moral
waywardness;[15] such generic signals appear at crucial junctures to
indicate the continuing fallibility of human nature before and after
the Fall. When Eve makes her appeal to Adam that they divide
their labors, she asks a question that sounds like Milton's famous
disparagement of "a fugitive and cloistered virtue" in *Areopagitica*
(728), until she slips into the values of romance with their premium
on solitary heroism. "And what is Faith, Love, Virtue unassay'd"
(9.335), she inquires—in complete harmony with the views of Milton's pamphlet, until the next line adds this modification: "Alone,
without exterior help sustain'd?" (336). Here Milton manages the
verse ending to highlight further the kind of mistake Eve's thinking
entails, which his previous description of Satan's journey as an
"uncouth errand sole" (2.827) most memorably encodes in the
terms of romance.

At the poem's end Milton draws upon the same verbal resources,
the language of what has become in its most notorious instance a
satanic genre, to present us with a final glimpse of our first parents:

"They hand in hand with wand'ring steps and slow, / Through Eden took thir solitary way" (12.648–49). The two of them are about to begin what, paradoxically, seems yet another in a series of "uncouth errand[s] sole." Only Milton's apocalyptic conviction that time must have a stop in our final doom and that those saved will return to the presence of God keeps this series from being the interminable sequence of romances envisioned by Tasso in his consideration of multiple plots. Milton's demonization of romance, the very genre that enables him to represent such a grim prospect of potentially uncontrollable activity, also enables him to contain it within the providential design of human history that presides in his poem. Certainly it was Tasso, as Milton would readily acknowledge, who helped him to understand the resources of genre and "what the laws are of a true epic poem" (*Of Education* 637) so he could thus employ them in his Protestant masterpiece of that kind.

Notes

"Romancing the Pope: Tasso's Narrative Theory and Milton's Demonization of a Genre" originally appeared in Italian as "Romanzare sul Papa: la teoria narrativa del Tasso e la demonizzazione miltoniana di un genere," in *Tasso e l'Europa,* ed. Daniele Rota (Bergamo: Centro Studi Tassiani, 1996), 47–56. This revised and expanded version is reprinted by permission of the publisher.

1. Roger Ascham, *The Schoolmaster* (1570), ed. Lawrence V. Ryan (Ithaca: Cornell University Press, 1967), 67. All references to *The Schoolmaster* are to this edition and are cited parenthetically in the text. For comparable sentiments from a later Elizabethan decade, cf. *Richard II* (*The Riverside Shakespeare,* ed. G. Blakemore Evans [Boston: Houghton Mifflin, 1974], 2.1.19–23), where York denounces

> Lascivious metres, to whose venom sound
> The open ear of youth doth always listen,
> Report of fashion in proud Italy,
> Whose manner still our tardy-apish nation
> Limps after in base imitation.

In Christopher Marlowe's *Edward II* (ed. W. Moelwyn Merchant [New York: Norton, 1967], 1.1.50–70), Gaveston likewise refers to the Circean allure of "wanton poets" and "Italian masques," though he is cynically appreciative of the spell they can cast and that he means to exploit.

2. Edmund Spenser, *The Faerie Queene,* ed. Thomas P. Roche, Jr. (New York: Penguin, 1978), 39.

3. D. H. Craig, *Sir John Harington* (Boston: Twayne, 1985), 22. See Sir John Harington, *The Letters and Epigrams of Sir John Harington, Together with "The Prayse of Private Life,"* ed. Norman E. McClure (Philadelphia: University of Pennsylvania Press, 1930), 77.

4. In her paper, "Harington's *Orlando furioso* in Ireland and His Irish Journal in England," Clare Carroll elaborated upon this thesis at the 1995 meeting of the

Renaissance Society of America. I adapt here a sentence from the abstract of her paper in the conference program.

5. John Milton, *Areopagitica,* in *John Milton: Complete Poems and Major Prose,* ed. Merritt Y. Hughes (New York: Odyssey, 1957), 725. Unless otherwise noted, all references to Milton's works are to this edition and are cited parenthetically in the text.

In the opening of his first antiprelatical tract, *Of Reformation,* Milton's censure of "the new-vomited Paganisme of sensuall Idolatry" prompts the editors of the Yale edition, Don M. Wolfe and William Alfred, to cite the Errour episode as "a parallel but substantially different appearance of this allegorical dyspepsia" (*Complete Prose Works of John Milton,* 8 vols., ed. Don M. Wolfe et al. [New Haven: Yale University Press, 1953–82], 1:520). Their phrase, "allegorical dyspepsia," is memorably felicitous, but another of their notes on this initial paragraph exemplifies the virtual interchangeability of the two churches that strikes me as in the offing, if you will, of the Spenserian passage. "Milton is speaking in his first two paragraphs of the Roman Catholic Church before Luther. But he nowhere mentions it by name and evidently means his readers to apply his description to the Anglican Church of Laud's day as well" (1:520).

6. Torquato Tasso, *Discorsi dell'arte poetica e del poema eroico,* ed. Luigi Poma (Bari, Italy: Laterza, 1963), 24. An English translation of *Discorsi dell'arte poetica* is available in Lawrence F. Rhu, *The Genesis of Tasso's Narrative Theory: Translations of the Early Poetics and a Comparative Study of Their Significance* (Detroit: Wayne State University Press, 1993), 99–153. See 119 for the passage on the potentially endless number of plots in a romance.

7. For a discussion of this phenomenon in Spenser's poem at greater length, see Lawrence F. Rhu, "Romancing the Word: Pre-Texts and Contexts for the Errour Episode," *Spenser Studies* 11 (1994): 101–9, reprinted Rhu, *Genesis,* 57–71.

8. Cited in Torquato Tasso, *Gerusalemme liberata,* ed. Lanfranco Caretti (Turin: Einaudi, 1971), 4.

9. See Judith Kates, "The Revaluation of the Classical Hero in Tasso and Milton," *Comparative Literature* 26 (1974): 299–317.

10. Milton's pointed association of dreamlike insubstantiality with Ariostan romance recurs in *Paradise Regained,* 4.541–43, where he thus describes the transit to the site of the Son's final temptation:

> So saying he [Satan] caught him [Christ] up, and
> without wing
> Of Hippogrif bore through the Air sublime
> Over the Wilderness and o'er the Plain.

Those familiar with the narrator's initial observation about the hippogriff in *Orlando furioso* can savor here an added irony: "Non e finto il destrier, ma naturale" (4.18.1, quoted from the edition of Lanfranco Caretti [Turin: Einaudi, 1971]).

11. Tasso, *Discorsi,* 36; Rhu, *Genesis,* 130–31.

12. See David Quint, "Tasso, Milton, and the Boat of Romance," in *Epic and Empire: Politics and Generic Form from Virgil to Milton* (Princeton: Princeton University Press, 1993), 248–67.

13. Tasso, *Discorsi,* 116.

14. Tasso, *Discorsi,* 6–7; Rhu, *Genesis,* 103–4.

15. The poet, it is important to note, very much includes himself and the project of composing his poem as potentially liable to such lapses. The initial query in

the proem to book 3 reveals his serious concern with his own fallibility: "May I express thee unblam'd?" (*Paradise Lost* 3.3). Further, since a series of *venture* epitomizes the characteristically episodic structure of romance, he pointedly deploys the code of that genre to indicate his liability to err when he refers to his "*advent'rous* Song" (1.13) and his attempt thereby to transcend his classical precursors or again when he describes his effort to "*venture* down / The dark descent" (3.19–20; emphasis mine). That his subsequent ascent requires a "*bolder wing*" (3.13; emphasis mine) affiliates him indirectly with Satan, whose "*bold words*" (1.82; emphasis mine) characterize him from the outset of the poem.

Building Pandemonium: Vitruvian Architecture in *Paradise Lost*

RICHARD J. DUROCHER

> And what will they at best say of us and of the whole English name, but scoffingly as of that foolish builder, mentiond by our Saviour, who began to build a tower, and was not able to finish it. Where is this goodly tower of a Commonwealth which the English boasted they would build to overshaddow kings, and be another Rome in the west? The foundation indeed they laid gallantly; but fell into a wors confusion, not of tongues, but of factions, then those at the tower of Babel; and have left no memorial of thir work behinde them remaining, but in the common laughter of Europ.

I begin with this excerpt from *The Readie and Easie Way* because it draws together a cluster of Miltonic preoccupations that are fundamental to my discussion of architecture in *Paradise Lost*. In the prose passage, alluding to Luke's Gospel and the Book of Genesis, Milton adduces images of towers from both the New and Old Testaments—in that characteristic, inverted order[1]—to chide his audience for their failure to advance "the Good Old Cause." While the passage seems primarily calculated to scold Milton's audience for their recent backsliding, the image of the "goodly tower," figuring a thoroughly reformed and reconstructed state, holds out the possibility of a positive future for England. In that sense the tower image has palpable rhetorical force, through its appeal to English pride to make good on their earlier boasting. Making good on a boast, one recalls from *Beowulf*, has long been a matter of honor for British speakers. Moreover, the image of the Commonwealth as a structure built to "overshaddow kings" is politically astute. On the occasion of the monarchy's impending restoration, Milton deftly sketches a tattling Europe in which a more or less thoroughly reformed England will find itself either a leader or a laughingstock. Looking behind the faltering Protectorate toward a glorious vision of the future, Milton reminds the builders of the Commonwealth that they had for England a yet unrealized ambition: to be "another

Rome in the west."[2] In *Of Reformation* (1641) almost twenty years earlier, Milton himself had advocated classical republican precedents for the political structure of the Commonwealth, including chiefly a theory of the "mixed state" that Polybius saw exemplified by the Roman republic.[3] Both versions of *The Readie and Easie Way* (February and April 1660) show Milton's enduring conviction that classical republican ideals are politically viable—though the later version upholds Roman virtues amidst increased reliance on Machiavellian practices.[4] For Milton as for many supporters of "the Good Old Cause," ancient Rome embodied the premier model of a flourishing culture and government that England, while watchful against papist corruption, ought still in the 1660s to emulate.

These same Miltonic preoccupations—typological treatment of Scriptures, architectural imagery, political briefing, classical Roman models—appear in a new configuration when Milton describes the building of Pandemonium in book 1 of *Paradise Lost*. The architectural part of that new configuration derives from the presence of another Roman author, Vitruvius Pollio, who in the first century before Christ was chiefly responsible for Augustus Caesar's public building campaign.[5] Vitruvius, in the ten books of his *De architectura* (circa 28 B.C.), expounds the essential principles that Milton invokes in the scene. This is not to say that Milton was ignorant of other architectural models or that his Pandemonium reflects nothing from architectural theory and practice among his near contemporaries such as Palladius, Leon Battista Alberti, Sebastiano Serlio, Giorgio Vasari, and Inigo Jones. A fuller, contextualized account of Milton's collective architectural inheritance than is possible here would surely enrich and complicate our understanding of Milton's notions of the art of building.[6] In any responsible account of Milton and architecture, however, I submit that Vitruvius would remain the central and primary figure. First of all, Vitruvius is the one architect Milton recommends by name. In addition to Milton's singling out Vitruvius in *Of Education*, Edward Phillips recalls in his brief life of the poet that Milton included "Vitruvius his *Architecture*" in the curriculum of his private tutorial during the 1640s.[7] While typically absent from academic curricula, the text of Vitruvius was often put to practical use by Renaissance builders. For example, one copy of Vitruvius published by Guinta in Florence, 1513, in a small octavo size, contains dozens of annotations of a practical, rather than a scholarly nature.[8] All of the Renaissance architects mentioned above regarded him as their chief authority and precursor. Breathtaking technical developments in single-point perspective and domed roofing, to name only two, are directly traceable to sentences in the text of Vitruvius. In short, Vitruvius was "highly valued by architects all over western Europe in the seventeenth century."[9] In this essay, I concentrate on one well-known Renaissance architect whose exposition of Vitruvius adds a fresh perspective on the Roman architect's theory.

To understand the building of Pandemonium, I maintain, requires a reading of its double possibility akin to the hermeneutic Milton focused on the tower imagery in *The Readie and Easie Way*. St. Augustine had provided the theoretical basis for interpreting signifiers in this compound way in his *De Doctrina Christiana* 3.25.36–37. There Augustine uses the example of lion imagery in Scripture to show that one thing might signify in two ways: *in bono,* "in a good sense," or *in malo,* "in an evil sense."[10] To put it simply, Pandemonium is designed to stand as an image of both good and bad building. Such a building is at once worse than the tower of Babel and better than the unfinished "goodly tower of a Commonwealth." When we read Pandemonium in this way, we stand to recover a sense of Milton's daring narrative strategy, inviting readers to marvel at demonic echoes of the architectural achievements of the high Renaissance.

We may begin with the more obvious sense in which Pandemonium is a negative image. Traditionally, one way of reading Pandemonium as an image *in malo* has been to regard the palace essentially as a locus of anti-Catholic satire. In an article published in *Modern Philology* in 1931, Rebecca W. Smith drew a sharp distinction between the "generalized summary of Roman architecture" presented in Satan's panorama in book 4 of *Paradise Regained* and the "individual scene, with vivid, precise details and a definite location" of Pandemonium.[11] For the latter, Milton supplemented his reading with personal recollections of St. Peter's, Smith argued. Her argument can be extended. For example, Milton's epic bee simile in *Paradise Lost* 1.768–75 does more than allude to literary precursors. When, during his travels through Italy in 1638–39, Milton visited the Barberini palace in Rome as a guest of the Cardinal, he surely would have seen the bronze sculptures of bees emblematic of Pope Urban VIII. The subtly unresolved question in Milton's simile of who controls the bees would have recalled Protestant and Catholic arguments over the pope's putative supremacy, arguments Milton had disputed with Salmasius in *A Defense of the English People*. Through specific references to ecclesiastical terms such as "conclave" (1.795),[12] by which Catholics designated an assembly to elect a pope, Milton in Smith's words "ascribes to the conferences of Satan and his peers the secrecy and dark designs that Protestants of his day denounced in the Church of Rome."[13] Taking Smith's analysis of the Roman church as the single, definitive source for Pandemonium, William Riley Parker best summarizes the satiric reading of the scene. Parker links the account of Pandemonium directly to Milton's visit to Rome in 1638: "Standing at last in St. Peter's, Milton must have felt it to be an architectural blasphemy, a perversion of true worship, a cathedral more fit for devils."[14]

The trouble with the satiric reading is not that it is false. Throughout his career Milton had rallied Protestant readers to his cause by mocking Catholic institutions. He does so most famously perhaps in his humorous indictment in *Areopagitica* of five imprimaturs conferring "in the Piatza of one Title page, complementing and ducking each to other with their shav'n reverences" (2:504). Certainly Pandemonium is a place, in Parker's phrase, "fit for devils." To the extent that the quintessential Catholic cathedral would signal to Milton's readers a perversion of true religion, Pandemonium delivers a satiric barb at the papacy. But would not Milton's "fit audience" (*Paradise Lost* 7.31) take for granted the corruption of the Roman church? Why would Milton lavish such painstaking attention on an image he wished only to explode? Simply regarding Pandemonium as the creation of demonic papists seems to distance and dismiss the scene too comfortably, in a way inconsistent with the troubling appeal of Satan himself in book 1.

Before asserting a positive view of Pandemonium, one ought perhaps to anticipate the objection that the iconoclast Milton would oppose such a positive view of any church edifice. The evidence of the Lady Chapel at Ely Cathedral, where Cromwell's soldiers literally defaced or where possible beheaded the stone statues of Roman Catholic saintly icons, points to a literal iconoclasm of church architecture that Milton—if he did not applaud— at least endured without recorded objection. Milton's assaults on nonscriptural forms of worship and government do seem at times consistent with Puritan attacks on false icons. Thanks to Paul Stevens, Sanford Budick, David Loewenstein, Lana Cable, Ronald W. Cooley, Michael Lieb, and others, Milton scholarship has come a long way from equating Milton's "icastic" treatment of images with either mere destructiveness or visual incapacity.[15] As an overview of this issue, W. J. T. Mitchell's summary best represents my position: "Milton's poetry is the scene of a struggle between iconoclastic distrust of the outward image and iconophilic fascination with its power."[16] In the opening invocation to *Paradise Lost*, Milton asserts that the Spirit prefers "Before all Temples th' upright heart and pure" (1.18); on a superficial reading, this line might be taken as a rejection of all houses of worship. Rather than denying that church buildings have any value, Milton's comparison treats "temples" as the standard dwelling place of the Spirit, a standard which the punningly "upright" heart nonetheless excels. To be sure, there are buildings as decadent as the cultures they represent: the Philistian temple in *Samson Agonistes* is the obvious example. Yet not even Samson's ultimate dismantling of the Temple of Dagon indicates that Milton views all building as vain or negative. After the tragedy, Manoa will bring Samson "Home to his Father's house: there will I build him / A Monument" (1733–34) that will commemorate Samson and rally "all the valiant youth" (1738), inflaming them "To matchless valor, and adventures high" (1740). However inward one regards Milton's ultimate turn in politics and poetry, he remains in dialogue with readers who are inspired by grand buildings. A cursory review of Milton's oeuvre presents several instances of the poet's fondness for impressive church architecture, from at least as early as the time he composed "L'Allegro" and "Il Penseroso." It is precisely the power of architecture to *impress* the observer, I shall argue, upon which Milton draws in *Paradise Lost*. And whereas the Son in *Paradise Regained* rejects Satan's offer of the panorama of imperial Rome, that epic culminates on the pinnacle of the temple, with the Son embodying a typological kind of architectural flourish, a figure in flesh mysteriously standing atop the Hebraic temple. *Paradise Regained* ends with the victorious Son quietly returning, in the poem's last line, "Home to his Mother's house" (4.639). Parallel to the "goodly" but incomplete tower in *The Readie and Easie Way* that could "overshaddow kings," the palace of Pandemonium does, as I will show, reflect sound aesthetic and architectural principles. That these positive features are weighted down, even perverted, by teleological misappropriation in no way cancels the architectural virtues of the edifice. Instead, such failings and exaggerations in demonic architecture may lead readers to reflect on the opportunities for appropriate building squandered by human architects. The Commonwealth, alas, was sorely in need of master builders.

The sequence by which Milton introduces Pandemonium to readers of *Paradise Lost* in book 1 hints at his double strategy of celebrating and undermining the structure. This doubleness is reflected in the two grammatical senses of "building": the gerund ("Building takes time.") referring to an unfolding process; the substantive ("What a fine building!") to a finished product. The satiric coloring of Pandemonium is applied to the finished structure only *after* we have seen the building process completed. For example, Milton's description of the assembly as a "secret conclave" (795) associates the devils' meeting with Catholic practice. This satiric designation, however, comes in the last sentence of the episode, after we have seen the magnificent building rise. Likewise, the bee simile linking the palace with the Barberini papacy appears only *after* the devils have assembled or "Swarm'd" (776) into the completed edifice. Preceding that simile is the narrator's celebrated correction of human error in ascribing the name "Mulciber" to the palace's demonic architect (730–51). Indeed the collective effect of these authorial comments is to undermine whatever admiration readers may have felt about the glorious scene of Pandemonium. Such a corrective strategy logically implies, of course, that an initially positive response to the place was expected and appropriate.

As a hinge between those later comments and the description of the actual scene of building Pandemonium, Milton describes the impressive effect the palace has on those who enter:

> The hasty multitude
> Admiring enter'd, and the work some praise
> And some the Architect: his hand was known
> In Heav'n by many a Tow'red structure high,
> Where Scepter'd Angels held thir residence.
>
> (730–34)

The devils universally admire, but their differing responses divide them into two groups: some admiring the craftsmanship ("the work some praise") and others "the Architect."

The doubleness in the devils' response may reflect the English Renaissance debate over the relative merits of architects and artisans. John Dee, in his 1570 preface to Euclid's *Elements*, had insisted on the gulf between the architect's intellectual achievement and the craftsman's handiwork. Paraphrasing Vitruvius, Dee claims that the architect is no mere "Artificer" but the "Hed, the Provost, the Director, and Judge of all Artificiall workes, and all Artificers."[17] Likewise, Sir Henry Wotton writes in his *Elements of Architecture* (1624) that the architect's chief "glory" consists "in the Designment and Idea of the whole Worke, and his truest ambition should be to make the Forme, which is the nobler Part (as it were) triumph over the Matter."[18] Specifically, Wotton cites on this point book 6, heading 2 of *De architectura*, which claims

that an architect's greatest care must be to find the exact mathematical proportion that determines a building's design.

In any case, Milton's verse paragraph makes one undeniable
point: the architect behind Pandemonium is the same architect
renowned for designing many magnificent dwellings in Heaven.
Those structures are described in unequivocally positive fashion.
The only note of discord in Milton's scene is the elegiac tone deriv-
ing from the past tense: "Where Scepter'd Angels *held* thir resi-
dence" (emphasis mine). Assuming that the architect's skill
remained constant from his tenure in Heaven to his relocation
to Hell, a reader gathers from this transitional passage evidence
attesting to the demonic architect's continuing mastery of the art.

A master architect's plan is likewise discernible in the initial
description of Pandemonium's rise. The principles of Vitruvius,
adumbrated by several Renaissance architects, pervade Milton's
description. To begin with, in describing the combining of various
materials into a single "mould" (706) for the building, he draws a
precise musical analogy: "As in an Organ from one blast of wind /
To many a row of Pipes the sound-board breathes" (708–9). In the
surviving manuscript of book 1 edited by Helen Darbishire, a
scribe alleged to be Edward Phillips has written "a row of" over
the crossed-out "an hundred" and added an "s" to Pipe.[19] The
change focuses Milton's simile on an organ, making it at once more
orderly and more visually accurate. The specific vehicle of Milton's
comparison, the organ's sounding board that conveys architectonic
unity and harmony, derives from Vitruvius. In discussing the design of theaters in book 5 of *De architectura,* Vitruvius tells how
ancient architects considered acoustics:

> et quaesierunt per canonicam mathematicorum et musican rationem,
> ut, quaecumque vox esset in scaena, clarior et suavior ad spectatorum
> perveniret aures. uti enim organa in aeneis lamminis aut corneis echeis
> at cordarum sonitum claritatem perficiuntur, sic theatrorum per har-
> monicen ad augendam vocem ratiocinationes ab antiquis sunt constitu-
> tae. (5.3.8)

> By the rules of mathematics and the method of music, they sought to
> make the voices from the stage rise more clearly and sweetly to the
> spectators' ears. For just as organs which have bronze plates or horn
> sounding boards are brought to the clear sound of string instruments,
> so by the arrangement of theaters in accordance with the science of
> harmony, the ancients increased the power of the voice.

Consistent with his notion of the perfect architect's knowledge of all arts and sciences,[20] Vitruvius articulates an architectural principle that depends upon music and mathematics. He takes the harmonic tuning of the sounding board as the standard for acoustic design; Milton's devils rely on this notion in laying the foundation of Pandemonium.

When we hear next in Milton's narrative how Pandemonium arose on its site, Vitruvian doctrine and demonic practice unfold inseparably. Describing the distinctive features of the building from bottom to top, Milton's single, sinuous sentence mimics the vertical rise of Pandemonium:

> Anon out of the earth a Fabric huge
> Rose like an Exhalation, with the sound
> Of Dulcet Symphonies and voices sweet,
> Built like a Temple, where Pilasters round
> Were set, and Doric pillars overlaid
> With Golden Architrave; nor did there want
> Cornice or Frieze, with bossy Sculptures grav'n;
> The Roof was fretted Gold.
>
> (1.710–17)

The generic term Milton uses to describe Pandemonium is a "Fabric." Vitruvius had used the Latin word *fabrica* to refer both to particular buildings and to the art of architecture. Accordingly, "fabrica," "fabric," or "fabrique" became the Renaissance terms of art for an architecturally composed building. Wotton routinely refers to buildings as "fabrics," pausing once to translate the term: "*Vna Fabrica ben raccolta:* as *Italians* use to speake of well united Workes."[21] Using the phrase "fabricke of man," Sir Thomas Browne in *Religio Medici* extends the architectural term to human anatomy, and thence to an argument for the inorganic nature of the soul.[22] The various architectural features of the fabric that Milton describes can all be traced to Vitruvius, but they can just as easily be illustrated by dozens of Renaissance structures. Above all, Pandemonium stands as "a Fabric huge": it presents to the eye a grand spectacle of imperial power and magnificence.

Milton takes particular care to point out that Pandemonium is "Built like a Temple." Smith emphasizes the negative implication of that description. Pandemonium is *not* a temple but a palace in temple style, she remarks, which provides a measure of the perversion the devilish building represents.[23] I suggest that the perversion Smith stresses coincides with an undeniably impressive aspect of Pandemonium. To say that Pandemonium is "Built like a Temple," or built in the style of an ancient temple, is to say that it resembles in its basic design the grandest and most celebrated Renaissance churches. William A. McClung has recently added the Temple of Jerusalem, a scholarly reconstruction of which was published at Rome in 1604, to the list of likely precedents for Pandemonium. McClung notes the tradition that the Vitruvian canon informing that temple had been delivered by God to the Hebrews.[24] I caution, however, against the positive identification of any single edifice with Milton's poetic image of Pandemonium. The ambiguity of Milton's poetic utterance "Built like a Temple," doubly indefinite through its use of simile and indefinite article, certainly creates space for a range of possible models. Rather than being modeled exclusively on St. Peter's, Pandemonium reflects any number of Renaissance churches built along Roman lines that Milton knew.

Here again the revival of Vitruvius in the Renaissance provides illumination for Milton's verse account. Cesariano's commentary in his 1521 edition of Vitruvius had issued a sharp challenge to aspiring architects. Domestic architecture is easy in comparison with designing a sacred building, Cesariano writes, "with its fitting parts proportioned and diligently harmonized."[25] The comment may reflect credit on the builder of Pandemonium, who previously had designed dwellings for the angels. In the opening chapter of the third book of De architectura, Vitruvius had introduced his famous observations on the proportions of the human figure, which are to be reflected in the overall proportions of temples. Vitruvius explains how the human figure with extended hands and feet fits perfectly into the two putatively perfect geometrical figures: the square and the circle. Fra Giocondo, in his 1511 Venice edition, provided woodcut illustrations of Vitruvius's "homo ad quadratum" and "homo ad circulum" (illustrations 1 and 2). "This simple picture," Rudolf Wittkower remarks, "seemed to reveal a deep and fundamental truth about man and the world, and its importance for Renaissance architects can hardly be overestimated. The image haunted their imagination."[26]

Indeed, Renaissance commentators on Vitruvius elaborated, in a variety of ways, upon this picture of the human form circumscribed and framed within a square. Cesariano's edition takes a graphic, mathematical turn by generating a circle within a grid of smaller squares inside a single square encompassing the human form (illustration 3). This geometric grid evokes a mechanistic view of the inscribed human being. Within Milton's poem, God's act of circumscribing the universe with "golden Compasses" (7.225), thereby casting God as divine architect, is the central—but by no means the only—reflection of Vitruvius's geometrical anthropomorphism.

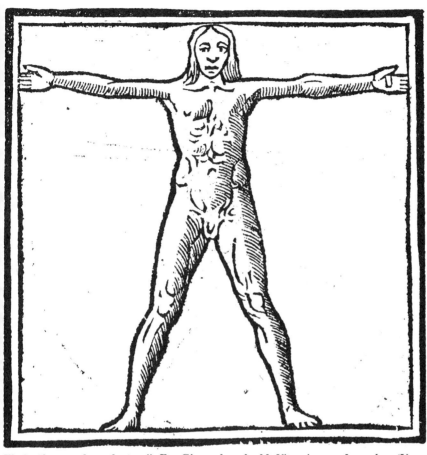

Ill. 1. "homo ad quadratum". Fra Giocondo, ed., *M. Vitruvius per Jocundum* (Venice, 1511). Photo courtesy of The Newberry Library, Chicago.

Ill. 2. "homo ad circulum". Fra Giocondo, ed., *M. Vitruvius per Jocundum* (Venice, 1511). Photo courtesy of The Newberry Library, Chicago.

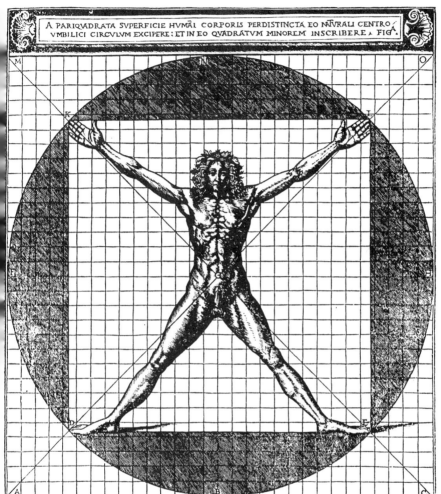

Ill. 3. Vitruvian figure. Cesariano's *Lucio Vitruvio Pollione de Architectura* (Como: Gotardus de Ponte, 1521). Courtesy of Special Collections and Rare Books Dept., University of Minnesota Libraries.

Yet the ambiguous vision of Milton's poem for which I have been arguing resists the definite mechanism of Cesariano's illustration. When, for example, Satan escapes from the nether world and once again glimpses Heaven, his vision employs the geometric forms of circle and square, but he cannot resolve what he sees into one definite pattern. Satan beholds

> Far off th' Empyreal Heav'n, extended wide
> In circuit, undetermin'd square or round,
> With Opal Tow'rs and Battlements adorn'd
> Of living Sapphire, once his native Seat.
>
> (2.1047–1050)

After the Fall, Sin mockingly asserts the superiority of Satan's "Orbicular World" (10.381) to God's "quadrature" (10.381), assuming that the sphere is a more perfect form than the cube. Sin's opposition of these forms, however, overlooks the possibility of their fusion in the human form. During the Renaissance, the mathematical conundrum of squaring the circle came to symbolize the mysterious integration of spirit and matter in humankind; inevitably, it came to symbolize as well the mystery of the Incarnation.[27] Indeed from the sentence first naming Pandemonium, Milton has playfully associated both circle and square with the fallen angels. There the demonic heralds

> proclaim
> A solemn Council forthwith to be held
> At Pandæmonium, the high Capitol
> Of Satan and his Peers: thir summons call'd
> From every *Band* and *squared* Regiment
> By place or choice the worthiest.
>
> (1.754–59; emphasis mine)

The "Capitol" in Milton's sentence has an obvious Roman precedent as well, alluding to the Roman Capitol, where assemblies debated peace or war. As the dominating structure of Pandemonium itself, the Capitol has patent architectural significance.

Perhaps the illustration of Vitruvius most influential upon Milton's scene is also the most familiar. Behind Leonardo's immediately recognizable drawing of a circumscribed human figure at Venice, the text Leonardo illustrates is this same passage from book 3 of Vitruvius. Moreover, the matching of circular and square geometrical forms based on the human body reappears in Leonardo's sketches of various church designs. These sketches remind us that, in its most basic definition, architecture is the creation of interior spaces for human occupants. Among many composed structures, those sketches are magnificently realized in the church of Santa Maria della Consolazione at Todi, which embodies Vitruvius's combination of circle, square, and human form along the lines of Leonardo's sketches (illustration 4). Responding to this fusion of Renaissance artistry and ancient theory, Wittkower concludes: "How could the relation of Man to God be better expressed, we feel now justified in asking, than by building the house of God in accordance with the fundamental geometry of square and circle?"[28]

The Vitruvian background to Pandemonium that I have sketched in this essay should raise similar questions. Granted that the palace of Pandemonium amounts to a perverted temple, a place of self-worship, is it possible that it also reflects a spiritual urge for harmonic relation with God? Whatever else they have lost, the fallen in *Paradise Lost* nonetheless seek encounters with goodness and divinity. Milton refers to the devils assembled in Pandemonium as "A thousand Demi-Gods on golden seats" (1.796). Cesariano argues in his commentary on Vitruvius that master architects who can create the effects they desire appear *come semidei* [like demi-gods].[29] Blasphemy and divine aspiration are near in kind. While Puritan reformers rightly mocked the greed and corruption of the imperial Roman church, seen in the lavish expenditure on St. Peter's no less than in the "fretted Gold" crowning Pandemonium, can the architectural achievements of Leonardo, Brunelleschi, Alberti, and Palladio be likewise mocked as merely perverse? At the very least, should not a full response to Pandemonium also credit the impressive act of creation that its architect has left as a memorial?

The Miltonic narrator, by the way, includes a teacherly bit of commentary on Pandemonium aimed at ambitious architects. In accord with my argument for both positive and negative aspects of Pandemonium, the advice he gives to human builders is at once uplifting and humbling:

> Learn how thir greatest Monuments of Fame,
> And Strength and Art are easily outdone
> By Spirits reprobate.
>
> (1.695–97)

Notes

I wish to thank my colleagues Jolene Barjasteh, Sylvia Carullo, and Katherine Smith-Abbott for gracious assistance in obtaining permission to reproduce artworks from European collections.

Ill. 4. Aerial view of Santa Maria della Consolazione, Todi, 1508. Courtesy of the photo laboratory of Vincenzo Benigni, Todi, Italy.

The epigraph is from John Milton, *The Readie and Easie Way to Establish A Free Commonwealth*, in *The Complete Prose Works of John Milton*, 8 vols., ed. Don M. Wolfe et al. (New Haven: Yale University Press, 1953–82), 7:422–23. Unless otherwise indicated, all references to Milton's prose are to this edition and are cited parenthetically in the text.

1. Regina M. Schwartz (*Remembering and Repeating: Biblical Creation in "Paradise Lost"* [Cambridge: Cambridge University Press, 1988], 2–3) observes that Milton begins the opening proem of *Paradise Lost* with just such an inversion, a reversal of the biblical order of creation and fall that signals the continuing process of re-creation.

2. Andrew Barnaby ("'Another Rome in the West?': Milton and the Imperial Republic, 1654–1670," *Milton Studies* 30 [1993]: 67–84) argues that the allusion to the Roman republic here at once "establishes Rome as a model for England's godly task in history" and "associates Roman *imperium* with ungodly conquest." Such a notion of Rome's bifurcated status as a suspect yet successful model underlies my argument in this essay.

3. Z. S. Fink, *The Classical Republicans: An Essay in the Recovery of a Pattern of Thought in Seventeenth-Century England* (Evanston, Ill.: Northwestern University Press, 1962), 105–16.

4. Nigel Smith, *Literature and Revolution, 1640–1660* (New Haven: Yale University Press, 1994), 193–95.

5. For a summary of Vitruvius's life and work in the context of the Augustan age, see *The Cambridge History of Classical Literature*, ed. E. J. Kenney and W. V. Clausen, vol. 2, Latin Literature (Cambridge: Cambridge University Press, 1982), 493–94; and Frank Granger's introduction to *Vitruvius: On Architecture*, 2 vols., Loeb Classical Library (Cambridge: Harvard University Press, 1931), 1:xiii–xvi. Unless otherwise indicated, all references to the Latin text of Vitruvius are to this edition and are cited parenthetically in the text. I follow standard practice in citing *De architectura* by its book, section, and member numbers. The English translation is my own.

6. Anthony Johnson's *Ben Jonson: Poetry and Architecture* (New York: Oxford University Press, 1995) could serve as a useful precedent for such a comprehensive study.

7. John Milton, *Of Education*, in *John Milton: Complete Poems and Major Prose*, ed. Merritt Y. Hughes (New York: Odyssey, 1957), 634; Edward Phillips, *The Life of Milton*, in *John Milton: Complete Poems*, ed. Hughes, 1029.

8. This copy, recently displayed at the Newberry Library in Chicago, is in the private collection of Jeffrey Jahns, whose generosity in allowing me to examine the book I am happy to acknowledge.

9. *John Milton: Complete Poems*, ed. Hughes, 634 n. 34.

10. Augustine, in Sancti Aurelii Augustini, *De Doctrina Christiana*, ed. Joseph Martin, Corpus Christianorum Series Latina, Vol. 32 (Turnhout, Belgium: Brepols, 1962), 98–99. For a discussion relating this Augustinian tradition to English literature, see D. W. Robertson, Jr., *A Preface to Chaucer: A Study in Medieval Perspectives* (Princeton, N.J.: Princeton University Press, 1962), 295–99. Robertson sees Augustine's articulation of multiple signification as a key factor in the development of both scriptural and literary exegesis.

11. Rebecca W. Smith, "The Source of Milton's Pandemonium," *Modern Philology* 29 (1931): 187.

12. John Milton, *Paradise Lost*, *John Milton: Complete Poems*, ed. Hughes. All references to Milton's poetry are to this edition and are cited parenthetically in the text.

13. Smith, "The Source," 193–94.

14. William Riley Parker, *Milton: A Biography*, 2 vols. (Oxford: Clarendon, 1968), 1:172–73.

15. Paul Stevens, "Milton and the Icastic Imagination," *Milton Studies* 20 (1984): 43–73; Sanford Budick, *The Dividing Muse: Images of Sacred Disjunction in Milton's Poetry* (New Haven: Yale University Press, 1985), especially 7–8; David Loewenstein, *Milton and the Drama of History: Historical Vision, Iconoclasm, and the Literary Imagination* (Cambridge: Cambridge University Press, 1990); Lana Cable, "Milton's Iconoclastic Truth," in *Politics, Poetics, and Hermeneutics in Milton's Prose*, ed. David Loewenstein and James Grantham Turner (Cambridge: Cambridge University Press, 1990), 135–51; Ronald W. Cooley, "Iconoclasm and Self-Definition in Milton's *Of Reformation*," *Religion and Literature* 23 (spring 1991): 23–36; Michael Lieb, *Milton and the Culture of Violence* (Ithaca: Cornell University Press, 1994); and Lana Cable, *Carnal Rhetoric: Milton's Iconoclasm and the Poetics of Desire* (Durham, N.C.: Duke University Press, 1995).

16. W. J. T. Mitchell, *Iconology: Image, Text, Ideology* (Chicago: University of Chicago Press, 1985), 36.

17. John Dee, *The Mathematicall Praeface to the Elements of Geometrie of Euclid of Megara* (1570), intro. Allen G. Debus (New York: Science History Publications, 1975), d.iiij-v.

18. Sir Henry Wotton, *The Elements of Architecture, A Facsimile Reprint of the First Edition* (London: John Bill, 1624; reprint, Charlottesville: University of Virginia Press, 1968), 11–12. Two factors point to Wotton as the conduit for Milton's awareness of this issue: Milton's cordial relationship with the English ambassador to Venice, attested by Wotton's glowing letter of introduction for the younger man; and their mutual reliance on Vitruvius, whom Wotton several times calls "our principal Master."

19. *The Manuscript of Milton's "Paradise Lost," Book I*, ed. Helen Darbishire (Oxford: Clarendon, 1931).

20. In the introduction to *De architectura* 1.1.3, Vitruvius argues that the master architect should be a man of letters, a skillful artist, a sound mathematician, and a diligent student of philosophy, as well as familiar with scientific studies, acquainted with music, not ignorant of medicine, learned in the writings of jurists, and familiar with astronomy. Such encyclopedic learning is the aim of Milton's educational scheme, as well as a corollary of his own ambition as an epic poet, in accord with the notion in the *Apology against a Pamphlet* "that he who would not be frustrate of his hope to write well hereafter in laudable things, ought himself to be a true poem, that is, a composition and pattern of the best and honorablest things" (2:354).

21. Wotton, *The Elements*, 68.

22. Sir Thomas Browne (*Religio Medici*, in *The Works of Sir Thomas Browne*, 4 vols., ed. Sir Geoffrey Keynes [Chicago: University of Chicago Press, 1964], 1:47) argues as follows:

In our study of Anatomy there is a masse of mysterious Philosophy, and such as reduced the very Heathens to Divinitie; yet amongst all those rare discoveries, and curious pieces I finde in the fabricke of man, I doe not so much content myselfe as in that I finde not, that is, no Organ or instrument for the rationall soule; for in the braine, which we tearme the seate of reason, there is not any thing of moment more than I can discover in the cranie of a beast: and this is a sensible and no inconsiderable argument of the inorganity of the soule, at least in that sense we usually so receive it.

For this reference I am indebted to William Howard of the University of Washington.

23. Smith, "The Source," 192–94.

24. William A. McClung, "The Architecture of Pandæmonium," *Milton Quarterly* 15 (1981): 109–12. Moreover, McClung refutes the notion, still heard occasionally, that Pandemonium is a monstrous melange of styles, a notion advanced by A. L. Turner in "Arts of Design, Milton and the," in *A Milton Encyclopedia*, 9 vols., ed. William B. Hunter et al. (Lewisburg, Pa.: Bucknell University Press, 1978), 1:90–102; and by Roland Mushat Frye, *Milton's Imagery and the Visual Arts: Iconographic Tradition in the Epic Poems* (Princeton: Princeton University Press, 1978), 134–35. But Pandemonium is not Chaos. That notion depends upon two misreadings: of "Roof" in line 717 as excluding the ceiling; and "arched" in line 726 as implying Gothic vaulting. Essentially, Pandemonium is constructed in the Doric order, with some reasonable departures, considering its supernatural context.

25. Cesariano, ed., *De architectura*, by Vitruvius (Como, 1521), 3.1.43.

26. Rudolf Wittkower, *Architectural Principles in the Age of Humanism*, 4th ed. (New York: St. Martin's, 1988), 22.

27. Alastair Fowler, ed., *Paradise Lost*, by John Milton (London: Longman, 1971), 527 n. x381. Cf. Fowler, *Spenser and the Numbers of Time* (New York: Barnes and Noble, 1964), 267.

28. Wittkower, *Architectural Principles*, 25.

29. Cesariano, ed., *De architectura*, 1.5.2.

Milton and Blake: Visualizing the Expulsion

CHERYL H. FRESCH

It has been forty years since Jean H. Hagstrum in *The Sister Arts* described Milton's pictorial abilities much as T. S. Eliot had a few years earlier: "Milton's visual touches . . . remain [touches and strokes], serving other larger aims. The iconic and pictorialist conventions do appear, but they are soon absorbed in intellectual conceits, musical resonances, or sublime epic movements. . . . One of the most characteristic motions of . . . [Milton's] imagination is to approach the pictorialist conventions and then to withdraw into other forms of expression."[1] While Hagstrum offered compelling support for such an argument, it is nevertheless firmly countered by such remarkable visual images as those which move *Paradise Lost* to its conclusion:

> In either hand the hastening angel caught
> Our lingering parents, and to the eastern gate
> Led them direct, and down the cliff as fast
> To the subjected plain; then disappeared.
> They looking back, all the eastern side beheld
> Of Paradise, so late their happy seat,
> Waved over by that flaming brand, the gate
> With dreadful faces thronged and fiery arms.

(12.637–44)[2]

Milton does not here approach, but then withdraw from "pictorialist conventions," nor does he permit those "pictorialist conventions" to be absorbed within "intellectual conceits." With this image, Milton rather effects new intellectual meaning; indeed, the "pictorialist conventions" that Milton here masterfully maintains do no less than involve the meaning of expulsion with the meaning of deliverance.

Those modern scholars concerned with the illustrated editions of *Paradise Lost* have done much to enhance our view of Milton's Michael leading Adam and Eve to the edge of Eden. While Roy Flannagan's recent edition of *Paradise Lost* now makes readily available the illustrations from the 1688 edition of the poem, Blake's early nineteenth-century illustrations to *Paradise Lost* have already focused most of the modern scholarly attention upon this image near the end of book 12.[3] Joseph A. Wittreich acknowledges, for example, that although Blake's illustration of Milton's Expulsion scene includes pictorial details missing from Milton's text, it nevertheless "constitutes an epilogue to Milton's poem and is, therefore, an epitome of its action."[4] Until we recover the pictorialist conventions that shape both Milton's and Blake's Expulsion scenes, however, we will remain but dimly aware of just how profoundly they serve as epitome and epilogue to the entire poem.

Henry Aldrich's *Expulsion,* which appeared in the first illustrated edition of *Paradise Lost* (1688), ignored the pictorial conventions of Milton's Expulsion scene. As Helen Gardner explained in 1956, "instead of studying his author," the first illustrator "was content with a bad imitation of Raphael's 'Expulsion' . . . itself derived from Masaccio's fresco in the Carmine in Florence."[5] Francis Hayman broke from the authority of the 1688 edition when he illustrated the Expulsion for Thomas Newton's 1749 edition of *Paradise Lost,* and by the turn of the century, Hayman's acknowledgment of Milton's text was seen to be continued both in the work of Edward Burney (1799) and—most remarkably—in the work of William Blake, who completed two series of *Paradise Lost* paintings (1807, 1808). (See illustration 1.) Both Burney and Blake, like Hayman, show Michael clasping Adam's and Eve's hands, and all three Expulsion scenes are basically frontal depictions of the angel flanked by the humans he leads out of Eden. A remarkably different tone characterizes Blake's illustration, however, as Merritt Hughes emphasized in 1965: "Blake was the first artist to conceive Milton's Expulsion with hope and love in the faces of Adam and Eve, and an unarmed Michael leading them by the hands, as Milton has him do."[6]

Marcia R. Pointon, elaborating upon Merritt Hughes's point, located the source of the tone of Milton's Expulsion scene in the theory of the Fortunate Fall: "It is upon the idea of the 'felix culpa' that Milton's conclusion to *Paradise Lost* depends. The expulsion for Milton is not a negative, tragic event but a positive and hopeful though still unhappy one. This ambivalence is essential to the poem."[7] The source of Blake's staging, rather than the source of Milton's tone for the Expulsion scene, moved Pamela Dunbar to suggest that the "one possible [pictorial] model" for Blake's depiction of Michael leading Adam and Eve out of Eden is *Lot's Escape,* a painting by Rubens, which Blake had engraved for the *Protes-*

Ill. 1. William Blake, "The Expulsion from Eden" (1808). Gift by Subscription. Courtesy, Museum of Fine Arts, Boston.

tant's Family Bible (1781) and which—in a nearly frontal presentation—has Lot holding his daughters' hands as they resignedly flee the burning Sodom over which lightning flashes.[8] More recently, Stephen C. Behrendt has seen another pictorial parallel for Blake's *Expulsion* in Blake's own 1807 painting *The Fall of Man.* (See illustration 2.) The central focus of that painting is Christ holding Adam and Eve by the wrists, leading them directly toward the viewer, and away from the pre- and post-lapsarian garden scenes balanced behind them. The three stride forward atop a hill within which Satan, with suffering lamenting human forms in a gated Hell to his left, sits upon a throne, just as in the upper plane of the three-tier painting the Father sits upon his throne.[9] Blake's *The Fall of Man* presents not the actual eating of the forbidden fruit, but rather the act of rescue by which divine love first responded to human sin, and the apocalyptic and ambivalent quality of this painting extends to Blake's Expulsion illustrations. The vision that Blake establishes in paintings of both The Fall of Man and the Expulsion in the *Paradise Lost* series is the vision that Blake himself perceived in Milton's depiction of the Expulsion in *Paradise Lost*, and the inspiration for the visionary force in Milton's Expulsion, I contend, is the traditional visual rendering of the *Anastasis*—the crucified Christ's rising and his simultaneous raising of Adam and Eve from Hell on Holy Saturday. Working with the pictorialist conventions of the *Anastasis*, Milton conceived and established an extraordinarily new image of the Expulsion from the Garden of Eden, an extraordinarily new image that Blake not only saw in the closing lines of *Paradise Lost* but that he also made visible in his own illustrations for Milton's epic.

The Son's offer to redeem humanity, seen fulfilled—for the visionary viewer—in the *Anastasis* illustrations we shall look at, is of central importance in *Paradise Lost* to both Milton and Blake. From the bard's invocation that the muse sing "Of man's first disobedience . . . till one greater man / Restore us" (1.1, 4–5), through the heavenly dialogue in which the Son actually volunteers to die— "on me let Death wreak all his rage" (3.241)—and continuing on to Michael's narration of the Crucifixion atop the visionary mountain, the reader of *Paradise Lost* is persistently reminded of the Christocentric nature of the epic. In the Expulsion scene, the Son's promise of redemption is yet once more recalled and further developed—now, however, with a closing vignette in which the promised word moves to enter time, and acts to shatter it for those whose eyes perceive Milton's visionary art.

Ill. 2. William Blake, "The Fall of Man" (1807). Victoria and Albert Museum.

While Behrendt somewhat similarly argues that "Every design in [Blake's] . . . *Paradise Lost* series elucidates some aspects of the Son's offer to redeem man, rediscovering and reemphasizing its significance by exploring its various aspects,"[10] he holds that Blake's illustration to book 11, *Michael Foretells the Crucifixion,* "represents the fulfillment of the Son's offer to redeem humanity."[11] Behrendt seems unaware that his emphasis on the Crucifixion illustration renders Blake's subsequent Expulsion illustration anticlimactic. Giving considerably more prominence to the Crucifixion than to the Resurrection, Behrendt's reading of Blake's illustrations separates into two the complex theological whole that, according to Anna D. Kartsonis, is the essence of the mystery of Redemption. Explaining that the Anastasis became the central image of the Resurrection for medieval Eastern Christianity, Kartsonis asserts that "Crucifixion and Anastasis are interpreted as the two interdependent facets of the scheme of Redemption."[12]

As she traces the development of the *Anastasis* image over a four-hundred-year period, Kartsonis identifies four variants on its central iconographical features. The first type of *Anastasis* image, clarified through the ninth century, shows Christ moving toward a kneeling Adam, who may be on either side, and lifting him, sometimes from a sarcophagus. Behind Adam, Eve raises her hands in supplication and is ignored. "The scene usually takes place in the upper part of the *tenebrae* . . . [and] [t]he broken gates of Hades are sometimes included." When represented, Satan is fettered, although he may be holding Adam's foot.[13] (See illustration 3.) The second type, dominant in the eleventh century, shows Christ dragging Adam behind him while holding the cross in his left hand.[14] The third type, also seen in the eleventh century, very significantly establishes the "strictly frontal figure of Christ,"[15] who stands upon or above the trampled head or body of Satan who lies on top of a hill. Christ is flanked by Adam and Eve and is often seen—again— lifting Adam by the hand. The fourth type of the *Anastasis,* and the latest to develop, combines elements of the second and third. Most significantly with the fourth type, however, not only does Christ pull Adam from the realm of Death, but "now Christ also pull[s] Eve by the hand, thus raising for the first time both Adam and Eve, who flank . . . him symmetrically."[16]

The basic arrangement of the three principal persons in the third and fourth types of the *Anastasis* is the same arrangement seen in both Milton's and Blake's Expulsion scenes: Christ or Michael is seen moving forward and down a hill, that is, while holding Adam and Eve by the hands. Another important and fairly constant ele-

Ill. 3. *The Anastasis.* The Pierpont Morgan Library, New York, M.639,f.1

ment in all of the *Anastasis* images is the trampled Satan. To recognize this feature is also to realize that Blake for the first time most remarkably brings the Miltonic representative of Satan—the Serpent—into an illustration of Milton's Expulsion, and while the Serpent is not trampled by Blake's Michael, he is certainly threatened by the angel's heel. Finally, almost invariably featured in the *Anastasis* images are the fires of Hell, which Milton and Blake recall by means of the "flaming brand" (12.643) that blazes behind Adam and Eve.

Despite the parallels between the image established in Milton's poem and the pictorial conventions of the *Anastasis*, Kartsonis's monumental study carries no evidence that the iconography of the *Anastasis* was available to Milton; the pictures that Kartsonis presents are by and large Byzantine. Furthermore, when opening her work, Kartsonis defines the *Anastasis* by contrasting it with the *Descensus ad infernos* tradition, which she claims was more popular in the Western Church:

> any designation of the subject matter of this [Anastasis] iconography as the Descent or harrowing of hell misrepresents and distorts the message of the chosen label Anastasis. The title and subject matter of this image refer, not to the Descent of Christ into Hell, Hades, Limbo, or Inferno, but to the rising of Christ and his raising of the dead. The concepts of rising and descending are obviously antonymous and therefore not interchangeable. Furthermore, the choice of the one over the other vitally affects the theological emphasis and interpretation of the image labeled Anastasis.[17]

A brief glance at medieval Western art—both literary and pictorial—suggests that Kartonis's distinctions here are perhaps more theoretical than actual, however, and that the icongraphy of the *Anastasis* was very much available to Milton.

While *The Descensus* rather than *The Anastasis* may be the title of the illustration from the *Latin Hours of Catherine of Cleves* (1440), for example, the image is that of the redeemed being hauled from Hell. (See illustration 4.) So too, the iconography of *The Harrowing of Hell* in the twelfth-century St. Albans Psalter, like the iconography of the similar scenes in the Avila Bible, the Winchester Bible, and the Exultet Roll is the iconography of the *Anastasis*—Christ, striding across or standing on Satan, the gates of Hell splintered about him, and fire blazing behind him, pulls Adam out of Hell. (See illustrations 5, 6.) Complementing these pictorial images, the literary arts also argue for the Western Church's force-

Ill. 4. *The Descensus,* in *The Latin Hours of Catherine of Cleves* (1440). The Pierpont Morgan Library, New York, M.945, f.107

Ill. 5. *The Harrowing of Hell*, St. Alban's Psalter. The Warburg Institute.

Ill. 6. Beatus initial from Psalm 1, Winchester Bible. The Dean and Chapter of Winchester. The Warburg Institute.

ful understanding of the vital association between the Descent and the *Anastasis*.

The medieval morality plays of England, for example, most obviously reveal a strong popular appreciation of the entire tradition. The Coventry "Harrowing," like "The Deliverance of Souls" in the Wakefield cycle, presents Christ calling Adam and Eve from Hell:

> Come forth Adam and Eve with thee,
> And all my friends that here-in be,
> To paradise come forth with me.[18]

> Come now forth, my children all,
>   Forgiven now what was amiss;
> With me now go ye shall
>   To joy and endless bliss.[19]

Even more remarkable for those readers with the concluding vignette from *Paradise Lost* in mind, both the Chester and the York "Harrowing" plays conclude with Jesus ordering Michael to lead Adam and the other Old Testament heroes from Hell. As he prepares to return to the tomb where his body remains, the soul of Jesus in the York "Harrowing" directs his followers:

> Adame and my frendis in feere,
> Fro all youre fooes come fourth with me.
> Ye schalle be sette in solas seere,
> Wher ye schall nevere of sorowes see.
> And Mighill, myn aungell clere,
> Ressayve thes saules all unto the,
> And lede thame als I schall the lere
> To Paradise with playe and plente.
> [*Michael Leads the Souls from Hell.*][20]

In the Chester *Harrowing of Hell,* Adam is led from Hell by both Jesus and Michael. Stage directions call for a stage image that shows anticipatory fulfillment of the subsequent words of Jesus:

> *Then Jesus shall take Adam by the hand.*
>   Peace to the, Adam, my darlinge,
>   And eke to all thy ofspringe,
>   That righteous were in eirth lyvinge;
>   From me you shall not sever.
>   To blis[se] now I will you bringe;
>   Ther you shall be without endinge.

At that point, however, Jesus turns to Michael: "Michael, lead these men singinge / To ioy that lasteth ever." Once again, then, the Chester play immediately moves visually to realize its verbal text, for Michael no sooner vows, "Lord, your will done shall be. / Come forth, Adam! come with me!" than the image of the *Anastasis* is delineated by stage directions: *"Then Michael shall lead Adam and the saints to Paradise."*[21]

Michael's assumption of the role of guide to Paradise or his sharing that role with Christ, as he does in these "Harrowing" plays, reflects the increasing importance of the angel throughout the Latin Middle Ages. During the fourth and fifth centuries the popular history of the angel's spirited involvement with human history moved Christians to emphasize his identity as *Quis ut Deus* [He who is as God]. The cult of Saint Michael throughout medieval Europe resuscitated the angel's importance in Hebrew Scripture and legend, and, explains Olga Rojdestvensky, he became widely celebrated as the "ange des morts," or the "angel of the dead" who guided the souls to the afterlife: "C'est dans un ordre d'idées un peu special que se développe sa fonction d'ange des trépasses, guide d'outre-tombe des ames mortes."[22] For the devout believer, of course, the angel who guides the soul to death also guides it out of death and into Paradise, and Christians have elaborated this tradition, adapted for the "Harrowing" plays, from the early centuries of the Christian era (even within apocryphal treatises such as *The Apocalypse of Paul*) to the *Roman Missal* still in use today in which "the standard bearer Michael [is asked to] lead them [the souls of the deceased] into [God's] holy light."[23]

While Michael shares with Christ the role of guide in the Harrowing episode in the *Gospel of Nicodemus*,[24] Christ alone functions as guide in what was probably the fullest, most important literary presentation of the Harrowing available to Milton, the Harrowing prophetically described in Passus 18 of *Piers the Plowman*. In *Piers*, both Satan and Jesus anticipate Christ's leading his beloved from Hell. Alerting his demonic comrades to the threat outside the gates of Hell, Satan explains, "If this kynge come in mankynde wil he fecche, / And lede it ther hym lyketh."[25] Repeating Satan's emphasis, Jesus soon thereafter declares that "Thus bi lawe . . . lede I wil fro hennes / Tho that me loved and leved in my comynge" (398–99). Finally, William recalls that the demons of Hell, not daring to look on Christ, "leten hym lede forth what hym lyked" (403–4). For those readers familiar with the traditional visualizations of the *Anastasis*, the Harrowing episode in *Piers the Plowman* also brings intriguing attention to the physical details of humanity's being led out of Hell.

During the heavenly debate among Mercy, Truth, and Peace, which precedes the actual Harrowing, Mercy says the "man shal from merkenesse be drawe" (135), and Peace then proceeds to explain that

> Mercy, my sustre, and I mankynde shulde save;
> And that god hath forgyven and graunted me, Pees, and Mercy,
> To be mannes meynpernoure for evere-more after.
>
> (181–83)

Literally translating "meynpernoure" as "taken by the hand," the *Oxford English Dictionary* tracks the term's currency from late thirteenth-century through late nineteenth-century legal writings in which "meynpernoure" means "A surety for a prisoner's appearance in court on a specified day." Legal interpretations of the nature of the responsibility taken on by the purchaser (or holder) of the surety for the prisoner varied considerably through the centuries, however. Approximately one hundred years after Hall's *Chronicles* (1548) explained "meyneperner" with the appositional "body for body," for example, the *O.E.D.* indicates that Nicolas Bacon qualified that meaning by arguing that "Mainperners are not to be punished as principals, unless they be parties or privies to the failing of the Principal" (1647).

More emphatically than in *Piers the Plowman,* this legal understanding of the "meynpernoure" is shown to assume profound theological significance in *Paradise Lost,* when the Father announces humankind's impending fall and calls for someone to "pay / The rigid satisfaction, death for death," someone "just the unjust to save" (3.211–12, 215). Volunteering, the Son announces his willingness to die for another, and also, therefore, to die for justice:

> Behold me then, me for him, life for life
> I offer, on me let thine anger fall;
> Account me man; I for his sake will leave
> Thy bosom, and this glory next to thee
> Freely put off, and for him lastly die
> Well pleased, on me let Death wreak all his rage.
>
> (3.236–41)

Sustained by his simple and unshakable faith in the Father—"by thee I live" (3.244)—the Son then quickly proceeds to glimpse the implications of his act:

> But I shall rise victorious, and subdue
> My vanquisher, spoiled of his vaunted spoil;
> Death his death's wound shall then receive, and stoop
> Inglorious, of his mortal sting disarmed.
>
> (3.250–53)

In his descent to death lies the Son's own individual triumph over Death through the Resurrection, but in the Son's descent is also guaranteed the triumph of redeemed humanity through the Harrowing of Hell.

Both typified by and implicated in this shared temporal triumph, however, is that eternal triumph to be established by the Last Judgment. Developing his revelation of the timeless implications of the Passion, the Son's voice irresistibly and ever more powerfully modulates into prophetic registers, collapsing into simultaneity and merging into identity the first separation of the redeemed from the damned, to be effected by the Harrowing, and the final apocalyptic separation of the redeemed from the damned, after which the Son

> through the ample air in triumph high
> Shall lead hell captive maugre hell, and show
> The powers of darkness bound.
>
> (3.254–56)

"Thou at the sight / Pleased, out of heaven shalt look down and smile" (256–57), he prophesies to the Father,

> While by thee raised I ruin all my foes,
> Death last, and with his carcass glut the grave:
> Then with the multitude of my redeemed
> Shall enter heaven long absent, and return,
> Father, to see thy face, wherein no cloud
> Of anger shall remain, but peace assured,
> And reconcilement; wrath shall be no more
> Thenceforth, but in thy presence joy entire.
>
> (258–65)

The association between the *Anastasis* and the Last Judgment, which Milton's Son prophetically establishes in *Paradise Lost,* is integral to the meaning of *Anastasis,* explains Kartsonis: "The fundamental interpretation of redemption as an act of Judgment whose catalyst was the Passion, and whose realization requires the Resurrection of the dead was responsible for the linking of these two themes."[26] As she has explained, "the *Suda,* a tenth-century dictionary, defines the Anastasis as an act of justice, and as 'the second rising to a standing position and the end of the patience of God.'"[27] Consequent to and also expressive of such associations are the pictorial conventions common to the *Anastasis* and the Last Judgment. The boldly frontal, central, and symmetrical presentation of the Judge-Redeemer is one feature of the common iconography, and, as Kartsonis explains, so too are the fires of Hell, some kind of representative of Satan, and angelic attendants such as Michael, who is also identified as "l'ange du Jugement," the angel who will call the earth to the Last Judgment and, for some church authorities, also weigh the souls of those being judged.[28] One of the most remarkable pictorial "icongraphic hybrids" resulting from the interinvolvements of the *Anastasis* and the Last Judgment, which Kartsonis discusses, is the three-tiered fresco on the west wall of the church of Santa Maria Assunta at Torcello in which visual parallels vertically associate the three horizontal bands of the Crucifixion, *Anastasis,* and Last Judgment.[29]

Unaware of the *Anastasis*-Last Judgment associations that Kartsonis presents, Blake and Milton scholars alike have nevertheless long noted the associations between the Expulsion in *Paradise Lost* and the Last Judgment. The tears that Adam and Eve wipe suggest the tears in Revelation: "And God shall wipe away all tears from their eyes" (21.4; also see 7.17).[30] In addition, what Milton's Adam and Eve turn back to see in *Paradise Lost* is not so much Paradise as "the flaming brand" (12.643), "dreadful faces . . . and fiery arms" (644); what lies before them is a new world, and the contrast between the old and lost, and the new and about-to-be-discovered once again suggests provocative associations with Revelation: "And I saw a new heaven and a new earth: for the first heaven and the first earth were passed away" (21.1). Furthermore, Michael, as the angel of Judgment as well as the angel of the dead, both anticipates and first fulfills the role of the angel in Rev. 20: "And I saw an angel come down from heaven, having the key of the bottomless pit and a great chain in his hand. And he laid hold on the dragon, that old serpent, which is the Devil, and Satan, and bound him" (1–2). Foremost among those scholars of Milton and Blake who associate Milton's Expulsion and the Last Judgment, Wittreich acknowledges that "the last lines of Milton's poem [contain] no horsemen, no stems of thorns, no thunderbolts . . . no coiled serpent. . . . Yet all these images figure in Blake's concluding illustration." Wittreich insists, however, that Blake's "four horsemen and the stems of thorns are faithful in spirit, if not in letter to the poem Milton wrote," for they anticipate both the first and the second coming of Christ who "will restore man to a paradise happier far than the one from which he was exiled."[31]

In fact, nowhere in *Paradise Lost* does Milton's visionary art delineate a sharper, steadier image than in the Expulsion scene at the end of book 12. Collapsing the Last Judgment and the Expulsion into apocalyptic simultaneity, Milton, however, shows his reader not "horror or terror," but deliverance and restoration, what Louis L. Martz has described as "an act of rescue."[32] In Milton's verbal art, Blake saw precisely this vision and made visible precisely this vision in his own pictorial art. What focuses, stabilizes, and colors this most extraordinary vision of the Expulsion for both Milton and Blake is the iconography of the *Anastasis* that draws the so-called first and second coming of Christ into prophetic conjunction by visualizing Christ's intermediate coming—after his mortal death—to liberate humanity from Hades.

Notes

1. Jean H. Hagstrum, *The Sister Arts: The Tradition of Literary Pictorialism and English Poetry From Dryden to Gray* (Chicago: University of Chicago Press, 1958), 127.

2. John Milton, *Paradise Lost,* ed. Alastair Fowler (London: Longman, 1971). All references to Milton's poetry are to this edition and are cited parenthetically in the text.

3. Roy Flannagan, ed., *John Milton: Paradise Lost* (New York: Macmillan, 1993).

4. Joseph A. Wittreich, *Angel of Apocalypse: Blake's Idea of Milton* (Madison: University of Wisconsin Press, 1975), 95.

5. Quoted by Merritt Hughes in "Some Illustrators of Milton: The Expulsion from Paradise," in *Milton: Modern Essays in Criticism,* ed. Arthur E. Barker (Oxford: Oxford University Press, 1965), 363.

6. Hughes, "Some Illustrators," 364.

7. Marcia R. Pointon, *Milton and English Art* (London: Manchester University Press, 1970), 15.

8. Pamela Dunbar, *William Blake's Illustrations to the Poetry of Milton* (Oxford: Clarendon, 1980), 87. Also see Stephen C. Behrendt, *The Moment of Explosion: Blake and the Illustration of Milton* (Lincoln: University of Nebraska Press, 1983), 175.

9. Behrendt, *The Moment,* 163–67.

10. Ibid., 130.

11. Ibid., 171–72.

12. Anna D. Kartsonis, *Anastasis: The Making of an Image* (Princeton: Princeton University Press, 1986), 149.

13. Ibid., 165.

14. Ibid., 205.

15. Ibid., 152.

16. Ibid., 8–9.

17. Ibid., 4.

18. *The Corpus Christi Play of the English Middle Ages*, ed. R. T. Davies (London: Faber and Faber, 1972), 328.

19. *The Wakefield Mystery Plays*, ed. Martial Rose (New York: Norton, 1969), 456.

20. *English Mystery Plays*, ed. Peter Happe (Harmondsworth, England: Penguin, 1975), 565.

21. *Chief Pre-Shakespearean Dramas*, ed. Joseph Quincy Adams (Cambridge, Mass.: Riverside, 1952), 189.

22. "It is in a category of somewhat special ideas that he develops his office as the angel of the dead, the guide beyond the grave of the dead souls" Olga Rojdestvensky, *Le Culte de Saint Michel et le moyen age latin* [Paris: Auguste Picard, 1922], xix).

23. *The Apocalypse of Paul*, in *The Apocryphal New Testament*, ed. J. K. Elliott (Oxford: Clarendon, 1993), 625. *The Roman Missal* is quoted by Alfred Rush, *Death and Burial in Christian Antiquity* (Washington, D. C.: Catholic University of America Press, 1941), 43.

24. *The Gospel of Nicodemus*, in *The Apocryphal New Testament*, ed. Elliott, 189, 195–96.

25. William Langland, *The Vision of William Concerning Piers the Plowman in Three Parallel Texts Together with Richard the Redeless*, ed. Walter W. Skeat (Oxford: Oxford University Press, 1969), 264–65. All references to *Piers the Plowman* are to this edition and are cited parenthetically in the text.

26. Kartsonis, *Anastasis*, 155–56.

27. Ibid., 154.

28. Rojdestvensky, *Le Culte*, xiii, xviii.

29. Kartsonis, *Anastasis*, 157.

30. All references to Revelation are to the King James Version and are cited parenthetically in the text.

31. Wittreich, *Angel of Apocalypse*, 95.

32. Louis L. Martz, *Poet of Exile: A Study of Milton's Poetry* (New Haven: Yale University Press, 1980), 187.

Hymns and Anti-Hymns to Light in
Paradise Lost

STELLA P. REVARD

Since Barbara K. Lewalski's work on genres within *Paradise Lost,* everyone recognizes the debt of the Hymn to Light in book 3 to the classical hymn tradition.[1] But the debt of Satan's address to the Sun in book 4 to this same tradition has not been acknowledged. Lewalski herself identifies it as a soliloquy rather than a hymn. Yet it too is founded on the classical hymn tradition that stretches from the ancient Homeric hymns to the hymns and odes of Callimachus and Pindar to the Renaissance hymns composed in imitation of these classical models. Satan's hymn-address to the Sun can be seen as an "anti-hymn" to light that inverts many of the traditions of classical hymn and in so doing contrasts with both the Hymn to Light in book 3 that precedes it and Adam and Eve's Morning Hymn in book 5 with its salute to the Sun that follows it, both of which, as Lewalski has shown us, are closely modeled on classical hymn. Its rejection of light and its negative treatment of the Sun that animates the world contrast with the treatment of light in both these hymns and also contrast with the treatment of light in the Neoplatonic and humanist hymns to Apollo or to the Sun that Milton as a Christian humanist would have known well.

Satan's address to the Sun, as we know from Milton's nephew Edward Phillips, is one of the oldest sections of *Paradise Lost,* composed when Milton still thought of his poem as an epic drama.[2] Its dramatic flavor is still evident. From the very opening address of this hymn, Satan puts himself in contest as the former Lucifer—the light-bearing star—with the Sun itself, a contest that echoes ironically Satan-Lucifer's own contest in the War in Heaven with the King of Heaven—the Son of God.

> O thou that with surpassing Glory crown'd,
> Look'st from thy sole Dominion like the God

> Of this new World; at whose sight all the Stars
> Hide thir diminisht heads; to thee I call.
>
> (4.32–35)[3]

To Satan this all-ruling Sun is both a classical sun deity—an Apollo who lights and rules the world from his sun chariot—and the symbol of the all-ruling Son of God, against whom he has revolted. As he addresses the Sun, he reveals the envy and prideful anger that in Heaven put him into contest with the Son of God. Satan resented God's crowning of the Son of God as king, and before his followers he accused the Son of scorning to share power with underlings.

> Another now hath to himself ingross't
> All Power, and us eclipst under the name
> Of King anointed.
>
> (5.775–77)

His address to the Sun, crowned also with surpassing glory, uses language similar to that he uses when he challenges the Son. In Satan's mind, the Sun, like the Son of God, is a king, even though of this lesser world; before him too the "stars," or angels, are diminished and must hide their heads. While he must acknowledge that the Sun—like the Son of God—holds *de facto* power and rules like the "god" or king over his world, Satan refuses to revere or worship him. Even as he begins his address to the Sun with a hymnlike opening, he refuses to bow his knee, just as in Heaven he had refused to bow to the Son of God.

His stance differs from that of Adam and Eve, who in book 5 address the Sun with due reverence. They recognize his position as a kind of "classical" deity, and they accord him respect as a "god" who shares rule with the other heavenly bodies. For Satan, however, the Sun's all-blazing majesty is not natural but tyrannical power, usurped and unshared. In a classical ode, such as Pindar's *Olympian l,* the sun is invoked as the highest and brightest of stars—unchallenged in his eminence over the other heavenly bodies. When the sun appears in the sky, says Pindar, lesser stars disappear.

> μηκέθ' ἁλίου σκόπει
> ἄλλο θαλπνότερον ἐν ἀμέ-
> ρᾳ φαεννὸν ἄστρον ἐρήμας δι αἰθέρος
>
> (5–7)

> Do not look for another star

in the day more blazing than the sun
in the solitary sky.[4]

Milton seems to be echoing Pindar's sentiment—echoing it, that
is, to invert it in Satan's mouth. Satan grudges the Sun both his
solitary eminence and his blazing splendor because the Sun's light
diminishes his own. He hates the Sun's beams, he says, for they
remind him of his own former magnificence. But, of course, this
too is a satanic evasion. Satan was never the "sun" of any world—
that role belonged to the Son of God. As Lucifer he was the star
harbingering the sun, the star whose head must be diminished in
the presence of a greater light. It is this role he has disclaimed.
His angry anti-hymn to the Sun is as much directed to the Son as
king of Heaven as it is to the earthly Sun, whose deity and lower
sphere he also envies.

As he refused in Heaven to recognize the Son's innate radiance
and majesty, Satan also repudiates the earthly Sun's glory, asserting that his splendor is sterile and his rule isolated and lowly.
The sphere he reigns over, Satan grudgingly remarks, is lower than
his [Satan's] former one. Declining to connect the Sun's light with
God's light or to acknowledge the Sun's proper function in illuminating and warming the world, Satan defies both Christian and
classical authority. Thus, he perverts not only the Christian Hymn
to Light, but also distorts the classical hymns to Apollo-Sun as
well as the Neoplatonic hymns to the Sun.

Critics have noticed how Satan's address to the Sun has inevitable links to Neoplatonic hymn and treatise. Both language and
attitude echo Proclus's fifth-century "Hymn to the Sun," Julian
the Apostate's treatise on the Sun, and more recent Renaissance
exemplars such as Michele Marullo's fifteenth-century "Hymn to
the Sun."[5] Like the hymns on which it is modeled, Satan's "hymn"
employs Neoplatonic terms to describe the Sun's kingliness and
eminence, while it refuses at the same time to laud this eminence.
Proclus's "Hymn to the Sun," for example, addresses the Sun as
"βασιλεύς" [king] and "αναξ" [Lord]—the ruler of the world—as
he is referred to in Satan's anti-hymn.[6] For Proclus, however, the
Sun is not merely the titular king but also the heart of the world.
Proclus defines the Sun's lordship in terms of the benefits that he
brings to earth—causing generation and bringing law, harmony,
and order. Important in his hymn is also the Sun's lordship over
song as well as light. Proclus's Phoebus-Sun is ruler of the Muses,
and through his music he inspires worship in human beings. As he
and the Muses strike the lyre, the choruses on earth respond,

inspired not only with Phoebus's law, but also with his harmony. Proclus's Phoebus-Sun is, as we shall see, similar to the sun described in other hymns in *Paradise Lost*. In Adam and Eve's Morning Hymn of book 5, for example, the Sun and the other heavenly bodies are not mute, but move "In mystic Dance not without Song" (5.178).

In his first words to the Sun, Satan has rejected the generative principle that is so important in Neoplatonic hymns. The rays of the sun bring warmth and life to the earth as well as light; they are the symbol of God's own generative power. Inevitably they must remind Satan that he was once part of the generative process, that he once stood in "bright eminence" (4.44) connected to God and his light. And for this very reason he denies them.

> to thee I call,
> But with no friendly voice, and add thy name
> O Sun, to tell thee how I hate thy beams.
>
> (4.35–37)

Having denied God and his generative light, Satan turns his back to the Sun's life-giving light, preferring its absence—the darkness. He begins his anti-hymn to Light by declaring his hatred for the very beams that the poet in the Hymn to Light of book 3 sought, despite his own blindness and his deprivation of light.

Thus, Satan's address to the Sun, although hymnic in form, differs in attitude from the so-called "pagan" hymns to Apollo-Sun. When Neoplatonic writers addressed the Sun or Phoebus Apollo, they were attempting to bring together Christian and classical "deities" of light and show their basic relationship; they were attempting to show how the ancient classical sun deity could be part of the larger Christian creative whole. By contrast, Satan's hymn to the Sun is an exercise in fragmentation rather than in syncretism. Satan refuses to grant to the Sun a "part" in the universal design. Even as he had refused to acknowledge his own "part" or connectedness to the Son of God, he refuses to associate the Sun of the world with the creative principles of the universe. For the fifth-century Neoplatonic hymnist Proclus, Apollo and the Sun and the Christ were essentially one in the creative light that connects them. For Satan discontinuity prevails. To deny the Sun is also to continue to deny God and the Son.

It is not just its opening hymnic invocation and the concepts that it draws from classical or Neoplatonic hymns that mark Satan's address to the Sun as modeled on these ancient literary forms.

Structurally, Satan's hymn is, like classical hymns, tripartite. It begins with an opening invocation, includes a digression, and concludes with a farewell—all well-recognized patterns both of classical hymns and of the Christian hymns of the Renaissance that imitated the classical exemplars. But even as it follows these hymnic patterns, it parodies the purpose of these hymns, which is to offer worship to a deity. When it abrogates offering either due worship or respectful homage or prayer to the Sun—either in his person as a classical deity or as the symbol of the radiant Son of God—Satan's hymnic address perverts the aim of a hymn. At the same time, Satan's anti-hymn to Light, placed at the beginning of book 4 of *Paradise Lost,* seems designed to recall structurally and thematically the Hymn to Light that opens book 3. Even as it employs its structure and echoes its patterns, it subverts the aims of the poet's address to Light.

Milton's Hymn to Light appears in *Paradise Lost* just at the point when light itself makes its first appearance on the scene, and the darkness visible of Hell begins to pall. As Satan emerges from Chaos, Milton tells us that "the sacred influence / Of light" (2.1034–35) at last makes its presence felt. Although Milton's "Hail holy Light" (3.1) seems at first as a Christian hymn to owe little to the classical hymn tradition and everything to the fiat in Genesis, "Let there be light" (1.3)[7] and to the Johannine celebration of Christ as "true light" (John 1.9), this is not so. The structure of the Hymn to Light, is, like Satan's hymn, tripartite, following that of the Homeric hymns and other classical hymnic poetry. It begins with an invocation to a "deity" it addresses in the second person, develops a "digressive" narrative of the poet's exclusion from light, and concludes with a prayer to light. Like classical hymns, Milton's hymn greets Light with the hymnic "Hail" (χαιρέ) and celebrates her through celebrating her genealogy—"offspring of Heav'n firstborn, / Or of th' Eternal Coeternal beam" (3.1–2). It endows her, like classical goddesses, with epithets, even though these epithets attempt in concrete terms to express the ineffable mystery of the divine presence in the created and uncreated light. Even the question, "May I express thee unblam'd?" (3), recalls the apology of the classical hymnist for attempting in mortal song to describe the nature and the exploits of the god.[8] As the hymn unfolds, Milton describes "Celestial Light" (51) in many of the same ways that classical and Renaissance hymnists had described Apollo-Sun. Like the Apollo-Sun of Proclus or of the fifteenth-century hymnist Michele Marullo, "Celestial" or "Holy" Light is a *protogonos,* or first being, who existed before the creation of the earthly sun: "before the Sun, / Before the Heavens thou wert" (8–9).

The Hymn to Light is carefully contrasted with the classical Orphic Hymn to Night, just as the celestial goddess, Light, is contrasted with the Stygian goddess, Night.[9] The poet, moreover, who has sung of Chaos and Night aspires now, he declares, to be a poet of Light. As Light is contrasted with Night, she is inevitably linked with Urania, the Muse, to be invoked in her own hymn in book 7. Like Celestial Light, the Muse also existed "Before the Hills appear'd, or Fountain flow'd" (7.8) and with her sister "Eternal Wisdom" (9) conversed and played "in presence of th' Almighty Father" (11).[10]

Milton critics have suggested that Milton's Urania and her sister Wisdom are connected with goddesses of Sapience that appear in Renaissance painting and poetry. These goddesses may also have influenced Milton's portrayal of Celestial Light. In the 1630s, the Italian painter Sacchi completed a fresco on the vault of the *salotto* of the Barberini Palazzo, a palace Milton visited during his trip to Rome later in that same decade.[11] In the ceiling fresco the goddess Divina Sapientia is enthroned in heavenly light. But there are also literary portrayals of Wisdom or Sapience that might have influenced Milton's description of the goddess, Celestial Light. Heavenly Beauty or Sapience is the divine goddess of Spenser's "Hymne of Heavenly Beauty" and is a deity radiant with light. Similarly, the Divina Sapientia of the neo-Latin poet, Casimire Sarbiewski, is a wisdom deity who is enthroned in the very bosom of God as a goddess of Light.[12] Like Spenser, moreover, Sarbiewski modeled his hymn to Divina Sapientia on the classical hymn. Milton's Celestial Light, like Spenser's Sapience and Sarbiewski's Sapientia, is inseparable from the light that is God.

In books 3 through 7, Milton has created a triad of heavenly goddesses—the Muse, Celestial Light, and Wisdom—all female abstract deities. Hymns had been addressed to similar deities since antiquity. Milton's triad of goddesses recall, moreover, the triads of deities depicted in classical hymns—the Horae, or Seasons, the Graces, and even the trio of abstract goddesses—Truth, Justice, and Peace that Milton appeals to in his Nativity ode. It is also surely significant that Milton in the original sketch he made of *Paradise Lost* as a drama proposed abstract goddesses as characters.[13] Celestial Light and the Muse and Wisdom seem to be descended from the abstract personages he proposed in this early sketch.

Another important part of the classical hymn or ode tradition is
the narrative digression. The digression can be mythic, historic, or
even personal. Imbedded in Milton's Hymn to Light is a narrative
digressive complaint (over forty lines in length)—a personal account of the poet who has "sung" hymns to "Chaos and Eternal
Night" (3.18) and who, having "Escap't the Stygian Pool" (14) to
revisit the realms of Light, cannot directly experience—because of
his blindness—the prime attribute of the goddess whom he would
celebrate.[14] The poet recognizes that he can only come to Light
through the intervention of her sister, the heavenly Muse, to whom
he has given his service. Through the Muse he can inhabit the
landscape that he cannot see—"Clear Spring, or shady Grove, or
Sunny Hill"(3.28)—and sing "darkly" like the nightingale of those
things he cannot experience directly. The poet complains that he
is cut off by his blindness from nature and from everything light
illumines.

> not to me returns
> Day, or the sweet approach of Ev'n or Morn,
> Or sight of vernal bloom, or Summer's Rose,
> Or flocks, or herds, or human face divine;
> But cloud instead, and ever-during dark.
>
> (3.41–45)

Light is that intermediary that connects human beings with God
(who is Light), with each other, and with their world that the Sun—
Light's Minister—not only illuminates, but also renews. In "Elegy
5," written in spring 1629, for instance, Milton described the generative power of Apollo-Sun, who through his warmth brings about
the return of spring. Light then is a force that both renews life and
conveys knowledge of the world and with knowledge, Wisdom (the
third of the heavenly sisters). Yet, as the poet complains, he is cut
off from Wisdom, the "Book of knowledge fair" (*Paradise Lost*
3.47) and presented with a "Universal blanc" (48). The goddess for
whom he would sing—Celestial Light—he cannot experience
directly.

The poet's closing prayer is a poignant request for inward light
to replace the denied outer light. Milton moves seamlessly from
the opening invocation to Light through the digression on his exclusion from light to this closing prayer. He carefully differentiates
earthly light from Celestial Light, both in the invocation and in the
closing prayer.

So much the rather thou Celestial Light
Shine inward, and the mind through all her powers
Irradiate, there plant eyes, all mist from thence
Purge and disperse, that I may see and tell
Of things invisible to mortal sight.

(3.51–55)

It is important that the Hymn to Light concludes with petition and prayer, and in this, Milton replicates both classical and Christian hymns. The classical hymn concludes by promising to remember the deity in another hymn and by requesting special favor from the deity. Milton's classical-Christian hymn internalizes the prayer— by making the favor requested the continual presence of the deity, Celestial Light, in the poet's life.

The Hymn to Light in book 3 is intimately related to the hymns the angels in books 3 and 7 sing to God and to the Son and to those hymns that Adam and Eve in books 4 and 5 offer to God. The angels in book 3 honor God and the only begotten Son by describing the invisible and visible light of their presence. Like the Christian Neoplatonists and early church fathers, Milton's angels describe God as a "Fountain of Light" (375) himself "invisible / Amidst the glorious brightness" (375–76). The hymnic epithets Milton's angels employ for the Son stress the bright or shining radiance of his visible, as opposed to God's invisible, light. The Son of God, as he is described in book 3, enthroned by the Father, has particular affinity with the classical god Apollo, whose epithet is Phoebus (the shining one), and with the creating *protogonos*— Apollo-Sun of Neoplatonic and Renaissance hymns. Like Phoebus Apollo, the son of Zeus, he is "radiant" (63) and "shines" (386) as he sits in Heaven as the Son of God at the right hand of the Father.[15]

As the angels glorify the Son in their hymns, they promise, as did the classical hymnist, to make his name the "copious matter of [their] Song" (3.413) and never to forget to praise him. Moreover, just as the Homeric hymnist or classical writer of ode did, the angels indulge in digressions, recounting the exploits of the hero Son—the creation of the heavens and Earth, the expulsion of the warring angels (which echoes Apollo's expulsion of the Titans), and finally the offer of grace and mercy to humankind. The hymns to the Son in books 6 and 7 also employ the formulas and digressive techniques of classical hymns and odes. In celebrating the Son's victory over Satan in the War in Heaven and his heroic achievement in creating the Earth, these songs might be regarded as mini-epinician, or victory, odes (6. 885–88; 7.602–32).

The evening and morning hymns of books 4 and 5 that Adam and Eve address to God the Creator—"The God that made both Sky, Air, Earth, and Heav'n" (4.722)—also praise the powers of light and call on these powers to protect them.[16] While these hymns are clearly grounded in Scripture, their form, as well as their descriptive techniques and some of their concepts, come, as Lewalski has shown, from classical hymn. Adam and Eve's morning and evening hymns are connected liturgically to the service of matins and evensong, and both are based on texts from Psalms, specifically Ps. 74.16 with its praise of Day and Night; Ps. 127.2, which gives thanks for God's gift of sleep; and Ps. 148, which calls on angels, stars, sun and moon, and all God's works to praise God— "Praise ye him, all his angels: praise ye him, all his hosts / Praise ye him, sun and moon" (Ps. 148.2–3).[17] Ps. 148, however, merely names the stars, sun, and moon and tells each to praise God; Adam and Eve's Morning Hymn describes each with epithet and interconnects stars, sun, and moon as entities, even as "gods" that praise the highest God. These heavenly bodies—the evening/morning star, the sun, the moon, the planets, as well as the elements of Earth that follow (Fire, Earth, Air, Water)—much resemble the planetary forces or gods that Marullo treats in his *Hymni Naturales,* for they have identity as heavenly bodies, as classical "gods," and as abstract forces of nature that interact one with another both scientifically and intellectually. Milton creates a symphony of heavenly and earthly divinities who speak praises for the highest God and in so speaking illustrate—in a way far above mere metaphor—the sentient life of the universe and the subordination of those sentient forces in planets and elements to the God that gave them life and light.

Light plays a significant part in the Morning Hymn of book 5 and in the briefer Evening Hymn of book 4 that precedes it, both of which correct Satan's anti-hymn to the Sun. In the Evening Hymn, Adam and Eve extol God as the maker of Day and Night and pray that he maintain the balance between the two. The Morning Hymn is in many ways a victory ode that celebrates the triumph of light over darkness. Milton presents us with a procession of heavenly lights (among them the Sun of Satan's hymn), who in offering praise to God demonstrate how his life-giving light conquers darkness and evil. We note particularly how each "light" has personality, place, and particular attribute. The angels are characterized as "Sons of Light" (160) who like stars "with songs / And choral symphonies, Day without Night, / Circle his Throne rejoicing" (5.161–63). Total entities of light, who know no darkness, the angels prepare the way for and imitate with their circuit about God's throne the orbits of the heavenly bodies that follow—the stars, sun, moon, and planets. The heavenly bodies add their voices to the angelic song and their light to the light of the angels in order to complete the divine conquest over darkness. Hesperus-Lucifer appears first, moving last in the train of night as the evening star or Hesperus, first in the train of Dawn as the morning star or Lucifer. In name—and in former function—the star recalls Lucifer-Satan, who once also heralded the Dawn and the Sun-Son. Satan now disclaims, as his anti-hymn demonstrates, the function either of "light-bearer" or of praiser of God. Hesperus-Lucifer, the "Fairest of Stars" (5.166), is, of course, as Milton knows, the planet Venus, as she functions, as she did in Renaissance hymns, both as deity and planet. A handmaiden to Aurora-Dawn, she comes smiling on, crowning her with a "bright Circlet" (169). She is, moreover, a beneficent deity not just of light, but also of fertility. In Renaissance hymns, she acts with Apollo-Sun to bring on not only day, but also spring.

In Adam and Eve's Morning Hymn, the Sun is described, as in Neoplatonic and humanist hymns, as the "Eye and Soul" of the "World":

> Thou Sun, of this great World both Eye and Soul,
> Acknowledge him thy Greater, sound his praise
> In thy eternal course, both when thou climb'st
> And when high Noon hast gain'd, and when thou fall'st.
>
> (5.171–74)

He also retains his role as the classical god, the ruler of the fiery chariot that makes its way through the sky, climbing until noon and then falling. But this ruler of the Earth, though the "Eye and Soul" of the "World," is subordinate to God, just as the Son is subordinate to the Father. Only Satan in his anti-hymn refers to the Sun as a ruler who reigns in sole dominion without reference to a greater. The Sun of the Morning Hymn functions with "the Moon" (175) and the "fixt Stars" (176), the "five other wand'ring Fires" (177)—the planets—to create a mystic dance of sound and light and motion. Sun, Moon, and planets bring both light and song, illuminating the universe with their vocal praise to God, "who out of Darkness call'd up Light" (179). The remainder of the hymn orders the elements of Earth, Air, and Water, who also offer benefaction to man and praise to God. No classical deity invades by name this Christian hymn. But, like the Renaissance hymnist, Mil-

ton has so animated and personified the elements of sky and earth
that he has given voice and life and distinct being to each. The
fires of Heaven and the elements of Earth join together to form a
classical chorus that praises the Creator. Significantly, the Sun has
a leading role in this hymn, offering praise to God, and receiving
praise in turn from God's other creatures, Adam and Eve, for his
part in bringing light.[18]

Satan's anti-hymn to the Sun in book 4 denies the Sun the honor
that the poet, the angels, and Adam and Eve have assigned to him.
Satan addresses the Sun without offering praise or making petition
either to the Sun, the Son of God, or God—something that the
classical hymn to the deity always does. Often classical hymns ask
not just for favor, but also for deliverance. Proclus's "Hymn to the
Sun" in particular seeks deliverance from afflictions. Satan's anti-
hymn begins with grudging invocation and concludes without petition. It is in some way an exercise in withheld praise and thwarted
petition. The long digressive personal section that occupies the
central part of the hymn—a section that resembles at the same
time it differs from the personal digression of the Hymn to Light—
demonstrates that Satan, like the poet of book 3, has need of deliverance. But while the poet turns to and petitions Celestial Light,
Satan neither petitions the Sun, whom he addresses in the second
person, nor God, whom he refers to as a more distant "he" (see,
for example, 4.42–43). His personal narrative is a self-absorbed
Ode to Himself that takes up one by one the motives for his fall and
meditates a possible petition for grace. It resembles a confessional
prayer without ever becoming one. Satan confesses that his own
"Pride and worse Ambition threw [him] down" (4.40) from that
sphere he once held: "Warring in Heav'n against Heav'n's matchless King" (41). In referring to "Heav'n's matchless King," is Satan
referring to God the Father, whom he appears to address, or to
the Son, whose elevation to kingship caused his revolt? If he is
referring to the Son, Satan is doing so for the first time in the epic,
now acknowledging, as he has refused to earlier, not only the Son's
rightful position above him, but also the Son's part in his creation,
"whom he created what I was" (43). In book 5, Satan denies that
the Son created him, pronouncing himself "self-begot" (860). Satan
also comes close to expressing the sentiments of a truly penitential
hymnist, that is, how due is the praise of the deity:

> What could be less than to afford him praise,
> The easiest recompense, and pay him thanks,
> How due!
>
> (4.46–48)

Yet, even as Satan recognizes that praise is the proper end of a hymn, he stops short of actually offering that praise. In the Hymn to Light in book 3, the poet yearns to approach the deity, yearns, despite his blindness, to come to God's light. But even as he bends upward toward the light, Satan feels the abyss of darkness open below him: "myself am Hell; / And in the lowest deep a lower deep / Still threat'ning to devour me opens wide" (4.75–77). Satan's personal digression leads him away from penitence and prayer. Asking whether there is "no place / Left for Repentance, none for Pardon left?", he produces his own irresolvable condition: "None left but by submission" (79–81). He had refused union with God and the Son when he first began his revolt; he now confirms that disunion. He began his Hymn to the Sun by proclaiming his hatred of the Sun's beams; he closes his digressive narrative by confirming his hatred of God and declaring reconcilement void "Where wounds of deadly hate have pierc'd so deep" (99).

Satan concludes his "classically correct" hymn with a section that uses the key hymnic word, "Farewell" (109). Typically in the final verses of a classical hymn, the poet salutes the god and says farewell (χαιρέ), promising to compose another hymn in his honor. χαιρέ in Greek can mean either "Hail" or "Farewell." When Milton employs this formula at the end of the Morning Hymn, Adam and Eve use the word "Hail" as they petition God for good and for the dispersal of evil, and salute his lordship:

> Hail universal Lord, be bounteous still
> To give us only good; and if the night
> Have gather'd aught of evil or conceal'd,
> Disperse it, as now light dispels the dark.
>
> (5.205–8)

By requesting good and by rejecting evil, Adam and Eve take part in the symbolic conquest of light over darkness that their Morning Hymn has itself enacted.

Satan's χαιρέ is a dismissal rather than a valediction, a dismissal that neither requests good, asks for protection against evil, nor salutes the deity. Refraining from saying farewell to the Sun, the deity he has invoked in his hymn, or to God whom he excludes from "granting . . . as I from begging peace" (4.104), Satan bids farewell to Hope, Fear, and Remorse—a trio of abstract goddesses. His farewell, however, makes no petitionary request of them. His only petition is not for Good, but for Evil as his Good:

So farewell Hope, and with Hope farewell Fear,
Farewell Remorse: all Good to me is lost;
Evil be thou my Good.

(108–10)

In the abstract world of Satan's mind where Evil and Good are
inverted and where Sin and Death—his daughter and son—are
personified deities, Hope, Fear, and Remorse are the final beneficent divinities that must be expelled. From ancient times they were
tutelary goddesses who were often addressed in hymn and ode,
often supplicated for assistance and comfort. Hope (Ελπίς) in Hesiod's *Works and Days* was the last comfort to humankind, left
from Pandora's emptied jar, and in Pindar, as Plato reminds us,
she is the nurse of old age (*Republic* 1.331a).[19] In the Roman pan-
theon she is the protective deity Spes (the Latin version of her
name), to whom classical and modern poets addressed hymns.
Richard Crashaw wrote a Latin hymn to Spes, and Crashaw and
Cowley composed twin English odes for and against Hope that
explored her different facets as a deity and as an allegorical concept.[20] Hope is also, of course, the second of the theological virtues, here dismissed by Satan, who has already forsaken her
sisters, Faith and Love. The abstract goddess Fear suggests the
Greek term for reverence or shame—Αἰδώς—the goddess who in-
structs human beings in the proper relationships both to God and
to their fellow human beings. Satan, however, demonstrates only
the wrong kind of "shame" when he fears that in repenting he will
be shamed before the angels he seduced. Remorse, the last of these
penitential sisters, Satan abandons when he turns away from God's
pardon. Ironically, Satan dismisses these goddesses with the code
word of the classical hymnist—"Farewell"—at the very moment
that he dismisses Good and determines that Evil shall be his Good.

It is important to recognize that Satan's speech to the Sun is not
simply an extended soliloquy but an anti-hymn that employs and
parodies the formulas of classical hymn. Milton has deftly placed
the parody, moreover, between two of his most exalted examples
of hymn—the Hymn to Light and the Morning Hymn. With invocation, praise, and petition, they fulfill the proper aim of hymn. But
even as his Evil has subverted Good and his Darkness the Light,
Satan's anti-hymn subverts the worship of the true hymn.

Notes

1. Barbara K. Lewalski, *"Paradise Lost" and the Rhetoric of Literary Forms*
(Princeton: Princeton University Press, 1985).

2. See Edward Phillips, "The Life of Milton," in *John Milton: Complete Poems and Major Prose*, ed. Merritt Y. Hughes (New York: Odyssey, 1957), 1034–35. Phillips remarks that these verses were intended by Milton for the very beginning of the tragedy.

3. John Milton, *Paradise Lost*, in *John Milton: Complete Poems*, ed. Hughes. All references to Milton's poetry and prose are to this edition and are cited parenthetically in the text.

4. Pindar, *Carmina*, ed. C. M. Bowra (Oxford: Oxford University Press, 1935), 1.

5. See Alastair Fowler, ed., *Paradise Lost* (London: Longman, 1971), 192 n. iv32–41.

6. The tradition of the philosophical hymn goes back to pseudo-Aristotle (second century A.D.) and Cleanthus (first century A.D.). Proclus follows in this tradition. The philosophical hymn was sung in honor of a mythological deity to which the common notions of the deity (that is, Apollo as son of God, master of the sun and light, prophet and establisher of the divine order) are added to a symbolic interpretation, which makes the deity serve as an abstract principle. See "Avant-Propos" in *Hymnes philosophiques, Aristote. Cleanthe. Proclus*, ed. and trans. Mario Meunier (Paris: L'Artisan du Livre, 1935), 12–13.

7. All biblical references are to the King James Version and are cited parenthetically in the text.

8. See, for example, the Homeric hymns "To Delian Apollo" (19–20) and "To Pythian Apollo" (207–8), both of which pose the hymnic question, "How can I sing worthily of you?" (*Hesiod, The Homeric Hymns, and Homerica*, ed. Hugh G. Evelyn-White [London: William Heinemann, 1914]).

9. Milton's interest in deities of light and darkness goes at least as far back as his college Prolusion 1, "Whether Day or Night Is the More Excellent" (545–602), in which he embraces completely the virtues of the deity Day and rejects the Stygian goddess Night, refuting Hesiod's genealogy that made Day a daughter of Night. Another goddess of night exists apparently in the Ludlow mask—a "Goddess of Nocturnal" sport to whom Comus frames a hymnic invitation (*Comus* 128). In suggesting that Celestial Light is a goddess, I am merely pursuing the pattern of Milton's own mythmaking.

10. For connections of the Light and the Muse and Wisdom, see William B. Hunter, "Milton's Urania," *SEL* 4 (1964): 35–42; William B. Hunter and Stevie Davies, "Milton's Urania: 'The Meaning, Not the Name I Call,'" *SEL* 28 (1988): 95-111; reprint, *The Descent of Urania* (Lewisburg, Pa.: Bucknell University Press, 1989), 31–45. Hunter suggests that the Hymn to Light is a hymn to the Son as the "Bright effluence" (3.6) of God's light and the second person of the Trinity, all three persons of which are suggested in the exordium of book 3.

11. See Margaret Byard, "Divine Wisdom—Urania," *Milton Quarterly* 12 (1978): 134–37. Also see John Beldon Scott, *Images of Nepotism: The Painted Ceilings of Palazzo Barberini* (Princeton: Princeton University Press, 1991), 34–44; Mindele Anne Treip, *Allegorical Poetics and the Epic: The Renaissance Tradition to "Paradise Lost"* (Lexington: University Press of Kentucky, 1994).

12. See Mathias Casimirus Sarbievius, "Carmen Saeculare," in *Lyricorum Libri IV* (Antwerp: Plantin, 1632).

13. See John Reichert, *Milton's Wisdom: Nature and Scripture in "Paradise Lost"* (Ann Arbor: University of Michigan Press, 1992), 205.

14. It is not unprecedented for Renaissance hymns to include autobiographical passages. Marullo's "Hymn to the Moon" includes a lament for his exile from

Florence (*Hymni Naturales*, in *Carmina*, ed. Alessandro Perosa [Zurich: Thesaurus Mundi, 1951]), 145–47.

15. For connections of Christ and Apollo in Milton and in other seventeenth-century poets, see Stella P. Revard, "Apollo and Christ in Seventeenth-Century Religious Lyric," in *New Perspectives on the Seventeenth-Century English Religious Lyric*, ed. John R. Roberts (Columbia: University of Missouri Press, 1994), 143–67.

16. Of the Morning Hymn, Lewalski (*Rhetoric of Literary Forms*, 203) comments:

> Formally, the hymn has the three-part structure of a Callimachan literary hymn. The exordium consists of an apostrophe to God with the expected catalogue of epithets—"Parent of good," "Almighty," "Unspeakable," "Wondrous." The body of the hymn expands upon all the epithets by calling upon all the works of God, whose beauty and power reflect his glory, to praise him. The peroration contains the formulaic "Hail" customary in the close of the Homeric and Callimachan hymns, along with a petition that also recalls those sources.

17. See Hughes (*John Milton: Complete Poems*, 295 n. 724–735, 306 n. 156–169) and Fowler (*Paradise Lost*, 238 nn. iv724–5, iv732–3, iv735, 265 n. v153–209) for commentary on the use of Scripture in these hymns. Also see Mary Ann Radzinowicz, *Milton's Epics and the Book of Psalms* (Princeton: Princeton University Press, 1989), 147–56.

18. Also see *Paradise Lost* 8.273–77. Adam addresses the Sun ("Thou Sun, said I, Fair Light") and the Earth as sentient beings, asking them how he came to be.

19. Plato, *The Republic*, ed. John Burnet (Oxford: Clarendon, 1902).

20. See Stella P. Revard, "Crashaw and the Diva," in *New Perspectives on the Life and Art of Richard Crashaw*, ed. John R. Roberts (Columbia: University of Missouri Press, 1990), 80–98.

Egyptian Gold: Milton's Use of Virgil in *Paradise Lost,* Books 11 and 12

DAVID J. BRADSHAW

Milton learned from Virgil the importance and the technique of emulating his epic predecessors, but it may well have been from Augustine that he acquired the strategy for adapting Virgil himself to Christian apologetics. Augustine, whose *De civitate Dei contra paganos* is predicated upon deliberate juxtaposition with classical texts, prime among which is the *Aeneid,*[1] offers in *On Christian Doctrine* the following admonition concerning how the faithful should respond to some aspects of the non-Christian tradition:

> If those who are called philosophers, especially the Platonists, have said things which are indeed true and are well accommodated to our faith, they should not be feared; rather, what they said should be taken from them as from unjust possessors and *converted to our use.* Just as the Egyptians had not only idols and grave burdens which the people of Israel detested and avoided, so also they had vases and ornaments of gold and silver and clothing which the Israelites took with them secretly when they fled, as if to put them to a better use. They did not do this on their own authority but at God's commandment. (Emphasis mine)[2]

Familiar with Augustine's exhortation to use Egyptian gold, that is, to employ well what was worthwhile in classical tradition, Milton offers a signal qualification to such a disposition when he notes that, in their adaptation of such material, the Israelites did not "scape / Th' infection [of idolatry] when thir borrow'd Gold compos'd / The Calf in Oreb" (1.482–84).[3] What was to be appropriated from classical writers was, for Milton, not altogether neutral in nature but potentially tainted, carrying the danger of infection; having been associated with those who failed to understand the proper relationship of Creator and creature, such gold was all too likely to tempt those susceptible of error to misuse it as the Israelites of the exodus had misused what they had taken. How, properly,

to convert classical learning to Christian use was very much a
problem for Milton, and, in Virgil particularly, with the heroism of
Aeneas so like that "better fortitude" (*Paradise Lost* 9.31) he was
bent to extol, Milton must have sensed the danger of lapsing into
a worship and an ethic that he ought not simply forsake but repudiate as false.

Not alone in the figure of Aeneas but also in much else that
Virgil offers would there have been problematic gold, especially in
those aspects of the *Aeneid* congruent with elements of Scripture
that Milton emphasizes. Notable here are patterns of exodus and
promise central to Milton's understanding of God's relation to his
creation.[4] A measure of what always had made Virgil attractive to
Christian writers was that the repeated exile and covenant informing Old Testament story comprise the central narrative of the
Aeneid, with the theme of a chosen remnant's putting a flawed past
behind in order to move forward to a redeemed future. If Abraham's obedience, submission, and faith predict the normative heroic virtues realized fully only in the antitype of Messiah, Milton
found those qualities already embodied in the hero of Virgil's
poem. How Milton works to deflect the force of such parallels tells
much about an anxiety to discriminate Christian from classical
virtues and much, too, about what he found limiting in Virgil's
depiction of the heroic.

The description of Abraham's response to the call of God reveals
the concerned consciousness Milton has of parallels between his
story and Virgil's. Michael tells Adam of "one faithful man"
(12.113) from whom will come the chosen race, the kings of Judah,
and the holy walls of Jerusalem; it is this Abraham whom

> God the most High voutsafes
> To call by Vision from *his Fathers house,*
> *His kindred and false Gods,* into a Land
> Which he will shew him, and from him will raise
> A mightie Nation, and upon him showr
> His benediction so, that in his Seed
> All Nations shall be blest; he strait obeys,
> Not knowing to what Land, yet firm believes:
> I see him, but thou canst not, with what Faith
> He leaves *his Gods, his Friends, and native Soil.*
>   (12.120–29; emphasis mine)

The intertextual evocation of Aeneas's similar call to leave the
doomed Troy is keyed by a repeated if varied anaphora: "his Fathers house, / His kindred and false Gods" and "his Gods, his

Friends, and native Soil." Such specific groupings constitute the subjects to whom the Virgilian hero is fast bound in ties of *pietas:* filial (and clan) loyalty is grounded in commitment to the *patria* and the gods of the fatherland, both *penates* and *magni dii.* The most well-known image of Aeneas may be that of the hero who subordinates his own will to redeem a flawed past and ensure a vital future: on his shoulders he carries his father Anchises to safety (Anchises holding the household gods and sacred vessels for which Aeneas's war-bloodied hands are unfit), while by his right hand he leads his son Ascanius toward the promise of life and high destiny (2.705–29).[5] Milton's Abraham recalls yet qualifies the Aeneas who leaves the old to found the providentially ordained city. Whereas Aeneas has only with great reluctance and after repeated admonitions heeded divine injunctions to leave Troy, Abraham "strait obeys" the call of God and, not knowing his destiny, "yet firm believes" in it. Whereas Aeneas takes with him the paternal gods, Abraham must see and forsake as false whatever the hand of man has made, for it cannot be God: what Virgil offers as instance of Aeneas's proper reverence Milton glosses as idolatry. Also, the "native Soil" that Abraham so unhesitatingly quits is the *patria* that only through grief and loss Aeneas comes to recognize as, not Troy, but rather the promised Lavinian lands: *hic amor, haec patria est* (4.347). Abraham's leave-taking, which replays the Expulsion from Eden and anticipates the exodus of Moses, is presented so that it recalls Aeneas's flight while suggesting crucial differences.

The story of Abraham is narrated to Adam by Michael, while Aeneas himself tells of the fall of Troy and his subsequent wanderings. Within his story, however, Aeneas recounts how he is offered an otherworldly vision, and in the interaction between Michael and Adam, Milton recasts this incident in deliberate fashion. As Troy burns and Aeneas, with an enraged mind (*furiata mente*, 2.588), revolves thoughts of killing Helen and dying with the *patria,* Venus admonishes him against such action, reminding him of his family and affording him a vision of the divine forces whose merciless vengeance (*divum inclementia,* 2.602) causes the destruction of the city. Venus grants such vision by purging the dimness from Aeneas's eyes so that he might actually see Neptune, Juno, Pallas, and Juppiter himself engaged in razing Troy. When Milton has Michael show Adam a portion of human history, the Archangel purifies, in similar fashion, the occluded vision of original man so that he, too, might see into the life of things: "Michael from Adams eyes the Film remov'd" (11.412).[6]

In certain ways, the similarities of the two situations are striking. Each human figure is trying to comprehend the extent of radical loss; each is about to go into exile from the home construed as synonymous with security and joy; each is being shown the truth of things in order that he might better understand cosmic purpose and so begin a life of labor in an unknown and insecure world. More instructive, however, are the dissimilarities, for they suggest why Milton recalls the Virgilian scene. Adam will see "supernal Grace contending / With sinfulness of Men" (11.359–60) as, through his projection of human history, Michael asserts eternal Providence. The major burden of the poem, the conviction that God foresees and provides for human failings, is summed up in the vision accorded Adam, and the proffered understanding of relations between mortal beings and the governing powers of the universe is, finally, a comforting one. By setting Adam's vision within the context of that afforded to Aeneas as he grasps the fact that he must leave Troy, Milton underscores how greatly the cosmic ordination described by Virgil differs from the Christian concern that he depicts. The gods whom Aeneas sees—and they include *ipse pater,* Juppiter, the father himself (2.617)—are angry and vengeful gods indeed; if they do not kill Trojans for their sport, they certainly take too little care for those who die supplicating divine help in defending home and family. Aeneas sees through to a vision of power at the center of things, but this power is capricious and inhumane, a matter that Milton emphasizes through his allusive recollection of the Virgilian text.

Yet it is not simply *Aeneid* 2 that is being recalled as Michael shows futurity to Adam. Also underlying this event are similar visions with which Aeneas is presented, and at stake is the understanding not only of what godhead is but also of what virtuous humanity should be. For, if at Troy Aeneas receives a most discomforting vision of divine antagonism, in the underworld and again by the Tuscan stream of Caere, he is offered the promise of favoring fates. The shade of Anchises reveals the line of Roman heroes whose cumulative efforts will, at length, restore a golden age in Latium and establish universal peace (6.756–886); on the shield of Aeneas forged by Vulcan are scenes that recapitulate Roman history and heroism (8.626–728). It is in clear imitation of Virgil that Milton fashions the similar scene with Michael and Adam.[7] Aeneas and Adam are shown their progeny with the ostensible hope that each might learn what comprises genuine heroic virtue, for their offspring are presented as moral exempla of either a positive or a negative sort. Aeneas's descendants are advanced as successful and largely virtuous, yet Aeneas apprehends less about them than might be expected; Adam's children are projected as failed because generally corrupted, yet Adam does, finally, discern the lesson of the pageant that he witnesses.

Why Milton would juxtapose the success of Romans with repeated failures of individuals within the Christian tradition has much to do with the nature of such success and with an understanding of human nature related to such failure. Peace, the Latin poet would have it, is realized through the labor of Aeneas's descendants, realized within the framework of historical discourse: what is predicted in the underworld and what is centrally depicted on the shield of Aeneas is the advent of a universal *pax* that is sociopolitical, and the virtues requisite to enact such peace are detailed by Anchises clearly:

> "excudent alii spirantia mollius aera
> (credo equidem), vivos ducent de marmore uultus,
> orabunt causas melius, caelique meatus
> describent radio et surgentia sidera dicent:
> tu regere imperio populos, Romane, memento
> (hae tibi erunt artes), pacique imponere morem,
> parcere subiectis et debellare superbos."
>
> (6.847–53)

> "For other peoples will, I do not doubt,
> still cast their bronze to breathe with softer features,
> or draw out of the marble living lines,
> plead causes better, trace the ways of heaven
> with wands and tell the rising constellations;
> but yours will be the rulership of nations,
> remember, Roman, these will be your arts:
> to teach the ways of peace to those you conquer,
> to spare defeated peoples, tame the proud."[8]

The ultimate success of Rome results from sustained effort through time and from enlightened control of self and others; it is embodied in the higher social good, although, as the career of Aeneas suggests, often at the expense of the individual.[9] Milton's readers may be sensitive to Virgil's interrogation of the ultimate worth of a communal security that comes at expense of the individual, and they may be alert to Anchises' indictment of the gods for jealousy over the *virtus* that makes Romans their rivals in power (6.870–71); however, such readers must find more striking the celebrated success of Aeneas's progeny standing in contrast to the failure of

Adam's, an issue underscored by Michael's echoing Anchises' skepticism about the merit of arts.

Anchises stresses the inferior status of the arts (casting bronze, sculpting marble, practicing rhetoric or science) to the ethical responsibilities of good government (the rulership of nations), and Milton, ever sensitive to the false claims of false art, has Michael share this bias when he juxtaposes the descendants of Cain with those of Seth. Cain's issue appear "studious . . . / Of Arts that polish Life, Inventers rare," but are "Unmindful of thir Maker" (11.609–11). Seth's offspring, however, seem "Just men,"

> and all thir study bent
> To worship God aright, and know his works
> Not hid, nor those things last which might preserve
> Freedom and Peace to men.

(577–80)

For all the sobriety of their appearance and intentions, however, these latter men are seduced by the daughters of Cain and fall to destruction (613–27). Unlike Anchises' Romans, the inhabitants of the world that Michael foresees cannot govern themselves and accordingly cannot rule others. Their failure repeats that of Adam and Eve and anticipates similar perversity in all future humanity. As Michael tells of subsequent attempts at governance, the repeated motif is that seen already in the careers of Satan and the primal parents—loss of freedom results from inability to control the passions, whether concupiscent or irascible; the Archangel summarizes this pattern when Adam expresses indignation at Nimrod's usurping from God authority over others:

> know withall,
> Since thy original lapse, true Libertie
> Is lost, which alwayes with right Reason dwells
> Twinn'd, and from her hath no dividual being:
> Reason in man obscur'd, or not obeyd,
> Immediately inordinate desires
> And upstart Passions catch the Government
> From Reason, and to servitude reduce
> Man till then free. Therefore, since hee permits
> Within himself unworthie Powers to reign
> Over free Reason, God in Judgement just
> Subjects him from without to violent Lords;
> Who oft as undeservedly enthral

His outward freedom: Tyrannie must be,
Though to the Tyrant thereby no excuse.

$$(12.82–96)^{10}$$

For Milton, the peace that at once rewards and confirms the life well-lived cannot be made authentic through the larger social order, and by setting Michael's articulation of the future against the predictions given to Aeneas, he emphasizes this point. Milton's own frustration that the English experiment in commonwealth government had failed not only to survive but more importantly to realize its own ideals no doubt contributed to his skepticism about the possibility of creating the good society,[11] but such skepticism was also an expression of his most deeply held religious beliefs. The success that Virgil extols pointedly relates to the City of Man, and, for Milton no less than for Augustine, final security and triumph can be achieved only within the City of God.[12]

The tension between the endorsement of the earthly city in the *Aeneid* and the rejection of it in *Paradise Lost* accounts for telling differences in the views of history that are offered within the poems. In the *Aeneid,* history is telic.[13] There is a movement, troubled and slow yet inexorable, toward the hard-won goal of the Augustan *pax,* a linear, cumulative effect of the actions of Aeneas's descendants outlined in Anchises' prophecy and on Aeneas's shield. In Michael's narrative, however, history is distinguished by repetitive cycles. This difference between Virgil and Milton is curious, for ordinarily, writers of the classical world construed the movements of history as cyclic, while Jewish and Christian thinkers, influenced by belief in a God whose mighty acts in history at once promise and enact salvation within or at some end of time, construed the movement of history as telic.[14] The vision that Michael affords Adam reveals Milton's redefining of the conventional Christian conception of history.

Michael's prophecy is episodic, yet the incidents Michael selects for narration reveal a somewhat arresting correspondence to each other and to the actions both of Adam and Eve and of Satan; the pattern evident in the individual happenings reveals them as repeated instances of a general rule, recurring motifs in a somewhat redundant score. Michael's analysis of the sinful quality of the activities of the kin of Jubal and Tubal-Cain (11.556–73) may be compared directly with what is sinful in Satan's or in the primal pair's actions: as have these other fallen individuals, the first musicians and artisans become "Unmindful of thir Maker" (611), failing to acknowledge him in order to assert themselves in his place (609–

12). Their sin is a repetition of the original sins committed in Heaven and Eden—a willful decision to live out of the creature rather than out of the Creator, desire for and assertion of illusory self-sufficiency.[15]

In addition to parallels between specific events that Michael tells of, moreover, there are parallels evident in the relationships between these events suggesting that human affairs follow repetitive rhythms. Specifically, the cyclic pattern of human behavior is revealed by the causal relations that connect opulence with moral dissoluteness and sin, the latter with warring factions and conquest, and this last with a repeated period of opulence that brings the process full circle.[16] Adam's first sons, the "Giants of mightie Bone" (11.642), their successors in the time of Noah, Noah's descendants in the time of Nimrod, the Israelites before the captivity, the Israelites following the return from Babylon, the "grievous Wolves" (12.508) who invade the Christian *ecclesia*—all conform to this specific schema. Social and political conduct, for Milton, follow a patterned norm of behavior from which there is no departing. The progress predicted in the political previsions of the *Aeneid* is seen by Milton as a possibility countermanded by the pervasive depravity informing human character. Fallen human beings are not free to act at all in one sense: they cannot advance, for they ever attempt to act out of themselves and so are limited to repeating the same mistakes, committing the same sins. The cumulative record of human actions therefore must display corresponding repetitive rhythms.

For Milton, then, history could reveal no progressive movement if only human agency were involved in events. Michael's exposition makes clear, however, that humankind is not the only or even the primary historical agent: rather, it is God, working in and through history, who directs a forward development, a soteriological progression, bringing good forth from man's evil. Michael's narrative develops a twofold conception of history. On the one hand, recalcitrant humanity, caught up in the limitations of its fallen nature, can produce only movements that conform to stereotypical and cyclical patterns; God, on the other hand, truly active and truly free, can introduce into history change and progressive development. Yet, however much Milton may have wished to emphasize the importance of God's mighty acts in history, he presents such actions as not efficacious *within* history, and this crucial difference from the prophecies offered in the *Aeneid* may explain why Milton develops the allusions to Virgil: the Christian God he presents as benevolently involved with creatures within time yet, unlike Juppiter or the Fates, concerned with an ultimate redemption beyond time. Providential guidance of events through intervention in history is, for Milton, always defeated within history by recurring patterns of creaturely depravity. Salvation, strangely enough for the commonwealth man of somewhat chiliastic belief, always lies not really at the conclusion of a providentially controlled segment of history, but, rather, beyond or apart from history altogether. The political pessimism evident in such a conception of the relationship of time and eternity may well stem from an adherence to the apocalyptic vision offered in Revelation. It might also, however, reflect an abhorrence of the "evil dayes" (*Paradise Lost* 7.25) and "evil tongues" (26) of the Restoration England that Milton found so oppressively dissolute and blasphemous (24–38); it might reflect, as well, the bitter disappointment of a man whose commitment to establishing a Christian commonwealth had been so frustrated as to erode any subsequent hope that justice and loving kindness could be sustained within the political world of contingent beings. However skeptical Virgil may have been about the human costs involved in the creation of an imperial peace, belief in the potential of such peace was possible for him, and he could nourish some hope for an Augustan culture that would sustain and be sustained by virtue. For Milton, whatever political hopes he may once have cherished, placing such hope in a quasi-utopian City of Man was the height of folly, the major lesson that he underscores by juxtaposing Adam's vision of the future with those accorded to Aeneas.

Notes

1. See Peter Brown's assessment of this expository strategy in *Augustine of Hippo: A Biography* (Berkeley: University of California Press, 1967), 306ff. Noting that, for Augustine, "'*Your*' Vergil" is consistently countered with "'*Our*' Scriptures," Brown asserts that "Juxtaposition . . . is the basic literary device that determines the structure of every book of the *City of God*. . . . The solutions of the new, Christian literature must 'stand out the more clearly' by always being imposed upon an elaborately constructed background of pagan answers to the same question."

2. Augustine, *On Christian Doctrine*, trans. D. W. Robertson, Jr. (New York: Bobbs-Merrill, 1958), 2.40.60. Pertinent scriptural passages include Exod. 3.22ff., 11.2ff., and 12.35ff.

See Peter A. Fiore (*Milton and Augustine: Patterns of Augustinian Thought in Milton's "Paradise Lost"* [University Park: Pennsylvania State University Press, 1981]) for consideration of the general influence that Augustine exerted upon all thinkers of the sixteenth and seventeenth centuries and especially upon Milton. Fiore addresses Milton's indebtedness to Augustine's interpretation of Christian

Scripture and does not touch directly upon Augustine's allusive engagement with non-Christian literature and ideas.

3. John Milton, *Paradise Lost,* in *The Complete Poetry of John Milton,* ed. John T. Shawcross (New York: Doubleday, 1963). All references to Milton's poetry are to this edition and are cited parenthetically in the text.

4. John Shawcross, in "*Paradise Lost* and the Theme of Exodus," *Milton Studies* 2 (1970): 3–26, establishes how central such patterns of exodus and promise are to Milton's thought. In *With Mortal Voice: The Creation of "Paradise Lost"* (Lexington: University Press of Kentucky, 1982), 119–38, Shawcross revisits ideas addressed in this essay.

5. P. Vergilius Maronis, *Aeneid,* in *Opera,* ed. R. A. B. Mynors (Oxford: Oxford University Press, 1969). Unless otherwise indicated, all references to Virgil's poetry are to this edition and are cited parenthetically in the text.

6. For brief but interesting comment concerning this and other Virgilian allusions in the concluding action of the poem, see John Banschbach, "Allusions to the *Aeneid* in *Paradise Lost,* Books XI and XII," *Proceedings of the Wisconsin Academy of Science, Arts and Letters* 74 (1986): 70–73.

7. K. W. Gransden addresses the parallels between *Aeneid* 6 and *Paradise Lost* 11 and 12 in "The *Aeneid* and *Paradise Lost,*" in *Virgil and His Influence: Bimillenial Studies,* ed. Charles Martindale (Bristol: Bristol Classical Press, 1984). See William Malin Porter (*Reading the Classics and "Paradise Lost"* [Lincoln: University of Nebraska Press, 1993], 97–105), for a sensitive treatment of the distinct verbal echoes that connect the last two books of *Paradise Lost* to *Aeneid* 6. Porter doubts whether similar specific connections to *Aeneid* 8 obtain (101–2), and his questioning seems apt. I suggest, however, that *Aeneid* 8 remains a general allusive referent for Milton as it did for others writing in the epic tradition; see, in this regard, David Quint (*Epic and Empire* [Princeton: Princeton University Press, 1993]), who devotes major attention to the role that imitation of the central scene on the shield of Aeneas plays in subsequent Western epics.

8. Allen Mandelbaum, trans., *The Aeneid of Virgil* (New York: Bantam, 1971), 6.1129–37. Mandelbaum's translation remains serviceable.

9. See Susan Ford Wiltshire (*Public and Private in Virgil's "Aeneid"* [Amherst: University of Massachusetts Press, 1989]) for extended consideration of this issue.

10. See *Paradise Regained* 2.466–80 for a similar passage: Milton has Jesus explore the relationship between moral self-control and the responsibility to teach (and by teaching truly to govern) others.

11. See Christopher Hill (*The Experience of Defeat: Milton and Some Contemporaries* [New York: Viking Penguin, 1984], especially chapter 10) for consideration of responses offered by Milton and other individuals of strong religious conviction to the failure of the English Revolution. See Quint, *Epic and Empire,* 41–48 and 248–340, for consideration of *Paradise Lost* and *Paradise Regained* as evidence that Milton saw himself and his cause as victims of an imperialist ideology that was most effectively inscribed within the discourse of epic itself.

12. The conclusion to book 2 of *De civitate Dei contra paganos* entails the most direct effort of Augustine to convince citizens of the empire that they should renounce a Virgilian earthly fatherland (*terrena patria*) for a spiritual fatherland (*caelestem* [*patriam*]), that they should conceive of heroic fulfillment not in the symbols of Roman imperial culture but instead in the realities of a transcendent Christian peace. The fact that Augustine employs a transmutation of Juppiter's promise to Venus that Romans will enjoy unlimited rule (*Aeneid* 1.278–79) indi-

cates how he, as did Milton after him, relied upon readers to perceive the larger cultural concerns and duties valorized in the *Aeneid* as types for the true experience of Christians who become citizens of the heavenly city.

13. See Philip Hardie (*Virgil's "Aeneid": Cosmos and Imperium* [Oxford: Oxford University Press, 1986]) for thorough consideration of Virgil's sense of history.

14. C.A. Patrides, in *Milton and the Christian Tradition* (Oxford: Oxford University Press, 1966), offers a thorough exposition of the opposing linear and cyclic conceptions of history as Milton would have received them in the seventeenth century. Isabel Rivers, in *Classical and Christian Ideas in English Renaissance Poetry* (London: Allen and Unwin, 1979), provides a brief but still helpful selection of various sixteenth- and seventeenth-century conceptions of history. John Shawcross, in chapter 10 of *With Mortal Voice,* but more particularly in "Stasis and John Milton and the Myths of Time," *Cithara* 18 (1978): 3–17, offers a clear analysis of how Milton works to adapt cyclic myths concerning human existence and action in time.

15. See book 14 of Augustine's *De civitate Dei contra paganos* for the source that probably had the strongest influence upon Milton's thought concerning the repetitive nature of sin within history.

16. Milton's pointing to this design of cyclic movement may be traced readily in selected passages of *Paradise Lost:* 11.712–18, 787–96, 12.315–20, 348–52. R. G. Collingwood (*The Idea of History* [Oxford: Oxford University Press, 1946], 23ff.) points to this same patterning as a characteristic theme in Greek poetry and history writing.

"Scarce-well-lighted flame": Milton's "Epitaph on the Marchioness of Winchester" and the Representation of Maternal Mortality in the Seventeenth-Century Epitaph

LOUIS SCHWARTZ

"An Epitaph on the Marchioness of Winchester" is not a poem that has occupied the full attention of Miltonists over the years. There have been a handful of essays on a few biographical riddles, some discussions of the influence of Jonson on Milton's early style, some discussion of a reference to Dante and of Milton's flirtation with the possibilities of patronage, but for the most part the poem has rarely occasioned more than a paragraph or passing aside.[1] The "Epitaph" is, however, worth further attention. It displays an ambitiousness and originality that have failed to register with critics because an important historical context has remained invisible: the high rate of maternal mortality suffered during the seventeenth century in London and among the upper and middle classes in various parts of the country. As this paper will show, Milton's "Epitaph" pushes at the boundaries of its genre to produce an aesthetic conciliation with maternal mortality. It is a rare, but significant, instance of such conciliation in the culture of seventeenth-century England.

Studies estimate that one woman died for every forty births in the seventeenth century among the English middle and upper classes, especially in London.[2] With a fertility rate of approximately one birth every eighteen to twenty-two months (an average of about eight to fifteen pregnancies from marriage to menopause), an upper-class married woman stood approximately a one-in-four chance of dying in childbed during her fertile years.[3] This also means that more or less everyone knew at least someone (a mother, a daughter, a sister, a wife, a friend) who had died giving birth.

These numbers are four to six times higher than most third-world countries today (and perhaps more than twice the rate in the British countryside at the time among the lower classes).[4] Poets were living, in other words, along with everyone else in the more privileged and consequently literate sectors of the population, in the midst of what can only be called a catastrophe. Under these conditions, one would imagine that poetry would be called upon regularly to provide a conciliation with the attendant pain.

In this essay I will discuss the reasons poetry was not, in fact, asked to do so very often. I will look at the ways in which maternal mortality presented a set of vexing theological, generic, and psychological problems that a poet could not easily confront and resolve by the merely conventional means of occasional verse. I will look closely at a poem by Michael Drayton that very starkly shows the difficulties posed by the occasion of a woman's death in childbed and that may have provided Milton with a model for his own more successful poem. I will conclude with a discussion of the importance of certain aspects of the "Epitaph" for an account of Milton's development. Some twenty or thirty years after writing this poem, Milton returned, in Sonnet 23, to the problems of maternal mortality in a painful and personal way. At that point, the original logic of his early achievement provided him with the means to explore those problems more complexly and in a far less conventional manner. He was then able to draw them into the allusive texture of *Paradise Lost*.

I

On 15 April 1631, Lady Jane Paulet, wife of Lord John Paulet, fifth Marquis of Winchester and daughter of Thomas, first Viscount Savage of Rock Savage, Cheshire, died giving birth to her second son. She was twenty-three years old, one month from her twenty-fourth birthday. According to two sources close to the family, her son was born dead and the difficult stillbirth seems to have been complicated by an infection from a lanced "impostume" (what we would today probably call an abscess) on her cheek.[5] She was delivered of her dead son before she herself died. As William Riley Parker notes, the story seems to have touched a number of people, for Lady Jane was mourned in verse by at least six poets whose poems survive: these include elegies by Ben Jonson, William Davenant, an obscure Roman Catholic poet named Walter Colman, and two even more obscure young men, a Mr. John Eliot, about whom almost nothing is known, and John Milton. There is also a short, anonymous Latin epitaph in William Camden's *Remaines concerning Britaine.*[6]

Milton's and Eliot's poems are the only two in this group that mention Lady Jane's dying in childbed, despite the fact that the general circumstances of her demise were, it seems, commonly known. Only Milton's is structured *entirely* around figures of tragic childbirth. (Eliot's develops only one conceit based on the manner of the Lady's death, and it is not integrated with any larger pattern of reference in the poem.) Milton, however, figures and refigures the Lady's death in a set of complex and complexly interrelated conceits, then concludes with an apotheosis that alludes to Dante, placing Jane where Dante placed Beatrice, next to Rachel in the heavenly rose.[7] He does so because Jane, like Rachel, died giving birth to her second son.

It is at once both odd and understandable that most of these poets should have chosen not to allude at all to the particulars of the Lady's death (also that they should pass up any one of a number of biblical allusions that were, like the one Milton used, ready-made for an epideictic conceit). It is odd because the simple poignancy of Lady Jane's death and its resonance with biblical commonplaces (not only Rachel, but portions of the Scripture as central as the Curse of Eve and the Nativity) make it seem a natural subject for formal epideictic poetry. The silence is understandable only because such silence is common. Parker suggests, in fact, that the poems about Lady Jane probably had more to do with religion and university politics than with the poignancy of her death. The Paulets were a prominent Roman Catholic family, but Jane seems to have had Protestant leanings and was a kinswoman of the chancellor of Cambridge.[8] Why Milton, who was probably subject to these same religious and political concerns, should have chosen to turn his attention, in addition, to the matter of maternal mortality remains a mystery. The youthful ambitiousness is not itself surprising, but the application of it to this subject matter is. Most of the few poems that have come down to us on the deaths of women who died in childbirth failed, like most of the others about Lady Jane, to make specific allusions to the manner of death at all, let alone make it a part of the logic of their consolations. Even poets like Eliot, who chose not to be silent about the nature of the Lady's death, tended to bracket the subject off when they treated it at all or confined themselves to one or two very commonplace figures.

There are a number of explanations as to why so few poets wrote about death in childbirth, despite its frequency in the period.[9]

Some of these explanations are obvious, but inadequate, some not so obvious, but I think central or dominant. For example, the silence may in part be due to the general tendency toward abstraction of the cause of death in conventional elegies. Writers of occasional verse turned more readily to poetic and mythic topoi than to physical particulars. This in turn may have been influenced by the vagueness of seventeenth-century medical diagnosis.[10] There were few specific names for what killed people, and the lack of specificity may have made it unlikely that an elegist would draw on particulars. Death in childbed, because it was usually understood as a medical matter (it is discussed in medical and anatomy texts and in the medically concerned sections of midwifery handbooks), may have, therefore, gone the way of most medical particulars when they were treated in the genre. Funeral elegies were, after all, highly conventional and abstract. When sickness was evoked at all, it tended to become an occasion for the elaboration of one of several generic topoi (for example, *contemptus mundi* and declarations of faith in God's power to heal the soul whatever might happen to the body) or, as in Jonson's poem on Jane Paulet, for satiric remarks about the ineffectuality or inadvertent cruelty of physicians.[11] The details were generally left behind. Fatal childbirth, as a medical particular, may have been abstracted out of the picture or treated simply as the "fever" or "consumption" it occasioned.

Another possible reason for the generic silence may have been that men usually had very little to do with childbirth, and men wrote most of the elegies we have. Under normal circumstances, except for the occasional male midwife, surgeon, or clergyman called in for emergencies, the entire process of birth and lying-in was taken care of by women and women only.[12] Most men, unless they made it their business to read medical or midwifery books, were largely ignorant of what went on in a birthing chamber. This lack of specific, firsthand experience must also be considered in relation to a problem of conflicting poetic decorums. It seems right, as we shall see, that an elegist might wish to portray the woman's death in relation to any one of a number of conventional themes and topoi (for example, as an instance of pity, an occasion for *contemptus mundi*, as a reminder of original sin, as a heroic deed on the part of the woman in the interest of future generations, or as a sacrifice to her husband's desires and the needs of a noble line). Poets would have thus had a reason for finding a decorous way of treating the subject in some specific way. The childbed, however, came curtained not just literally and by the female circle of attendants to the lying-in chamber; it also came curtained with vaguely articulated, though palpable, taboos about physical representation. Medical and midwifery books in the period had to themselves fight off the stigma of this taboo, often carrying prefaces from editors and authors warning against their use for prurient purposes.[13] It seems reasonable to assume that poets may have been loath to invite their readers into the chamber.

For two reasons, however, conventional abstraction, male ignorance, and decorous uneasiness are not completely satisfying explanations. First of all, they in some sense contradict one another. Given the clear generic tendency toward abstraction, men would not have needed to know what a real death in childbirth was like in order to write elegies that evoked such a death or discussed its implications. They would have needed merely to construct a set of decorous abstractions designed to signify the meaning of such an event, the lesson to be taken from it, its theological and perhaps social or to some extent psychological implications. None of this would have required firsthand knowledge. Exceptions like Milton's poem actually show that the poetic tradition was perfectly capable of suggesting the necessary abstractions, thereby conveying some of the pitiful ironies of a death in childbed in ways that fit the epideictic and consolatory purposes of the genre.

There is something else, however, that is peculiar about childbirth. When other causes of death (such as sickness, battle, or drowning) could be specified in an elegy, and they afforded an occasion for praise or the amplification of some commonplace, they very often were clearly specified.[14] Sickness, as Jonson's poem on Lady Jane shows clearly, provided an occasion for a set of appropriate conceits of satire and *contemptus mundi*. Many of the hundreds of poems written in honor of Prince Henry refer to his death by plague.[15] It is not uncommon for a man who died in battle to have that fact made much of in his epitaphs,[16] and things like drownings at sea are commonly made mention of or become the crux of important figures.[17] These are all treated abstractly in one way or another, but they make their presence known. Despite the fact, however, that women were dying in childbirth at an alarming rate, childbed death, unlike these other more general and/or masculine forms of death, never became the source of any really widely used conceit.

This fact requires more complex explanations than the ones I have mentioned so far, and at least two more will concern me here. First, the very decorous topics that, as I mentioned before, could be used to accommodate childbed death to the conventions of the genre, carried with them a burden of theological and ideological paradox. They required a complex discourse on the need for sacrifice, on the fragility of noble lineages, on a web of biblical texts, and on the nature of original sin, particularly its guilt-laden gender specificity (that, for example, men had to struggle to support and feed future generations, but women *died* to bring them forth). A seeming symmetry (that men might, for instance, die on trading missions or in war) takes on a peculiar psychological weight and asymmetry when one considers, in addition, the relationship of childbed death to sexual intimacy with men. And this takes on a further social and ideological complexity when one considers the role played in reproduction by male desires and dynastic hopes, as well as by rape and seduction outside wedlock and across class lines. These all suggest very vexed questions of theology and sociability that require more complex forms of theodicy and social reflection than could normally be offered in an occasional poem.

My second, more satisfactory, explanation for the silence of poets concerns one of the key conventional rhetorical resources of the genre itself. An evocation of death in childbed actually brought certain conventional elegiac motifs into conflict with one another. These are, broadly speaking, motifs derived from epithalamia, on the one hand, and from funeral imagery and ritual, on the other (the former were used as part of the consolation, the latter as part of the complaint). This second problem, more specifically rhetorical, is another reason the genre had a hard time reaching toward the more complex discourses that might have enabled it to confront death adequately in childbed. Elegies made use of motifs derived precisely from the very two human rituals (wedding and funeral) that collide in the childbed, where the "end" of marriage (physical love and procreation), becomes literally its end in death. This presented yet another conventionally insoluble paradox.

Milton offered a solution to the latter of these problems as a means of solving the former. In his "Epitaph," he used allusions to the ritual forms and poetry of funeral and wedding in an ambitious attempt to resolve the social, theological, and, to a lesser extent, psychological difficulties that normally would have compromised the logic of conventional consolation in an elegy that evoked death in childbed. He, in addition, resolved the problem of competing decorums by maintaining a high level of mythopoeic abstraction that was itself aimed at those very social and theological difficulties. We can see this process at work clearly if we compare Milton's "Epitaph" to Michael Drayton's "Upon the Death of Mistris Elianor Fallowfield." Milton may have known Drayton's poem and may have used it as a model, but even if he did not, the comparison will allow us to see him ambitiously solving a problem that Drayton courted, but could not solve, one that has implications not only for our understanding of Milton but also for our understanding of seventeenth-century notions of poetic value and vocation.

II

The following passage from Michael Drayton's "Upon the Death of Mistris Elianor Fallowfield" provides an indication of some of the anxieties that underlay the subject of childbed death and put strange demands on a funeral elegy that attempted to deal with it. Drayton's poem comes closer than any other poem of the period (with the exception of Milton's) to confronting the larger social and theological anxieties that attended death in childbirth, making remarkably explicit use of generic motifs associated with marriage and death, ones that Milton would put to more successful and rhetorically integrated use.

The woman of Drayton's poem has not been identified. It is possible, given the suggestiveness of her name, that she is an invention of the poet. The poem appeared in 1627, four years before Milton wrote his "Epitaph."[18] Drayton begins with an attack on death for taking the young and healthy rather than the old and already sick and dying. Mistress Fallowfield was particularly ill-suited for death, the poet tells us, for she was not only young, but "teeming." Drayton begins the third verse paragraph of the poem with what sounds like a threat:

> But cruell Death if thou so barbarous be,
> To those so goodly, and so young as shee;
> That in their teeming thou wilt shew thy spight.
>
> (23–25)[19]

At this point one is likely to expect a threat, perhaps a statement like the one Shakespeare's speaker makes in the final lines of Sonnet 19. Perhaps the poet will immortalize his subject or perhaps he will give way to *contemptus mundi* occasioned by the death of a young mother-to-be. This could lead to praise of her virtues and a consoling apotheosis. Something quite different, however, actually ensues, and in fact keeps the poet from ever constructing such an apotheosis.

The poet, it turns out, has no intention of threatening death with the eternal power of poetry, or even of drawing some consoling meaning from this particular death.[20] Instead, he begins to warn death of the consequences of his actions, not for death itself but for the social world of human beings:

> Either from marriage thou wilt Maides affright,
> Or in their wedlock, Widowes lives to chuse,
> Their Husbands bed, and utterly refuse,
> Fearing conception; so shalt thou thereby
> Extirpate mankinde by thy cruelty.
>
> (26–30)

This imagining then becomes the occasion for a remarkable turn on conventional generic figures that are often used not only in funereal verse but also quite appropriately—though here horrifically—in epithalamia:

> If after direfull Tragedy thou thirst,
> Extinguish Himens Torches at the first;
> Build Funerall pyles, and the sad pavement strewe,
> With mournfull Cypresse, & the pale-leaved Yewe.
> Away with Roses, Myrtle, and with Bayes;
> Ensignes of mirth, and jollity, as these,
> Never at Nuptials used be againe,
> But from the Church the new Bride entertaine
> With weeping Nenias, ever and among,
> As at departings be sad Requiems song.
>
> (31–40)

This "anti-epithalamium," drawing on motifs in Ovid and Apuleius (the weddings of Orpheus and of Psyche) and unfolding in the midst of a funeral elegy, makes explicit the generic similarity between elegies and epithalamia noted by Celeste Schenck (an imaginative intimacy that here serves a painful purpose and one that Drayton makes full use of).[21] It also makes explicit what Heather Dubrow has said about the marriage poems of the period themselves, that an association of death and sex preoccupies their authors for very basic reasons: "[Death] deeply threatens the occasion and the values they are celebrating. The bride might produce stillborn children and die herself in the process. The very hopes that epithalamia express might themselves be stillborn."[22] Drayton's evocation of virgin fears and his extraordinary equation of sexual refusal with widowhood followed by the imagining of the funereal wedding is a forceful, and for this occasion, very appropriate attempt to express fully the anxieties that feed the anti-epithalamic traditions that Drayton is himself drawing on, anxieties that were regularly combated rhetorically by the authors of commissioned epithalamia.[23] In those poems, the poet often incants a charm to protect the couple from baleful influences, enclosing them in a space in which God and various mythic patronesses of fertility can be invoked.[24] In Drayton's poem, death pervades, has in fact invaded, the poet's imagination because the catastrophe that marriage poems attempt to charm away has overwhelmed one marriage, and now, because all flesh is heir to this same natural shock, it threatens to overwhelm all future marriages.

Such a catastrophe demands that the poet give full voice to the threat to marriage posed by female fear of death both before and within nuptial union. Because actual marriages are here ending in funeral, all marriage becomes proleptically funereal, and the ceremony Drayton describes mourns the destruction of both the marriages that will not occur because of virgin refusal and those that will be destroyed by wives who, "fearing conception," will now refuse their husbands' beds and live like widows, figuratively killing their spouses as spouses. Drayton's use of anti-epithalamic motifs in an elegy that specifies death in childbirth throws the threat posed to the institution of marriage by its very own ends (sexual union and procreation) into bold relief, requiring that the twin and yet antithetical modes be used in tandem, but not in the ways they normally work together. Normally the one is a foil for the celebration of the other, acting like an anti-masque to a masque. In this case, the one, in effect, cancels out the other's ability to repair its damage or charm away its worries. Normally, as Schenck observes, epithalamic conventions come into play in the consolations of most funeral elegies, providing the consoling, figurative counter-ceremony to the funeral procession of their poems' lamentations.[25] In the conventional epithalamia, however, death and lament serve as foils for the nuptial celebration. They are invoked only to be displaced from the ritual of union and exiled to its margins. As Dubrow notes, they may also find oblique expression in laments about the passing of youth or maidenhood.[26] But they are never allowed to maim the rite of marriage or to stain it with real tears.

The purpose of the evocation of such things at all in a marriage poem is, as Dubrow puts it, to "control" and "subdue" the elegiac, making room for celebration *and* assuring all concerned that the couple will enjoy both long life and numerous progeny (despite the fact that these often proved incompatible).[27] This is not so far from the funeral elegy's purpose of using epithalamic motifs to control grief and make possible an argument for consolation. However, the actual evocation of childbed death in a funeral elegy for a woman who died that way weights the generic frame with a complex and unbearable crossing. In fact, it hobbles Drayton's poem, which never manages to generate much of a consolation at all. Drayton moves from the funereal wedding to a complaint against Lucina, Roman goddess of childbirth, for not coming to Mistress Fallow-field's aid, and then on to an inconclusive philosophical debate over whether "fortune" or "nature" is to blame (47–54). Then a reiterative meditation on the fact that death takes all leads to a four-line eternizing conceit, and the poem never confronts the terrifying question of what we are supposed to feel in the face of the tragic irony the poem has presented. Such inconclusive offers of poetic immortality are, however, no comfort at all. Drayton sees that the occasion demands the release of the elegiac subcurrents of traditional epithalamia, but can do nothing much in the face of them.

When Milton sat down to write his "Epitaph," he was faced with the same problem, and perhaps he had read Drayton's poem. He also makes use of the topos of the funereal wedding; he too invokes Lucina; like Drayton he uses the commonplace image of death's destroying both a plant and its seed or flower. However, Milton extends these conceits as he found them, perhaps in Drayton, perhaps elsewhere, with further fabling. He takes care to weave the topoi intricately with genealogy, communal and institutional mourning, personal compliment, and biblical comparison, to produce what has emerged in my research as one of the most ambitious and successful poems on maternal mortality produced in the period.

In his "Epitaph," the fatal conjunction of Orpheus' and Psyche's weddings with Rachel and the attendant conflation of elegy and epithalamium, genealogy, gardening, birth, myth, and pastoral also allows Milton to express himself on important vocational themes. Milton's conjunction of Orpheus/Psyche and Rachel itself might be the height of the genre's mythical and typological reach in this particular occasional context, and nothing in the tradition of elegy comes close to its ambition, even if the quality of the young Milton's execution seems to us immature when we read it after putting down a well-worn copy of *Paradise Lost*.

III

Milton's "Epitaph" moves through a series of classical, biblical, and literary allusions, climaxing in the allusion to Rachel via *Para-*

diso 32.7–10. The choice to end with an apotheosis is conventional, and this one is usually faulted for being forced. However, Milton's manner, along with the motive behind his choice of figures and allusions, makes his figure operate in a wholly original and complexly appropriate way. Just before the apotheosis he had addressed himself directly to the deceased ("Gentle lady may thy grave / Peace and quiet ever have") and directly tied the cause of her death to the nature of her salvation ("Sweet rest seize thee evermore, / That to give the world increase, / Shortened hast thine own life's lease"). The analogy between Jane's experience and Rachel's, along with the fact that she now sits next to Rachel in the heavenly hierarchy, therefore serves to reinforce those gestures by suggesting 1) that Jane is not only saved, but the form of her self-sacrifice has achieved for her a place of particularly high glory, and 2) that her manner of death has typological resonance. Milton makes the analogy, not just the ascent itself, at once the tragic and recuperative conclusion of his poem.

In the sequence of its allusions, Milton's poem is an earlier version of the strategy he would later employ in Sonnet 23, whose octave has long been understood as structured typologically. That poem moves from Alcestis to the Israelite women of Leviticus, who then suggest Mary and Elizabeth in Luke, allowing the lines to come to a pause just over the line of the octave/sestet break in an expression of Christian "trust" in a future redemption and reunion of husband and wife. A similar scheme determines Milton's use of Rachel here. Like the ladies of Leviticus in the sonnet, Rachel suggests Christian consolation typologically, here again as in the sonnet, via Mary, but in a more directly literary context, via Dante's Beatrice (to whom some people have long thought the sonnet refers as well). It is Mary whom Dante is gazing at when he is told by Benedict that the radiant women he sees just below the Virgin are, first, Eve, who "opened" and "pierced" the "wound which Mary closed and anointed." Then, below Eve, next to Beatrice, is Rachel, and below her in gradations are Sarah, Rebecca, Judith, Ruth, and then all the Hebrew women "who follow in succession, dividing all the tresses of the flower"(32.1–18).[28] This line divides the seats of the Rose between those who "believed in Christ yet to come" and "those who turned their faces to Christ already come" (22–27). As a pre-Christian Israelite who is later saved (and here appears in heaven), Rachel can suggest the fate of woman after the Curse of Eve (she is a woman who gave birth in pain and danger and died). By her position in the Rose, she can also suggest the one birth that makes it possible to transcend this Curse, that of Mary, who according to tradition gave birth without sin and therefore without pain or danger, and whose child made it possible for those who suffer in faith to be redeemed from their suffering.[29] Milton's allusion to Dante's arrangement of figures in the Heavenly Rose, his specificity about where Jane is sitting in the Rose, suggests that Milton may have considered the arrangement significant from the point of view of childbed death. Placing Jane at Rachel's side, on the Christian side, makes her occupy a position in the Rose that is on the cusp between the two dispensations, the line that both divides and makes them one (both piercing and closing the wound). Rachel is there below Eve (and, oddly, before Sarah), not just because she—as the earlier dream of *Purgatorio* 27 tells us—represents contemplation but also because in motherhood she represents the wound of painful fallen existence. Rachel's death in Genesis is a wound that never quite gets healed in the course of the Hebrew Scriptures, but it is healed for Christians by Mary.[30] Rachel is, for this reason, also a significant biblical touchstone in discussions about painful and dangerous birth in the midwifery handbooks of the period.[31] Her appearance at so important a point in Milton's poem is, for all these reasons, more deeply integrated with the poet's larger purposes than has so far been suggested.

Gayle Edward Wilson, for example, has perceptively noted that Milton treats Jane's giving birth to two children (dying in the birth of the latter), along with her marriage, under the topos of praise for laudable deeds.[32] The Marchioness is treated as mother, and motherhood is seen as a form not only of laudable but also, given the dangers, perhaps even of heroic action. This is reinforced by Milton when, as I said before, he wishes the Lady eternal rest after her hard travail for the sake of future life.

Wilson also rightly associates Milton's attention to the birth with the figures of genealogy that properly begin the poem, and that, as he says, function as a unifying theme. However, when Wilson comes to the issue of Milton's decision to treat the birth explicitly—including the reference to Rachel—he merely explains the choice as determined by decorum. Milton chose it, he argues, simply as the most appropriate and decorous figure to focus on. In a note, he even takes the letters of Pory and the Duchess of Buckingham as suggesting that it was indeed the "impostume" that killed Jane and that Milton knew this but decided instead to emphasize the birth because it was the decorous thing to do.[33]

As useful as Wilson's attention to rhetorical decorum is, there are a number of limits to his line of interpretation. The other poets, who were no more ignorant of the requirements of decorum than

Milton, actually chose *not* to focus their poems in this way. This is because death in childbirth, though not in itself an indecorous thing to focus on, was still something that required far more from the machinery of conventional consolation than models ready to hand could provide.

Wilson's reading, and in this he is not alone, also ignores certain facts about childbirth in the period:[34] for example, it was common for relatively minor ailments like an "impostume" to become fully blown critical conditions, not in addition to, but *because of*, the specific physical pressures exerted by dangerous childbirth.[35] The very presence of a surgeon who could have lanced her abscess argues that the usually exclusively female world of the lying-in chamber had already allowed in a man who, unlike a midwife, would have had the tools and expertise to have performed one of several invasive maneuvers to remove the stillborn infant. Surgery was common in such cases because the action of a living infant was thought necessary for birth to occur. Stillborn infants that could be identified as such by a good midwife or surgeon were often extracted through the vagina after being partially dismembered in utero with special cutting tools and hooks. This procedure, which was performed—as was everything in the period—under very septic conditions, was often primarily responsible for the severe infections that killed many women. These infections were often exacerbated by the fact that the infant had been dead inside the womb long enough to putrefy. Milton's decision to focus on the birth need not have been the product, therefore, of a turning away from a less poetic material to a more poetic one, abstracting, as he would have to, its grotesque and pitiable physicality into a set of decorous figures. Instead, he may have seen the practical connection between the two related causes of the Lady's death and treated them as of a piece. Such connections were, in any case, part of the general suffering that surrounded childbirth in the era and made it so loaded a subject for poetic description. The treatment by figurative abstraction was a difficult thing to pull off and would not have occurred to him as simply and naturally decorous in Wilson's sense.

Milton's choices, seen the way I am suggesting and seen in light of my reading of Drayton's poem, show that he chose deliberately and against convention to deal with the consequences of birth under contemporary conditions. The choices cannot simply be explained by recourse to inherited rhetorical theory, although—and this is the heart of Wilson's argument—the theories and topoi Milton learned so well were the scaffolding upon which he built the poem. This is, of course, the case with everything Milton wrote. The "Epitaph" is neither an exception to the rule of his following convention nor to the rule of his bending it ambitiously to his own purposes. As the allusion to Rachel shows, even at this early stage, in what is ostensibly only a piece of occasional verse, Milton is aiming at some point just above the peak of the Aonian Mount.[36]

Above all, it is this aiming high that determines his choice of Rachel, the funereal wedding, and the entire complex of images related to birth that structure the poem. The invocation of Lucina, the coming of Atropos with her shears, the pastoral fable of the "unheedy swain" (38), the "slip" (35) and "carnation train" (37) described in that fable, the two epitaphic figures of the "fruit and tree" (30) and the "womb" (33) as "tomb" (34), the lines about Jane's giving her life for the sake of future life and her fleeing in "pangs . . . to felicity" (68): all of these figures have more far-reaching implications than that Milton was adept already at marshaling decorous and rhetorically integrated comparisons. These choices were, in fact, the product of a conscious plan and were from the start integrated with the opening materials on genealogy. And they serve not only to reinforce the requirements of praise but also are designed to suggest a confrontation with social realities very like the ones we saw in Drayton, as well as with the medical realities of which Milton, or indeed anyone, could easily have been aware, even if he or she had no firsthand experience of them. The urgencies of these confrontations are resolved, as they are not in Drayton, by the ambitious typological formula I described above.

We can see that Milton had the centrality of genealogical tensions in mind, for example, from the start by looking at the one major revision we have. The manuscript version of the "Epitaph" contains in some canceled lines an accurate bit of biographical information that also determined Milton's use of Rachel.[37] For lines 15–23 of 1645, the 1631 manuscript has the following:

> Seauen times had the yeerlie starre
> in euerie signe sett vpp his carr
> Since for her they did request
> the god that sitts at marriage feast
> when first the earlie Matrons runne.

The poem then picks up with a line that is a match for line 24 of 1645: "to greete her of a lovely sonne." Jane, like Rachel, not only died giving birth to her second son but was also married for seven years before she gave birth to her first child. It seems likely that the manuscript version derives from an earlier version of the poem, and that at some point between that composition and his decision to include the poem in his first book of poems, Milton thought better of mentioning this detail. Rachel was barren during the first seven years of her marriage to Jacob, years full of humiliation for her. Milton notes or implies in the midst of his comparison that, like Rachel, Lady Jane also experienced "years of barrenness" (64 [1645]). (That line is in both versions, but only has that meaning clearly in the manuscript.) Jane was only fourteen years old when she married John Paulet, so the delay in her first birth may not have been *entirely* due to reproductive problems. Still, seven years and a first child at twenty-one hint, perhaps, at some problem more difficult than the extended period of nonsexual wardship that often began noble marriages between very young women and older men. (John Paulet was twenty-four when they married.) Milton may have at some point decided that the canceled lines, which reinforced the specific reference to Jane's possible barrenness, seemed too indecorous. That the poem reached some stage of completion and found its way into someone's hand with the canceled lines intact shows, however, that Milton had seriously contemplated full integration of the Rachel comparison with the images of birth, death, and lineage that dominate the first half of the poem. This adds some force to the defense of the last lines suggested by Wilson and others: that Milton's elevation of Jane to the status of "queen" (74) not only suggests Mary but also is a thematic continuation of description of titled lineage with which he begins the poem.[38]

In the place of the thematically integral, but possibly indecorous, lines in reference to Lady Jane's seven years of barreness, in the 1645 version Milton added something related to lineage in a more acute though less personal way, using the topos of the funereal wedding:

> Her high birth, and her graces sweet,
> Quickly found a lover meet;
> The virgin choir for her request
> The god that sits at marriage-feast;
> He at their invoking came
> But with a scarce-well-lighted flame;
> And in his garland as he stood,
> Ye might discern a cypress bud.
> Once had the early matrons run. . . .
>
> (15–23)

In these lines, Milton suggests something far more difficult to develop a consolation for than long, but finally alleviated, barrenness
(although that, too, contains its own particularly painful irony in
that relief from barrenness only brings death, an irony at the heart
of what makes the story of Rachel so hauntingly painful and so
appropriate here). This passage's direct invocation of the marriage
reminds us that it is *marriage,* after all, that brings about this kind
of death (or at least sex in or out of marriage). In addition, coming
at the end of an opening that traces Jane's noble line and reminds
us that it was her "high birth" as well as her virtue that brought
her "a lover meet," the passage suggests the anxieties attending
the survival of noble lineages and their considerable material in-
heritances. In other words, the elegy quite appropriately echoes
the concerns that Dubrow has shown haunt many epithalamia in
the period. John Paulet was "meet" because he too was the product
of a long noble line, which of course also depended upon the continued production of heirs. The pastoral imagery Milton later develops of "carnation trains" and slips of one sort of tree being cut
and grafted onto another reinforces these implications, since in
this case the ongoing project of noble hybridization has failed.
Once we note this, we cannot help but also hear in "lover meet"
an echo of the description of Eve in Genesis as "a help meet for"
Adam (2.18),[39] and along with this comes to mind the creation of
sexual difference and the fulfillment of the imperative to "Be fruitful and multiply" (Gen. 1.28), which these noble families (in their
economically and politically determined way) are continuing to
fulfill.

By replacing the earlier passage in the 1645 edition, Milton draws
into his poem the same sorts of questions and threats that Drayton
confronted in his, with the added complexity of dynastic succession.[40] He too brings the catastrophic weddings of Orpheus and of
Psyche into his poem and suggests the fatal conjunction in which
a wedding actually leads to a funeral. The invocation of Orpheus
would also seem to suggest a poetry of lament and irrecoverable
loss. This is an implication that Drayton's poem never recovers
from. Milton, however, works very hard and with some very ambitious materials (Dante, the Bible) to provide a consolation meet
for this catastrophe.

Milton must have intuited that the machinery of Dante was more
or less up to the task of making the right connections between
Old and New Testament, allowing him to associate the deceased
typologically with Mary and the Nativity via Eve and Rachel. The
passage on the funereal wedding, therefore, with its "scarce-well-

lighted flame" and "cypress bud," sets up and tries to solve a central human problem: in the seventeenth century what made the fulfilling of human dynastic ambition and personal love possible often led to what most deeply threatened them, that is, death in the midst of the human body's coping with the typically inevitable outcome of heterosexual love and marriage—at least in the absence of birth control. Milton's poem is far more conventional than Drayton's and also more controlled and effective in its basic aims. But those aims are unfolded in a larger literary and theological context in order to provide ceremonially for the restoration of meaning and value. This, after all, is the task of the funeral poem. Drayton expressed certain social anxieties more directly and could not control the outcome rhetorically. Milton courted the same anxieties and found a way to deal with them. According to the statistics, it is at least possible that about 20 to 25 percent of all elegies written about married women in the period were about women who died in childbirth. I would suggest that the main reason most of these poets say nothing about that fact is that, unlike Milton, they were unable to imagine what to say.

IV

Milton never actually discarded his early interest in maternal mortality. In fact, he later became the author of one of the most compelling poems on the subject written in the century (Sonnet 23). He also makes use of motifs of catastrophic childbirth at two important points in *Paradise Lost* (the birth of Death in book 2 and Adam's description of the creation of Eve in book 8).[41] In those instances he also finds ways of confronting the horrific medical realities that get abstracted out of the "Epitaph" (though they perhaps find oblique expression in the shears of Atropos). Milton's continued interest is perhaps due to the fact that childbed death unfortunately called upon his direct attention on two occasions later in his life. In 1652 Milton's first wife, Mary Powell, died three days after giving birth to her fourth child, and in 1658 his second wife, Katherine Woodcock, died of a "consumption" contracted in childbed just three months after giving birth to her first child (and barely a year after their wedding). There is therefore something chillingly prescient in the choices Milton made in constructing his early exercise in Jonsonian verse (though one need not have been a seer to understand the likelihood of maternal mortality). There is also something surprisingly sensitive and searching in these choices, something, in fact, that bore fruit years later as he meditated on his personal pain in the context of the Fall and remembered with an understandable vividness, and perhaps with no small temptation to bitterness, God's sentencing of Eve: "In sorrow thou shalt bring forth children" (Gen. 3.16).

Milton's "Epitaph" should be read, therefore, as an early attempt to provide an allusive structure capable of handling the theological and personal ironies involved in maternal and infant mortality. It is, like Sonnet 23, extraordinary in its method, and it remains unique among seventeenth-century epitaphs for its attempt to bring poetic strategies to bear on a circumstance particularly acute for Londoners and upper-class English men and women of the day. As a poem it is not as successful in this attempt as the later sonnet. By comparison its torch is scarcely well-lit. This is because, like most elegies—and by all conventional codes they ought to do this—it works very hard toward erasing the complexities and pains it presents. It aims ultimately for a consoling conclusion, taming the experience of grief, rather than complicating it by confronting, even courting despair. Sonnet 23, because of its much more personal occasion and above all the particular poetic concerns of the poet in the late 1650s, could not have helped courting such despair. The problems it confronts are, after all, too complex to be neatly resolved in fourteen lines. For that task Milton would need full epic machinery.

Notes

1. See, for example, Gayle Edward Wilson, "Decorum and Milton's 'An Epitaph on the Marchioness of Winchester,'" *Milton Quarterly* 8 (1974): 11–14. Most of the other earlier criticism is surveyed in A. S. P. Woodhouse and Douglas Bush, eds., *A Variorum Commentary on the Poems of John Milton*, 4 vols. (New York: Columbia University Press, 1970–75), 2 : 194–95. G. W. Pigman very briefly discusses the poem in his survey of Renaissance attitudes toward grief, *Grief and the English Renaissance Elegy* (Cambridge: Cambridge University Press, 1985), 106–7. Scattered comments can also be found in Gerald Hammond's *Fleeting Things: English Poets and Poems 1616–1660* (Cambridge: Harvard University Press, 1990), 145–53. John Peter Rumrich has included some brief and interesting remarks about the poem in relation to childbirth danger in his recently published *Milton Unbound: Controversy and Reinterpretation* (Cambridge: Cambridge University Press, 1996), 78, 97.

2. For statistics on maternal mortality, see Audrey Eccles, *Obstetrics and Gynecology in Tudor and Stuart England* (Kent, Ohio: Kent State University Press, 1982), 125. She gives the number as 25 deaths per 1,000 births, but I have reduced the numbers for the sake of clarity. Other studies cite statistics slightly below or well above this mark. See Adrian Wilson, "Childbirth in Seventeenth-

and Eighteenth-Century England" (Ph.D. diss., University of Sussex, 1982), 309; Thomas Forbes, *Chronicle from Aldgate: Life and Death in Shakespeare's London* (New Haven: Yale University Press, 1971), 106. Roger Schofield argues for a significantly lower national rate, but notes that the rates in London were much higher than in the rest of the United Kingdom. See "Did Mothers Really Die? Three Centuries of Maternal Mortality in 'The World We Have Lost,'" in *The World We Have Gained: Histories of Population and Social Structure*, ed. Lloyd Bonfield, Richard Smith, and Keith Wrightson (Oxford: Basil Blackwell, 1986), 231–60.

3. On fertility rates, see Roger Finlay, *Population and Metropolis: The Demography of London 1580–1650* (Cambridge: Cambridge University Press, 1981), 133–50, and Dorothy McLaren, "Marital Fertility and Lactation 1570–1720," in *Women in English Society 1500–1800*, ed. Mary Prior (London: Methuen, 1985), 22–53.

4. For comparison with present-day rates, see the *United Nations Statistical Yearbook,* 38th ed. (New York: United Nations, 1993), 164, 167, and World Bank, *World Development Report 1993: Investing in Health* (Oxford: Oxford University Press, 1993), 300–301. While the rate sometimes breaks 1,000 deaths per 100,000 births, it is quite rare for a nation to experience a rate higher than 700 or 800 per 100,000. Translated into the larger numbers used by present day demographers, the rate in seventeenth-century London would be 2,500 per 100,000.

5. See letters of 16 April from Katherine, Duchess of Buckingham, to her father and 21 April from John Pory to Sir Thomas Puckering. A full account of the biographical context with relevant quotations from the letters can be found in William Riley Parker, *Milton: A Biography,* 2 vols. (Oxford: Clarendon, 1968), 1:94–96, 2:766–68; and "Milton and the Marchioness of Winchester," *Modern Language Review* 44 (1949): 547–50. John Pory may have been the biographical connection that occasioned Milton's composition of the poem and provided him with the detailed biographical information he seems, on the evidence of both versions of the poem, to have had. The John Pory of the above letter may have been related to Milton's longtime schoolmate (at both St. Paul's School and Christ's College), Robert Pory. Masson suggests that John was Robert's uncle. See David Masson, *The Life of John Milton,* 7 vols. (London: 1859–94; reprint, Gloucester: Peter Smith, 1965), 1:244. There has been no confirmation of this. Parker speculates that the friendship between Milton and Robert Pory was very close. Indeed, after Charles Diodati left St. Paul's, he may have been, according to Parker, Milton's closest friend at school. They matriculated together at Christ's, chose the same tutor, and Parker believes it is at least possible that Milton chose to go to Christ's because Pory was also going there (Parker, *Milton: A Biography,* 1:722).

6. William Camden, *Remaines concerning Britaine,* 7th ed. (London, 1674), 439. John Carey, ed. (*John Milton: Complete Shorter Poems* [London: Longman, 1971], 127), reports an elegy by William Strode to be found "in BM MS Sloane" 1446 (where the manuscript version of Milton's poem appears). I do not find it there, but there is an anonymous poem on page 128 of the manuscript entitled, "On an Infant unborne and the mother Dyinge in travell." It may pertain to Lady Jane, but it contains no recognizable biographical references beyond the occasion of the death in childbed of both mother and infant. I have written to Professor Carey, but he does not recall the poem he was referring to. No such poem appears in the only published collection of Strode's verse nor among the surviving manuscripts and published texts of sermons and speeches that I have seen to date.

7. This allusion was first noticed by James Holly Hanford, ed., *The Poems of John Milton*, 2nd ed. (New York: Ronald Press Company, 1953), 79.

8. Pory's letter states that her death "is lamented as well in respect to her other virtues, as that she was inclining to become a Protestant" (Parker, *Milton: A Biography*, 1:94–95). In his 1785 edition of Milton's poems, Warton claimed to have heard of a volume of Cambridge verses but doubted that such a volume was ever actually published (qtd. in Parker, 767). If it existed, it has never been found. Masson thought that the existence of the manuscript version of Milton's poem (in BM MS Sloane 1446) suggested that it may have circulated in some printed form before Milton published it in 1645 (1:246). This need not have been the case. The poem could well have circulated in manuscript, although other copies have been lost if they existed. Parker points out that student expectations about a volume of dedicatory verses might have alone sufficed to move Milton to write his elegy, particularly given that line 59 proclaims that the poem was sent "from the banks of Came." Alberta T. Turner ("Milton and the Convention of the Academic Miscellanies," *Yearbook of English Studies* 5 [1975]: 86–93) warns, however, that student expectations of a volume may have been unlikely, given that Cambridge had not by 1631 published very many miscellanies for private persons. In addition, such expectations are unnecessary for an explanation of the existence of the poem. It was customary for students to write funeral verses to tack on the hearse and the walls of the college or to recite at gatherings. All of Milton's Cambridge funeral verses could have been produced for this purpose. It is possible that the poem came into the hands of the Sloane manuscript compiler via the walls of Christ's.

9. There are remarkable exceptions to the general silence, but they are rare. See, for example, the discussion below of Michael Drayton's "Upon the Death of Mistris Elianor Fallowfield." Others include poems by Robert Herrick, Lady Jane Cavendish, George Wither, Nicholas Grimald, and several anonymous elegies. I am presently at work on a study of these and other representations of catastrophic childbirth in the context of contemporary practices and lore.

10. On diagnosis in the period, see Nancy Siriasi, *Medieval and Early Renaissance Medicine: An Introduction to Knowledge and Practice* (Chicago: University of Chicago Press, 1990), 123–33.

11. Jonson discusses the presence of surgeons at Lady Jane's bedside. He knew the Duchess of Buckingham and therefore could easily have known about the impostume, but he does not suggest that the Lady had been the subject of obstetric surgery, despite the fact that her stillbirth, as I argue later in this essay, suggests she was in fact subject to some such procedure, and it probably played a far greater role in her death than the lancing.

12. Birth and lying-in could often, in fact, mean over a month of separation between man and wife. See Adrian Wilson, "Participant or Patient? Seventeenth-Century Childbirth from the Mother's Point of View," in *Patients and Practitioners: Lay Perceptions of Medicine in Pre-Industrial Society*, ed. Roy Porter (Cambridge: Cambridge University Press, 1985), 129–44. Wilson's interpretation of the rituals surrounding childbirth in the period have undergone some changes in recent years, and he has done more work on the subject than anyone else. It is therefore important to see both his more recent essay, "The Ceremony of Childbirth and Its Interpretation," in *Women as Mothers in Pre-Industrial England: Essays in Memory of Dorothy McLaren*, ed. Valerie Fildes (London: Routledge, 1990), 68–178, and part 1 of his even more recent book, *The Making*

of Man-Midwifery: Childbirth in England 1660–1770 (London: University College London Press, 1995), 11–62.

13. See Audrey Eccles, "The Early Use of English for Midwiferies 1500–1700," *Neuphilologische Mitteilungen* 78 (1977): 377–85.

14. This is particularly true from the 1590s on, when in the wake of the outpouring of poems on Sir Philip Sidney's death, specificity of all kinds became more common in elegiac verse. Earlier specific poems that do so, however, also exist. Dennis Kay surveys the development of the sixteenth-century English epitaph in *Melodious Tears: The English Funeral Elegy from Spenser to Milton* (Oxford: Oxford University Press, 1990), 10–17.

15. Probably the most remarkable of the poems that make use of sickness is Chapman's elegy for Prince Henry, an adaptation of Politian's elegy on Albierta Albitia, which contains mythic treatment of Febris, Goddess of Fever. See O. B. Hardison's extended discussion of the poem in *The Enduring Monument: A Study of the Idea of Praise in Renaissance Theory and Practice* (Chapel Hill: University of North Carolina Press, 1962), 131. The coming of Febris to the bed of the young Albierta might be related to the replacement of Lucina with Atropos in Milton's poem.

16. There are many famous examples of this—see, again, those about Sidney. Other examples of elegies that specify and celebrate warfare as the manner of death include Henry Howard, Earl of Surrey's epitaph on the death of Thomas Clere during the siege of Muttrell; Andrew Marvell's "An Elegy on the Death of my Lord Francis Villiers." William Davenant also wrote several specific elegies: "Elegie on B. Haselrick, slaine in's youth in a Duell," "Written, When Collonell Goring Was beleev'd to be slaine, at the siege of Breda. His death lamented by Endimion, Arigo," and "An Elegy on the Duke of Buckingham's Death." I mention these because of all the poems we have on Lady Jane, Davenant's is perhaps the most abstract and least specific.

17. This is, of course, the case with *Lycidas* and many of the other elegies published on the death of Edward King in the commemorative volume, *Justa Eduardo King*, (1638).

18. It appeared in the volume, *The Battaile of Agincourt* (London: Printed for William Lee, 1627), as the last poem in the last section of the volume, entitled "Elegies vpon sundry occasions." I know of no reason Milton should not have owned a copy, although this essay is the first to argue any explicit connection between the volume and Milton's work. See *The Works of Michael Drayton*, 5 vols., ed. William Hebel (Oxford: Oxford University Press, 1961), 3:242–43.

19. All references to Drayton's poetry are to Hebel's edition, *The Works of Michael Drayton*, and are cited parenthetically in the text.

20. It is remarkable how long it takes Drayton to take up one of these strategies. He finally chooses to immortalize Mistress Fallowfield, but not until the last two lines of a sixty-three-line poem. It is one thing for Shakespeare to hold off until the couplet of the sonnet, but fourteen lines are a different matter from sixty-three lines. And when Drayton finally employs the conceit, its effect is strangely anticlimactic. Rather than offering consolation, it seems an afterthought, or something the poet says just to bring the poem to a close, fulfilling a generic obligation without the proper rhetorical preparation.

21. Celeste Marguerite Schenck, *Mourning and Panegyric: The Poetics of Pastoral Ceremony* (University Park: Pennsylvania State University Press, 1988), 7, 10–16. The term "anti-epithalamium" was coined by Virginia Tufte in *The Poetry of Marriage: The Epithalamium in Europe and Its Development in England* (Los

Angeles: Tinnon-Brown, 1970). As Schenck observes in her introduction—and my example from Drayton bears her out—the term should in no way be confined to examples of full-blown parody like John Donne's "Epithalamion Made at Lincoln's Inne," but should be used to refer to the quite serious use of antithetical motifs in conventional marriage verses, funeral elegies, and all sorts of what she calls "poems of pastoral ceremony." The category includes a wide range of poems of initiation and transition. For interesting readings of the tensions expressed by anti-epithalamic motifs, see Heather Dubrow's discussion of Richard Crashaw, *A Happier Eden: The Politics of Marriage in the Stuart Epithalamium* (Ithaca: Cornell University Press, 1990), 121–22. Also see Schenck, *Mourning and Panegyric*," 73–83, on Donne and Crashaw.

22. Dubrow, *A Happier Eden*, 120. The quotation continues: "It is no accident that the marriage ceremony in the Book of Common Prayer juxtaposes a reference to heirs with the hope that the couple will enjoy long lives: 'We beseech thee assist with thy blessing these two persons, that they may both be fruitful in procreation of children, and also live together so long in godly love and honesty, that they may see their children's children.'" Dubrow is quoting *The Book of Common Prayer, 1559: The Elizabethan Prayer Book*, ed. John E. Booty (Charlottesville: University Press of Virginia for the Folger Shakespeare Library, 1976), 296. Dubrow makes two other direct references to childbirth (39, 86). While she notes that obstetric catastrophe is one of the sources of deep anxiety in the Stuart epithalamia, the issue is ancillary to her argument, which explores sexual and dynastic anxieties at length. She deals with poetry and obstetrics in more detail in *Echoes of Desire: English Petrarchism and its Counterdiscourses* (Ithaca: Cornell University Press, 1995).

23. "Funereal wedding" is J. Arthur Hanson's translation of Apuleius's *funerei thalami* (*Metamorphoses*, 2 vols., ed. and trans. J. Arthur Hanson [Cambridge: Harvard University Press, 1989], 1:247). The motif has a long history in anti-epithalamia and has its roots in both elegy and myth. See Schenck, *Mourning and Panegyric*, 73–74.

24. See, for example, stanzas 19 and 20 of Edmund Spenser's "Epithalamion."

25. Schenck, *Mourning and Panegyric*, 10–16.

26. Dubrow, *A Happier Eden*, 121–22.

27. Ibid., 122.

28. Dante Alighieri, *Paradiso*, in *The Divine Comedy: Paradiso*, trans. Charles S. Singleton (Princeton: Princeton University Press, 1975). All references to *Paradiso* are to this edition and are cited parenthetically in the text.

29. Singleton notes the commonness of a Latin pun on "Ave," as in "Ave Maria," as the reverse of "Eva." On this thematic material in *Paradise Lost* see Louis Schwartz, "'Conscious Terrors' and 'The Promised Seed': Seventeenth-Century Obstetrics and the Allegory of Sin and Death in *Paradise Lost*," *Milton Studies* 32 (1995): 63–89.

30. Rachel appears again in Jacob's grief and again in the Lamentations of Jeremiah, weeping for her children.

31. See for example Jane Sharp, *The Midwives Book* (London, 1671), 169–70. A facsimile of Sharp's book is available in the Garland series *Marriage, Sex, and the Family in England 1660–1800*, ed. Randolph Trumbach (New York: Garland, 1985). Milton is not the first to make use of Rachel for mourning the death of a woman in childbed. See, for example, the Latin epitaph, "EPITAPHIVM fæminæ lectissimæ D. Elizabethæ Crashaviæ in puerperio heu mortuæ," in *The Honor of Virtue or the Monument erected by the sorowfull Husband, and the Epitaphes*

*annexed by learned and worthy men, to the immortal memory of that worthy
Gentle-woman Mrs Elizabeth Crashawe who died in child-birth and was buried
in whitchappell: Octob. 8. 1620. In the 24 yeare of her age* (London, 1620), B3,
which, like the sermon published in the same volume, refers to the death of
Phinehas's wife at 1 Sam. 4.19–22.

32. Wilson, "Decorum," 11–12.

33. Ibid., 14.

34. Studies have plainly shown that in the seventeenth century, women during
their childbearing years, especially during the last months of pregnancy and
through their recovery from giving birth, experienced highly accelerated rates of
morbidity as well as mortality. See Lucinda McCray Beier, "In Sickness and in
Health: A Seventeenth-Century Family's Experience," in Porter, *Patients and
Practitioners*, 103–7; Alan Macfarlane, *The Family Life of Ralph Josselin, A
Seventeenth-Century Clergyman: An Essay on Historical Anthropology* (Cambridge: Cambridge University Press, 1970), 81–89; Wilson, "Childbirth"; and
Schwartz, "'Conscious Terrors,'" especially 70–71.

35. Pory's letter, in particular, can clearly be seen as expressing no real distinction between the lancing and the birth as conditions contributing to the Lady's
death. Pory does say, in line with common humoral explanations of the nature of
infections, that it was the humor from the impostume falling down her throat that
"despatched" her, but he clearly associates this with the fact of her obstetric
condition, saying that the humor "quickly despatched, being big with child" (Parker, *Milton: A Biography*, 2:767). Impostumes were thought to be collections of
harmful humors. See, for example, book 7, Chapter 1, of *The Workes of that
famous Chirurgion Ambrose Parey, Translated out of the Latin and compared to
the French by Tho: Johnson* (London, 1649), 195.

36. The comparison to Rachel has not fared well in the critical literature. See,
for example, Cleanth Brooks and John E. Hardy, eds. *Poems of John Milton: The
1645 Edition with Essays in Analysis* (New York: Harcourt, 1951), 120–22. Parker
thought it perhaps impoverished the Lady herself. He bids us remember that
Benjamin lived and that Jacob had other children by Leah and his various maid-
servants (*Milton: A Biography*, 1:96). Wilson argues that the figure is appropriate,
again in the context of decorum, but mainly because its "straining" is in line with
Quintilian's dictate that hyperbole should always exhibit an "elegant straining of
the truth" and that such "youthful fondness for comparisons," as Parker (*Milton:
A Biography*, 1:96) blames Milton for, is appropriate to the rhetorical need he
felt to express his ethos as a speaker characterized by his youth and status as a
university student (Wilson, "Decorum," 12).

37. The manuscript has the very explicit title, "On the Marchioness of Winchester whoe died in Child bedd. Ap:15. 1631." Wilson and Parker both take note
of the manuscript changes but make little of them. Wilson believes that they show
Milton's consciousness of "the *topos* of descent" from an early stage ("Decorum,"
11), Parker that they show Milton had more specific biographical information than
the 1645 version implies ("Milton and the Marchioness," 549).

38. Wilson, "Decorum," 13.

39. All biblical references are to the King James Version and are cited parenthetically in the text.

40. It is possible that the idea of using the generic tension between ceremonial
tropes and modes found in epithalamia was suggested to Milton by Drayton's
text, but we do not know at what point Milton made the change I have pointed
out. Parker notes that it is too substantive and clearly related to the poem's other

thematic concerns to have been the product of a copyist's hand ("Milton and the Marchioness," 549). Unlike Drayton, Milton moves into the topos by invoking Jane Paulet's actual wedding. He even follows it, as does Drayton, with the invocation of Lucina, here tragically crossed with Atropos. The passage on Lucina also deserves some attention. Milton here is alluding not only, perhaps, to Drayton but also, perhaps, to *Cymbeline* 5.4.43–44: "Lucina lent me not her aid, / But took me in my throes" (William Shakespeare, *Cymbeline*, in *The Riverside Shakespeare*, ed. G. Blakemore Evans [Boston: Houghton Mifflin, 1974]); to Sandys' Ovid 10.507: "Nor could she call Lucina to her throwes" (*Ovid's Metamorphosis Englished, Mythologized, and Represented in Figures by George Sandys*, ed. Karl K. Hulley and Stanley T. Vandersall [Lincoln: University of Nebraska Press, 1970]); and/or to *The Faerie Queene* 2.1.53 and 3.6.27 (Edmund Spenser, *The Faerie Queene*, ed. A. C. Hamilton [London: Longman, 1977]).

41. See Schwartz, "'Spot of child-bed taint': Seventeenth-Century Obstetrics in Milton's Sonnet XXIII and *Paradise Lost* 8.462–78," *Milton Quarterly* 27 (1993): 98–109, and Schwartz, "'Conscious Terrors.'"

From Temperance to Abstinence: The Argument of *Comus* Revisited

J. MARTIN EVANS

The argument I refer to in my title is not the overall theme of the mask, as in A. S. P. Woodhouse's famous article,[1] but rather the debate between Comus and the Lady at its center. Comus begins the argument by observing that since Nature pours forth her wealth in such overwhelming abundance, those who follow the Stoics and Cynics in praising "the lean and sallow abstinence" (709)[2] are not only acting ungratefully; they are courting ecological disaster. In order to prevent a vast and destructive surplus from building up, he concludes, we should consume Nature's gifts without restraint:

> if all the world
> Should in a pet of temperance feed on pulse,
> Drink the clear stream, and nothing wear but freise,
> Th' all-giver would be unthank't, would be unprais'd,
> Not half his riches known, and yet dispis'd,
> And we should serve him as a grudging maister,
> As a penurious niggard of his wealth,
> 'And live like natures bastards, not her sons,
> Who would be quite surcharg'd with her own waight
> And strangl'd with her wast fertility.
>
> (720–29)

Comus offers, in other words, only two possible courses of action: on the one hand, unrestrained self-indulgence, on the other, total self-denial.

The main burden of the Lady's reply is that there is a third alternative: moderation, or, as she calls it, temperance. This response to Nature's bounty, which Comus has falsely equated with abstinence, is now shown to consist in consuming "but a moderate and beseeming share" (769) of what Nature has to offer, as opposed to the "vast excess" (771) enjoyed by "som few" (771) in "lewdly-pamper'd Luxury" (770). It is the "swinish gluttony" (776) of the

224

unjust, she points out, that causes just men to pine "with want" (768). To remedy the situation, she proposes that the human race should share Nature's full blessings "In unsuperfluous eev'n proportion" (773). The Lady thus refuses to accept Comus's parody of temperance as total abstinence and insists that moderation is the key to achieving a healthy balance between production and consumption.

The terms of this debate derive, of course, from the Aristotelian concept of virtue, which is defined in the *Nicomachean Ethics* as a mean between two opposing extremes, one of defect, one of excess:

> The nature of moral qualities is such that they are destroyed by defect and by excess. . . . The same applies to self-control, courage, and the other virtues: the man who shuns and fears everything and never stands his ground becomes a coward, whereas a man who knows no fear at all and goes to meet every danger becomes reckless. Similarly, a man who revels in every pleasure and abstains from none becomes self-indulgent, while he who avoids every pleasure like a boor becomes what might be called insensitive. Thus we see that self-control and courage are destroyed by excess and by deficiency and are preserved by the mean.[3]

According to Aristotle, then, virtue is primarily a matter of accurate calculation, for the mean is not necessarily the exact midpoint between the extremes of excess and defect. It is rather, Aristotle insists, a "median relative to us . . . an amount neither too large nor too small, and this is neither one nor the same for everybody" (2.6.42). As the Lady observes, the mean is determined by the laws of "proportion"; all that is required is that each person receive a "beseeming share," not necessarily an equal share, of Nature's blessings.

So far so good. In all this the Lady is clearly and unequivocally in the right. The problems begin to arise when we try to reconcile this level-headed and thoroughly humane position with the Lady's response to the two concrete temptations with which she is faced: Comus's persuasions to drink of the cup, and his subsequent attempt to seduce her. To begin with the former, that she is tired and thirsty we know by the evidence of her earlier speeches and those of her brothers. Indeed, the very reason she finds herself in her present predicament is that they had gone off to find her some much needed refreshment while she rested:

> My brothers when they saw me wearied out
> With this long way, resolving heer to lodge
> Under the spreading favour of these pines,
> Stept as they sed, to the next thicket side
> To bring me berries, or such cooling fruit
> As the kind hospitable woods provide.
>
> (182–87)

So when Comus suggests that she has been "tir'd all day without repast" (688), he is describing her situation quite accurately. Unlike Comus's earlier victims described by the Attendant Spirit in his opening speech, the Lady would be drinking from his cup not as a result of "fond intemperate thirst" (67) but out of genuine need. When her host offers her his cordial julep, therefore, it might seem quite reasonable for her to accept it, provided that in accordance with the principle of moderation she does not partake of it greedily or intemperately. We in the audience know, of course, that the cup is enchanted and that even one sip would be fatal, but the Lady does not share our knowledge, and she is consequently hard-pressed to find an argument for refusing it.

The real trouble starts, however, when we try to reconcile the Lady's doctrine of temperance with her reaction to Comus's suggestion that she "be not coy, and be not cozen'd / With that same vaunted name virginity" (737–38). Without accepting the conclusion that she should be wholly promiscuous, the Lady could very well have replied that in sexual matters temperance consists in monogamous marriage, that although she hasn't the slightest intention of spending "natures coyn" (739) indiscriminately, she doesn't intend to hoard it either. But in fact she says nothing of the kind. Instead we hear:

> To him that dares
> Arm his profane tongue with contemptuous words
> Against the Sun-clad power of Chastity,
> Fain would I somthing say, yet to what end?
> Thou hast nor Ear, nor Soul to apprehend
> The sublime notion, and high mystery
> That must be utter'd to unfold the sage
> And serious doctrine of Virginity.
>
> (780–87)

Virginity or chastity—the terms are interchangeable in *Comus* as this passage, among others, demonstrates—has displaced temperance as the virtue the Lady feels called upon to defend.[4] Against the principle of sensual pleasure represented by Comus stands the principle of virginity represented by the Lady.

As a result, one of the major problems in the interpretation of *Comus* has always been how to reconcile the "holy dictate of spare temperance" (767), which the Lady advocates in the middle of the temptation scene, with the "sage / And serious of doctrine of Virginity," which she defends twenty lines later. It would be hard to improve on A. E. Barker's account of the difficulty:

> Comus strives to overcome her resolution by representing her virtue as an absurd and unlovely extreme. He ridicules the inflexible abstinence which uncompromisingly rejects nature's gifts, and cites the Lady's virginity—with its repudiation of the powers of youth and beauty—as a prime example of this repressive doctrine. In answer to the first part of this attack the Lady develops, with considerable effect, the doctrine of the mean. The extremes of undisciplined indulgence and of rigid abstinence are alike reprehensible; true virtue begins with temperance—the moderate and proportioned use of nature according to reason. But to the second part of the attack she replies with a categorical and cryptic assertion of the "sun-clad power of chastity" and an obscure reference to "the sage and serious doctrine of virginity." . . . And she does not indicate, as in the case of abstinence she has clearly indicated, at what point Comus's estimate of virginity is in error. We are left with the uncomfortable feeling that his interpretation of it as a perverse repudiation of powers with which nature has endued the Lady remains unrefuted.[5]

At one moment virtue is being defined as a mean between extremes; at the next it is being defined *as* one of the extremes.

The contradiction becomes even more striking when we consider the textual history of the mask, for the Bridgewater Manuscript, far from defending virginity, hardly mentions it at all. If, as most critics believe, the manuscript represents the version of *Comus* that was actually staged at Ludlow Castle in 1634, then the only references to chastity that the Earl of Bridgewater and his companions heard were the Elder Brother's speech on the efficacy of sexual purity and the Attendant Spirit's invocation of Sabrina. The Lady's famous vision of "Faith," "Hope" (213), and "Chastity" (215), Comus's leering allusion to the Lady's "dainty limms" (680), and his more direct attempt at persuading her to share with him in "mutual and partak'n bliss" (741), together with the Lady's steadfast defense of sexual abstinence (780–89), were either omitted from the acting version or added later. The theme of the 1634 text, then, was quite uncomplicated. It was temperance pure and simple. As Balachandra Rajan has put it, Milton staged at Ludlow "a straightfoward disputation between Comus and the Lady restricted to temperance and the right use of nature."[6] The Attendant Spirit announces in his opening speech that those who drink of Comus's cup are victims of "fond intemperate thirst," Comus derides the notion that all the world "should in a pet of temperance feed on pulse," and the Lady retorts by defending "the holy dictate of spare temperance." What is more, the ideal of temperance is implicit both in the Younger Brother's praise of divine philosophy as "a perpetual feast of nectar'd sweets, / Where no crude surfet raigns" (479–80) and in the Lady's criticism of the peasants' "riot and ill-manag'd merriment" (172). Most important of all, the Lady wins her victory over "sensual folly, and intemperance" (975) by refusing to drink from a cup symbolizing intemperance. Her virginity has never been implicitly or explicitly threatened, and the philosophical contradiction between abstinence and temperance that Barker pointed out is completely absent.[7]

The mask of temperance became the mask of virginity only in the 1637 printed text, in which Milton restored the lines omitted for the Ludlow performance and added another thirty-five or so on the same subject. It is in the printed text of 1637, not the performed (Bridgewater) text of 1634, that virginity emerges as a major issue in the temptation scene. Why, then, did Milton not only reintroduce but reinforce the fundamentally incompatible theme of virginity? How are we to account for the presence in *Comus* of two radically contradictory definitions of virtue?

The answer, I believe, is to be found in a deep-seated tension within the concept of temperance itself. As we have seen, the Aristotelian doctrine of the mean attempts to locate virtue along an essentially quantitative axis, at one end of which lies defect and at the other, excess; the ideal of moderation is at heart a matter of accurate calculation. Seen from a qualitative point of view, however, the mean is itself an extreme, a moral virtue opposed to the twin vices of defect and excess. In Aristotle's words, "in respect of its essence and the definition of its essential nature virtue is a mean, but in regard to goodness and excellence it is an extreme" (2.7.44). Faced with a choice between good and evil, a moral person would obviously be mistaken to seek out an intermediate position between them in accordance with the doctrine of the mean. And indeed, no one was more aware of this than Milton himself. The doctrine of the mean, he declared in *Of Reformation*, "is a fallacious Rule, unlesse understood only of the actions of Vertue about things indifferent, for if it be found that those two extremes be

Vice and Vertue, Falshood and Truth, the greater extremity of Vertue and superlative Truth we run into, the more vertuous, and the more wise we become" (3:66).[8]

Now drama, and especially drama with its roots in the English tradition of the morality play, tends to deal precisely in such polarities. To a greater extent than any other literary form, perhaps, it operates in terms of "Falshood and Truth," "Vice and Vertue," salvation and damnation, antitheses between which the middle way can only be a pallid form of accommodation. The task of characters like Everyman, Mankind, and their Renaissance successors is not to navigate between the personified vices and virtues that seek their allegiance but to choose the right side. By its very nature, drama invites us to apprehend human experience in qualitative rather than quantitative terms, and as a result, moderation is one of the least dramatic of the virtues. Indeed, in practice it can often look dangerously like a policy of moral compromise—just as the policy of moral compromise can all too easily be misrepresented as the practice of moderation. "I observe," wrote Milton in *An Apology Against a Pamphlet*, "that feare and dull disposition, lukewarmnesse & sloth are not seldomer wont to cloak themselves under the affected name of moderation, then true and lively zeale is customably dispareg'd with the terme of indiscretion, bitternesse, and choler" (3:281). When good faces evil or truth confronts falsehood, the middle of the road is neither the best nor the safest place to be.

What is more, as Aristotle originally noted, the mean is only rarely equidistant from the extremes that frame it: "In some cases it is the deficiency and in others the excess that is more opposed to the median. For example . . . in the case of self-control it is not the defect, insensitivity, but the excess, self-indulgence, which is more opposite" (2.8.49). The reason for this, he went on to argue, has to do with a fundamental characteristic of human nature:

> The more we are naturally attracted to anything, the more opposed to the median does this thing appear to be. For example, since we are naturally more attracted to pleasure, we incline more easily to self-indulgence than to a disciplined kind of life. We describe as more opposed to the mean those things toward which our tendency is stronger; and for that reason the excess, self-indulgence, is more opposed to self-control than is its corresponding deficiency. (2.8.49)

This tendency to transform the tripartite structure of the theory of the mean into a simple binary opposition has a consequence that Aristotle did not note however. For since the mean allies itself with the extreme closest to it against the extreme farthest from it, the mean inevitably takes on something of the character of its extremist ally. Self-control becomes increasingly difficult to distinguish from insensitivity as they make common cause against self-indulgence. And this alliance is reinforced by their opponents' habit of lumping them together. In Aristotle's words, "people at the extremes each push the man in the middle over to the other extreme: a coward calls a brave man reckless and a reckless man calls a brave man a coward, and similarly with the other qualities" (2.8.48). A self-indulgent character is thus likely to call a self-controlled person insensitive—hence Comus's equation of temperance with abstinence.

The natural conclusion of Aristotle's analysis is that "the first concern of a man who aims at the median should . . . be to avoid the extreme which is more opposed to it" (2.9.50). A writer who wishes to exemplify the virtue of fortitude is likely, therefore, to put all the emphasis on the threat posed by cowardice rather than recklessness, and a writer whose theme is the virtue of moderation will almost certainly identify its major antagonist as over-indulgence rather than insensitivity. As a result, characters like Spenser's Sir Guyon and Milton's Lady who represent the virtue of temperance find themselves tempted from only one direction, the extreme of excess. No one in the *Faerie Queene* tries to persuade Sir Guyon to reject the pleasures of the world in order to become a hermit, for instance, and no one in *Comus* attempts to convince the Lady of the desirability of becoming a nun. Attacked on one flank only, the exemplars and defenders of the *via media* are thus driven further and further toward the opposite extreme of defect. So although Sir Guyon approves of Medina (the golden mean) in theory, under the pressure of resisting those temptations embodied exclusively by Perissa (excess), he moves inexorably towards the opposite extreme of Elissa (deficiency) in his encounters with Mammon, Phaedria, and Acrasia. We can see the process taking place particularly clearly, I think, in Milton's retrospective interpretation of Sir Guyon's temptation in *Areopagitica,* where the patron of temperance is exposed to the bower of earthly bliss so that "he might see and know, and yet *abstain*" (4:311; emphasis mine). In much the same way, the internal dynamics of the temptation scene in *Comus* virtually guarantee that the defender of temperance will abandon the middle ground and turn into a militant defender of abstinence. However inconsistent the coexistence of the two values might appear to be from a strictly logical point of view, psychologically and morally the shift from the one to the other is entirely plausible.

Notes

1. A. S. P. Woodhouse, "The Argument of Milton's *Comus*," *University of Toronto Quarterly* 11 (1941): 46–71.

2. John Milton, *A Mask*, in *The Complete Poetry of John Milton*, ed. John T. Shawcross, rev. ed. (New York: Doubleday, 1971). *A Mask* will be hereafter referred to as *Comus*; all references are to this edition and are cited parenthetically in the text.

3. Aristotle, *Nicomachean Ethics*, trans. Martin Ostwald (Indianapolis: Bobbs Merrill, 1962), 2.2.35–36. All references to Aristotle's *Ethics* are to this translation and are cited parenthetically in the text. Ostwald consistently renders the Greek *sophrosyne* as "self-control." In all the Latin translations of Aristotle's treatise that I have consulted as well as in the English translations available in the Renaissance, *sophrosyne* consistently appears as *temperantia*, or "temperance." In the body of this paper, therefore, "temperance," "moderation," and "self-control" are used interchangeably.

4. Several critics, notably E. M. W. Tillyard (*Studies in Milton* [London: Chatto and Windus, 1930]) and A. S. P. Woodhouse ("The Argument") insist that Milton is making a crucial distinction between chastity and virginity. Although such a distinction was certainly available to him, John Demaray and Robert Adams clearly show that the text of *Comus* uses the two terms as synonyms. See John G. Demaray, *Milton and the Masque Tradition* (Cambridge: Harvard University Press, 1968), 93, and Robert M. Adams, *Ikon: Milton and the Modern Critics* (Ithaca: Cornell University Press, 1955), 9.

5. Arthur E. Barker, *Milton and the Puritan Dilemma* (Toronto: University of Toronto Press, 1942), 10–11.

6. Balachandra Rajan, *The Lofty Rhyme* (Coral Gables: University of Miami Press, 1970), 35.

7. The primacy of temperance is even clearer in Milton's original version of the temptation scene in the Trinity Manuscript where the invitation to drink Comus's cordial julep came at the end rather than the beginning of his encounter with the Lady. The tempter's theoretical arguments were only the prelude to the concrete temptation of the enchanted cup, which thus became the moral focus of the entire scene. In Milton's revisions, however, it became a mere preliminary to the attack on abstinence and the attempted seduction.

8. John Milton, *Of Reformation*, in *The Works of John Milton*, 18 vols., ed. Frank Allen Patterson et al. (New York: Columbia University Press, 1931–38). All references to Milton's prose are to this edition and are cited parenthetically in the text. Comus's cup, of course, was not "a thing indifferent," and that is why the Lady cannot drink from it even in moderation.

The Geometry of Choice: Chaos Theory and *Areopagitica*

MARY F. NORTON

Chaos often breeds life, when order breeds habit.
—Henry Adams

If Oscar Wilde is as right as he usually is, and "art is nothing more than an intensified mode of overemphasis,"[1] then Milton's poetry and prose overemphasize endings: the ending of monarchy, the ending of marriage, the ending of a sovereign Church, the ending of Paradise. Milton's sense of an ending is, however, a sense of beginnings. The forces of stability interacting with forces of instability and the movement from order to disorder and from disorder to order reveal how endings bring change. Change is necessary to know truth, but truth changes, so endings are necessary for beginnings. Such a perspective parallels that of contemporary chaos theory, wherein intrinsic instability within a system enables evolution of new orders, growth, and change. *Areopagitica* insists on individual free will and on a civic system that protects it, one in which individuals are granted "liberty to know, to utter, and to argue freely according to conscience, above all liberties."[2] Free will guarantees that human action and morality will be dynamic—that human beings will not be automatons, mere Adams "in the motions" (733). The presence and force of free will render the world unpredictable, yet "the pure and solid law of God,"[3] which is manifest in the conscience, can give order and coherence to human action. *Areopagitica* presents a world intrinsically complex and paradoxical, both unpredictable and orderly. Conscience is, paradoxically, both a principle of order and a force for disorder, for it is neither involuntary nor static, only a beacon that can guide the individual toward truth. It is a center that can hold, but only if the individual chooses to acknowledge and live by it.

Similarly, chaos theory perceives individuals "as dynamic processes that contribute to the determination of their course."[4] Milton insists in virtually all of his works, however, that an individual's liberty and choice are not synonymous with license to live independent of divine order and natural laws. Conscience makes the difference between absolute indeterminacy and true moral freedom, between unrestrained license and the responsibilities of liberty, and by analogy, between complete randomness and the patterns of chaos. Milton's epistemology does not try to subdue the forces of disorder and change, but like that of chaos theory, instead recognizes an inherent tendency of all things toward change, and thus, as does chaos theory, interprets "disorder and order not as antitheses but as complements."[5] Contemporary chaos theory offers a specific analogue for such an epistemology: Milton's moral system based on free will parallels chaotic systems classified as nonlinear, meaning that the system contains patterns, but the system is not fundamentally stable nor are its motions measurable to infinite precision. Further, the ways in which individuals reassemble pieces of dismembered Truth parallel a central component of chaos theory, fractal generation. Finally, conscience is analogous to a strange attractor, a point in a chaotic system's patterned but ultimately unpredictable movement that attracts systemic action.

Critics, however, widely dispute Milton's presentation of the moral character of Chaos, some claiming its inherent goodness,[6] some claiming its neutrality,[7] and some claiming its unequivocal evilness.[8] Criticism that has concentrated on the "ritualized repetition" and "patterns of birth and regeneration"[9] in Milton's works has not fully explored the deeper complexity of such patterns. Only recently has it been posited that Chaos is a force for indeterminacy that is simultaneously good *and* evil, productive *and* destructive.[10] I have argued elsewhere that, in *Paradise Lost*, Chaos as a realm, character, and principal is integral to the evolution of "increasingly complex moral systems" in the poem, and I have shown that chaos theory illuminates Milton's treatment of chaos, disorder, complexity, and unpredictability as forces of physical, moral, and intellectual generation and evolution.[11] Because of Milton's emphasis on the role and necessity of individual free will, the perspective of chaos theory does not undermine Milton's monism, but rather can be used to reveal his sense of the dynamism of the providential design wherein freedom is both implicit and necessary to its functioning. Chaos theorist David Porush contends, "Just because something is organized and systematic does not mean it is mechanical and has lost its freedom."[12]

Aereopagitica's injunction not to let truth "sicken into a muddy pool of conformity and tradition" (739) requires that the individual be neither intellectually nor morally static in the search for Truth. When Milton portrays Truth's metaphorical dismembering, from a "perfect shape most glorious to look on" (741) into "a thousand pieces . . . scattered . . . to the four winds" (742), he graphically illustrates the fractured nature of Truth, and because Truth is multidimensional and discernible only in fragments, Milton mandates Truth's reassembling as humanity's abiding quest. In the postlapsarian world, Truth can assume a variety of outward shapes: "it [is] not impossible that she may have more shapes than one" (747), and the assembling process demands that all pieces of Truth be utilized: "To be still searching what we know not by what we know, still closing up truth to truth as we find it . . . this is the golden rule in theology as well as in arithmetic" (742). Milton describes a building process like that of fractal geometry, a process that helps express graphically the structural variations of a shape. Fractal geometry, of which Benoit Mandelbrot was the mathematical inventor, demonstrates the evolution of increasingly intricate structural variations and patterns. The Latin verb *fractus*, "to break," denotes creation of irregular fragments that give increased dimensionality to an original figure: as new coordinates are added to a shape, a more intricate composite will evolve.

Like fractal geometry, which reveals multidimensionality and recognizes its significance, Milton's works similarly recognized the exigency of complexity and the essentiality of process rather than product, emergence rather than stasis, journey rather than destination. *Aereopagitica* argues that *not* utilizing the many pieces of Truth, even when they are controversial or ostensibly immoral, will hinder the quest to assemble the whole of Truth: "it will be primely to the discouragement of all learning and the stop of truth, not only by disexercising and blunting our abilities in what we know already, but by hindering and cropping the discovery that might be yet further made both in religious and civil wisdom" (720). Complexity is thus both an underlying necessity in the quest for Truth and a characteristic of Truth itself: "Yet is it not impossible that she may have more shapes than one. What else is all that rank of things indifferent, wherein Truth may be on this side, or on the other, without being unlike herself?" (747). Such complexity and multidimensionality reveal Milton's sense of the fundamentally dynamic composition of Truth.

Where "fractals describe the roughness of the world, its energy, its dynamical changes and transformations,"[13] likewise, the building of Solomon's temple in *Areopagitica* describes how multidimensionality and complexity are integral to its construction:

> And when every stone is laid artfully together, it cannot be united into a continuity, it can but be contiguous in this world; neither can every piece of the building be of one form; nay rather the perfection consists in this, that out of many moderate varieties and brotherly dissimilitudes that are not vastly disproportional, arises the goodly and the graceful symmetry that commends the whole pile and structure. (744)

Like stones for a temple, diverse ideas, choices, and opinions become fractals comprising a composite of Truth. Stevie Davies notes that Milton's description reveals the "many-sidedness of Truth," and John Peter Rumrich observes that the "structure includes disorder and disproportion."[14] Multiple facets or fragments of Truth must be discovered and amassed, not suppressed or disregarded in favor of a simpler or more habitual version of Truth.[15] Milton further insists that "there be pens and heads . . . sitting by their studious lamps, musing, searching, revolving new notions and ideas wherewith to present . . . others as fast reading, trying all things" (743). A multiplicity of political, moral, and intellectual positions can be constituent parts to be integrated into Truth, not forces that disintegrate Truth. Hence, "much arguing, much writing, many opinions" is creative, not destructive, for like the generation of fractals, "knowledge [is] in the making" (743).

Milton instead sees as destructive those who are intolerant of divergent opinions or "moderate varieties," for "They are the troublers, they are the dividers of unity, who neglect and permit not others to unite those dissevered pieces which are yet wanting to the body of Truth" (742). Unity does not mean simplicity, but rather coherent complexity, and Milton reproaches thus those who would reject schisms, as "Fool[s]" who "[see] not the firm root, out of which we all grow, though into branches" (744). Contradictions and "dissimilitudes" are implicit in and fundamental to the composition of Truth. Because *Aereopagitica* presents Truth as volatile and transient, and because the discovery of one truth may lead to the discovery of another truth, the quest for Truth is not teleological, though it can possess a sequentiality.

I have previously indicated that, as Milton states in *Aeropagitica*, God even "disseminates Truth in degrees and increments, in levels of its own verity":[16]

> For when God shakes a kingdom with strong and healthful commotions to a general reforming, it is not untrue that many sectaries and false

teachers are then busiest in seducing; but yet more true it is that God
then raises to his own work men of rare abilities and more than common industry, not only to look back and revise what hath been taught
heretofore, but to gain further and go on some new enlightened steps
in the discovery of truth. (748)

The process of looking back, revising, and going "on some new
enlightened steps," is necessary because truths can contain facets
of other truths, and truths can be enfolded within other truths,
just as fractals are "images of the way things fold and unfold, feed-
ing back into each other and themselves."[17] The *peroratio* of *Areopagitica* thus reiterates the fact that the process of discovering
Truth must be as multidimensional and complex as the composition
of Truth. As Ali Bulent Cambel maintains, "looking at complexity
as a hierarchical sequence implies the evolution of complexity."[18]
For Milton, the evolution toward Truth is the evolution of complexity. The process of constructing Truth, though not necessarily linear or even chronological, renders "dissimilitudes" generative and
productive, and Milton's emphasis, like that of fractal geometry,
is on the processes and productivity of change.[19]

The central notion of fractal geometry, that diversity yields
multidimensionality, is often also illustrated with images of lightning, root systems, or a tree branching into leaves whose patterns
are increasingly intricate but interrelated. Yet, "regardless of the
scale of magnification, structure is apparent."[20]

Self-similarity, an essential attribute of fractals, is likewise implicit in Milton's tolerance of "those neighboring differences" that
can be maintained within a "'unity of spirit'" (747). Without such
coherence, the search for Truth would be random and would lead
only to individual and civic anarchy, not to a commonwealth comprised of moral individualists "governed by the rules of justice and
fortitude" (739). Milton, like chaos theorists, finds "order at the
heart of disorder"[21]—the "firm root" of which Milton has spoken—
God in the hearts of humanity. He emphasizes neither the assurance nor absolutism of that presence but instead the process of
decision making that can be guided by it.

Chaos theorists use "bifurcation" to describe the juncture at
which a decision is made, when the course of action can be altered,
when the veins of the leaf branch into a new vein. The bifurcation
point is the point at which the system is, "in effect, being offered
a 'choice' of orders."[22] It marks the point where a decision has been
made and a new direction has been pursued, and consequently, a
new order established. Bifurcation points are, therefore, "mile-

stones in the system's evolution."[23] Milton's entire plea to the members of Parliament depends upon their changing their course, reversing their decision about pre-censorship, changing the direction of the future, following a new path. He urges Parliament not to allow the government to rest, static and immutable, as if civic stability were the only or even the ultimate goal of the government; he incites them instead toward the more complex goal of wisdom and true liberty: "For this is not the liberty which we can hope, that no grievance ever should arise in the Commonwealth—that let no man in this world expect; but when complaints are freely heard, deeply considered, and speedily reformed, then is the utmost bound of civil liberty attained" (718). In encouraging Parliament to admit dissension, he asks its members to admit complexity and instability into their governing—forces that engender reform, change in the direction of law and government, and consequently evolution to new levels of order. He emphasizes their ability to change courses if they are "willing to repeal any act of [their] own setting forth, as any set forth by [their] predecessors" (719). He insists in his *exordium* that separation from past actions or decisions can lead to new progress and evolution in the quest to compose Truth. He additionally posits himself as an example of the same kind of evolution he seeks from the Parliament, whose members, like him, should "freely magnif[y] what hath been nobly done and [fear] not to declare as freely what might be done better" (718). He exhorts them to recognize the juncture at which they stand and to see that the possibility for new direction lies only in a dynamic system directed to the progress toward reassembling whole Truth. He asks them to "be more considerate builders, more wise in spiritual architecture, when great reformation is expected" (744).

While bifurcation points illustrate "the irreversibility of time" because "one future was chosen and the other possibilities vanished," chaos theorists also assert that "the dynamics of bifurcations reveal that time is irreversible yet recapitulant."[24] Milton likewise iterates such irreversibility in moral terms: "'Tis true, no age can restore a life, whereof perhaps there is no great loss; and revolutions of ages do not oft recover the loss of a rejected truth, for the want of which whole nations fare the worse" (720). The consequence of one bifurcation may be lost time, lost progress in the quest for Truth, but while the past stands, it does not, nor should it, deter progress of the present toward the future.[25] Milton's insistence that no construct of order be absolute is reinforced by his insistence on the primacy of free will: "We ourselves esteem not of that obedience, or love, or gift, which is of force" (733), and as he declares later in *Paradise Lost,* neither humanity nor God "serve[s] necessity"(3.110).[26] He rejects tyranny in any form because, as an excess of authority, tyranny is its own form of lawlessness, one that denies the freedom and generative capacities of individual reason that can lead to change and evolution. Ironically, while civic or ecclesiastical systems should protect individual freedom, such systems can never stand entirely secure nor be permanently stable precisely *because* of that freedom. Free will guarantees that a moral system will be, in scientific terms, "nonlinear": unpredictable and intrinsically unstable.

Nonlinear mathematical equations reveal a system's intrinsic complexity and mutability, where, conversely, linear equations reveal a system's surface stability and order. Nonlinear equations are, further, unsolvable equations expressing episodes of instability within stable periods, and thus, "in fluid and mechanical systems, the non-linear terms tend to be the features that people want to leave out when they try to get a good, simple understanding."[27] An early and lucidly accessible explanation of chaos theory, James Gleick's *Chaos: Making a New Science* (1987), exemplifies nonlinearity:

> Without friction, a simple linear equation expresses the amount of energy you need to accelerate a hockey puck. With friction the relationship gets complicated, because the amount of energy changes depending on how fast the puck is already moving. You cannot assign a constant importance to friction, because its importance depends on speed. Speed, in turn, depends on friction. That twisted changeability makes non-linearity hard to calculate.[28]

As friction makes an equation nonlinear, free will makes moral systems nonlinear. Through its focus on how, why, and when choice functions, *Aereopagitica* reveals that neither discursive nor intuitive reason is static or schematized. Free will means that the choices and activities of individuals are intrinsically unpredictable, and so, by consequence, will civic systems be intrinsically unstable. Milton sees this, however, as preferable to a static moral order, one in which the outcomes of choices are invariable and citizens are ruled by "tyranny and superstition" (718). Instead, God "trusts [humanity] with the gift of reason to be his own chooser"; just as the government is the individual "writ Large" ("On the New Forces of Conscience Under the Long Parliament," 145) and the "government holds its authority from the governed,"[29] so "God commits the managing so great a trust, without particular law or prescription, wholly to the demeanor of every grown man" (727).

Though one can possess uncertainties, recognize mysteries, have doubts, see evil, "and yet abstain" (729), reason needs guidance. Milton's argument that books are living things, "lively" and "vigorously productive" (720), depends upon the will being free to choose a virtuous path and not being subjected to an aggressive or tyrannical external control even though a government must itself be guided and led by ethical and moral principles: "I am certain that a state governed by the rules of justice and fortitude, or a church built and founded upon the rock of faith and true knowledge, cannot be so pusillanimous" (739). Nonetheless, such a civic system must be fundamentally dynamic, else it is merely an undesirable anachronism that nullifies the "privilege of the people" (739) so that they "grow ignorant again, brutish, formal, and slavish" (745). And though Milton clearly "rejects a system of morality that is incoherent,"[30] nonlinearity is not to be confused with incoherence. Nonlinear systems are not entirely random, though their actions do not repeat themselves exactly. They instead possess patterns, replicating the same theme with variations. In Milton's chaotic, nonlinear moral system, there is an intrinsic force for structure and order: conscience. It is the self-determining control over unrestrained individual will that thus prevents systemic randomness and meaninglessness: "knowledge cannot defile, nor consequently the books, if the will and conscience be not defiled" (727).

Though perhaps unpredictable, human action is not for Milton entirely autonomous, for "the high providence of God" (733) renders actions meaningful in moral terms: they are either virtuous or not. Hence "though [God] command us temperance, justice, continence," he simultaneously "pours out before us, even to a profuseness, all desirable things, and gives us minds that can wander beyond all limit and satiety" (733). Human beings do not always or even consistently choose the way the conscience might direct, though in Sonnet 22, Milton assures that each individual is sufficient to stand and able to "bear up and steer / Right onward" (8–9). In Milton's nonlinear system, conscience is a strange attractor within the moral system of human choices and action. It is not a fixed point, but it does attract movement toward it. As Cambel posits, "Dynamical systems are attracted to attractors the way fireflies are attracted to light. And just as a firefly can come from most any direction and be attracted to bright lights, so a system can start from different sets of points in phase space and still wind up at the same attractor region, called the *basin of attraction*. The totality of basins makes up the phase space."[31] As N. Katherine

Hayles explains in *Chaos Bound,* whereas "truly random systems show no discernable pattern when they are mapped into phase space [a way of turning numbers into pictures], chaotic systems contract to a confined region and trace complex patterns within it."[32]

As in fluid systems where finite space contains an infinite number of paths, in Milton's dynamic moral system, human action is not entirely random because humanity "acts rightly and wrongly in relation to God."[33] Yet, as David Steenburg emphasizes in *The Harvard Theological Review,* "although the process will proceed within the parameters of the pattern . . . one cannot predict precisely where the next step will appear in the pattern."[34] Unpredictability does not, however, mean arbitrariness. Movement is contained within a recognizable pattern, which in Milton's moral terms is confined to a field of contraries in which "good and evil . . . grow up together almost inseparably" (728). Because meaning is determined within this field, Milton argues, "Wherefore did [God] create passions within us, pleasures round about us, but that these rightly tempered are the very ingredients of virtue?" (733). Because conscience attracts actions into patterns relative to contraries, actions are not random, but meaningful and interpretable within a larger moral context of good in relation to evil. Hence, in trusting conscience, Milton trusts that freedom will not become mere license, liberty not mere anarchy.[35] The strange-attractor component of chaos theory can be seen as the basis of Milton's relationship between consciousness and conscience and serves as the basis for Milton's argument for a system of ethics rather than a system of dogma: "A little generous prudence, a little forbearance of one another, and some grain of charity might win all these diligences to join and unite into one general and brotherly search after truth; could we but forego this prelatical tradition of crowding free consciences and Christian liberties into canons and precepts of men" (744).

The conscience should guide the will toward Truth and in conduct,[36] but it is both an independent and deterministic principle: it is both free and bound to God. Like Aquinas, Milton presents the conscience as an application of Christian faith to the business of life; it is the voice of God within humanity. Just as Paul compares conscience and faith in Rom. 13.5 and 14.1–23, Milton compares conscience and the law of nature in *Christian Doctrine,* when he defines that law as "a set of moral absolutes identical with the will of God. . . . The law of nature was 'in the hearts of all mankind' (*CD* 16:101)."[37] The individual's conscience both guides the will and is controlled by the will, and therefore, one can obey conscience or not: "reason is but choosing" (733). Precedent to application, it is a moral foundation upon which all decision making is based. As the "ultimate ethical imperative,"[38] it renders "a discreet and judicious reader" (727) capable of managing the exposure to "any books whatever come to [his] hands" (727). With conscience as substructure and the fundamental force influencing reasoning and choosing, Milton can confidently urge the "prudent spirit" of each Parliamentarian to "[acknowledge] and [obey] the voice of reason from what quarter so ever it be heard speaking" (719). Milton wants this concept to extend to a civic system based on an individual's freedom to follow that inward knowledge and guidance rather than some external legal or theological absolutist authority, "law and compulsion" (727). For Parliament to deny individuals freedom of conscience is tantamount to any (of the then) recent Roman Catholic form of tyranny, such as "the Council of Trent" or "the Spanish Inquisition" (724). Nonetheless, in his explanatory survey of "little else but tyranny in the Roman empire'[s]" attempts to suppress heresy (723), Milton posits as exemplary the "primitive councils and bishops [who] were wont only to declare what books were not commendable, passing no further, but leaving it to each one's conscience to read or lay by" (723). Acknowledging the political and ecclesiastical constructs that inhibit conscience, Milton warns also against humanity's general inability to trust, and withhold judgment of, others. Conscience therefore becomes more imperative because it ironically both engenders Christian charity and yet depends upon it: "How many other things might be tolerated in peace and left to conscience, had we but charity, and were it not the chief stronghold of our hypocrisy to be ever judging one another" (747). As a strange attractor, conscience reveals the patterns into which the liberty of individuals shapes itself. The attractor of human reason and choosing, conscience must be allowed free movement, exercise rather than suppression, so it can guide individuals and governments to virtue, prudence, wise deliberation, and thus true civil liberty.[39]

Perhaps Milton so overemphasizes endings because they reveal the power of disorder, and disorder is an inevitable result of freedom. Yet chaos theory enables us to concentrate on how disorder is also a catalyst for new order. As chaos theorist Ilya Prigogine's insights into chaos "highlight the difference between a mechanical view of nature and a holistic one,"[40] in highlighting the dynamics of choice and unpredictability, *Aereopagitica* reveals the complex interactions of order and disorder. Milton's epistemology of chaos is implicit and fundamental, deep within his view of reality, and *Areopagitica* envisions and anticipates chaos theory's perceptions about how this world works. In such a vision of reality, free will and choices make new civic orders possible, and multidimensionality is a form of freedom that will lead us closer to reassembling fractured Truth. Order therefore should be neither static nor tyrannical because endings impel new beginnings, because implicit complexities of this world will reveal mysteries enfolded within many dimensions.

Notes

The epigraph is from Henry Adams, *The Education of Henry Adams,* ed. Ernest Samuels (Boston: Houghton Mifflin, 1973), 249.

1. Oscar Wilde, "The Decay of Lying," in *Critical Theory Since Plato,* ed. Hazard Adams (New York: Harcourt, 1971), 678.

2. John Milton, *Areopagitica,* in *John Milton: Complete Poems and Major Prose,* ed. Merritt Y. Hughes (New York: Odyssey, 1957), 746. All references to *Areopagitica* are to this edition and are cited parenthetically in the text.

3. John Milton, *Christian Doctrine,* in *Complete Prose Works of John Milton,* 8 vols., ed. Don M. Wolfe et al. (New Haven: Yale University Press, 1953–82), 3:505.

4. David Steenburg, "Chaos at the Marriage of Heaven and Hell," *Harvard Theological Review* 84 (1991): 457.

5. N. Katherine Hayles, ed., *Chaos Bound: Orderly Disorder in Contemporary Literature and Science* (Ithaca: Cornell University Press, 1990), 9.

6. A. S. P. Woodhouse, "Notes on Milton's Views on the Creation: The Initial Phases," *Philological Quarterly* 28 (1949): 211–36.

7. Michael Lieb, *The Dialectics of Creation: Patterns of Birth and Regeneration in "Paradise Lost"* (Amherst: University of Massachusetts Press, 1970); Robert M. Adams, "A Little Look into Chaos," in *Illustrious Evidence: Approaches to English Literature of the Early Seventeenth Century,* ed. Earl Miner (Berkeley: University of California Press, 1975).

8. Regina Schwartz, *Remembering and Repeating: Biblical Creation in "Paradise Lost"* (Cambridge: Cambridge University Press, 1988); Harinder Singh Marjara, *Contemplation of Created Things: Science in "Paradise Lost"* (Toronto: University of Toronto Press, 1992); A. B. Chambers, "Chaos in *Paradise Lost,*" *Journal of the History of Ideas* 24 (1963): 55–84.

9. Schwartz, *Remembering and Repeating,* 4; Lieb, *The Dialectics of Creation.*

10. John Rogers, "Chaos and Consensus: The Liberal Science of *Paradise Lost*" (paper presented at the Milton Seminar, Franklin and Marshall University, spring 1993); Stephen M. Fallon, "'To Act or Not': Milton's Conception of Divine Freedom," *Journal of the History of Ideas* 49 (1988): 425–29; John Peter Rumrich, "Milton's God and the Matter of Chaos," *PMLA* 110 (1995); Mary F. Norton, "The Praxis of Milton's Truth: *Proairesis* and Qualification in the Civil Liberty Tracts," *Milton Quarterly* 28 (1994): 47–55.

11. Mary F. Norton, "'The Rising World of Waters Dark and Deep': Chaos Theory and *Paradise Lost*," *Milton Studies* 32 (1995): 91–110.

12. David Porush, "Literature as Dissipative Structure: Prigogine's Theory and the Postmodern 'Chaos' Machine," in *Literature and Technology: Research in Technology Studies, Volume 5*, ed. Mark L. Greenberg and Lance Schachterie (Bethlehem, Pa.: Lehigh University Press, 1992), 291.

13. John Briggs and F. David Peat, *Turbulent Mirror: An Illustrated Guide to Chaos Theory and the Science of Wholeness* (New York: Harper, 1989), 23.

14. Stevie Davies, *Harvester New Readings: Milton* (New York: Harvester Wheatsheaf, 1991), 38–39; Rumrich, "Milton's God," 1040.

15. In his broader discussion of gender discourse, Joseph Wittreich agrees that Milton "stands free of the illusion that new truth is the whole truth," a notion that, albeit in a different context, nonetheless fundamentally recognizes the necessity of constant action ("'Inspir'd with Contradiction': Mapping Gender Discourses in *Paradise Lost*," in *Literary Milton: Text, Pretext, Context*, ed. Diana Treviño Benet and Michael Lieb [Pittsburgh: Duquesne University Press, 1994], 136).

16. Norton, "The Praxis of Milton's Truth," 48.

17. Briggs and Peat, *Turbulent Mirror*, 23.

18. Ali Bulent Cambel, *Applied Chaos Theory: A Paradigm for Complexity* (Boston: Academic Press, 1993), 30.

19. Marjara observes that "Milton's world is dynamic as well as vast, and the action of *Paradise Lost* is replete with motion" (*Contemplation*, 145). His analysis of Chaos and the Creation also recognizes the emphasis that Milton places on the processes of change and generation (186).

20. Steenburg, "Chaos at the Marriage," 448.

21. Ibid.

22. Briggs and Peat, *Turbulent Mirror*, 143.

23. Ibid., 144.

24. Ibid., 144–45.

25. F. Cramer (*Chaos and Order: The Complex Structure of Living Systems*, trans. D. I. Loewus [Weinheim: VCH-Verlagsgesellschaft, 1993], 3) notes that "Order in living systems is not a static phenomenon comparable to crystallization. On the one hand, life is a dynamical creation of order and is always accompanied by decay, the transition to chaos. On the other hand, life *is* decay. The evolution of species could not be understood without a principle of selection; that is, the emergence of new species is accompanied by the extinction of others."

26. John Milton, *Paradise Lost*, in *John Milton: Complete Poems and Major Prose*, ed. Merritt Y. Hughes (New York: Odyssey, 1957). All references to Milton's poetry are to this edition and are cited parenthetically in the text.

27. James Gleick, *Chaos: Making a New Science* (New York: Viking, 1987), 24.

28. Ibid.

29. "Tyranny," in *A Milton Encyclopedia*, 9 vols., ed. William B. Hunter et al. (Lewisburg, Pa.: Bucknell University Press, 1978–80), 8:103.

30. Onno Oerlemans, "The Will to Knowledge and the Process of Narrative in *Paradise Lost*," *English Studies in Canada* 16 (1990): 2.

31. Cambel, *Applied Chaos Theory*, 59. Cambel adds that

Phase space is the playing field of dynamic phenomena. Systems move in all sorts of directions, execute strange patterns, and sometimes stop. For example, a children's swing will come to rest in a vertical position unless it receives pushes . . . or consider a grandfather clock and its pendulum. The pendulum will come to rest at a stable vertical position when the mechanism stops. Such stable equilibrium points are called *fixed point attractors*. The term "attractor" derives from the observation that if a system in phase space is near an attractor, it tends to evolve towards the state represented.

32. Hayles, *Chaos Bound,* 9–10.

33. Fallon, "'To Act or Not,'" 448.

34. Steenburg, "Chaos at the Marriage," 452.

35. In later works, Milton's concept is consistent with what he purports in *Areopagitica.* For example, he says in *Paradise Lost:* "And I will place within them as a guide / My Umpire Conscience" (3.194–95), agreeing with St. Paul's claims in 1 Cor. 10.27–30 and 2 Cor. 1.8–13 that conscience is a corrective power. In *Paradise Lost,* "conscience wakes despair" in Satan (4.23) and causes Adam to fear both the present and the future: "O Conscience, into what Abyss of fears / And horrors hast thou driv'n me" (10.842–43). In *Paradise Regained,* "Conscience" is "tormentor" (4.130).

36. Timothy Potts (*Conscience in Medieval Philosophy* [Cambridge: Cambridge University Press, 1980]) cites the origin of the complexity of conscience as a concept. He notes, perhaps most pertinently, that conscience has both private and public expression.

37. "Law of Nature, The," in *A Milton Encyclopedia,* 4:209.

38. In *The Idea of Conscience in Renaissance Tragedy* (London: Routledge, 1990), 8, John S. Wilks presents shifts in the role of conscience from medieval scholastics to the plays of the Tudor and Jacobean dramatists. His final section offers an illuminating study of the "theme of moral choice" and the relationship of motive to action in the drama of Christopher Marlowe, John Webster, Philip Massinger, and John Ford.

39. For further discussion of conscience, see Meg Lota Brown, *Donne and the Conflict of Conscience in Early Modern England* (New York: E. J. Brill, 1995).

40. Briggs and Peat, *Turbulent Mirror,* 153.

Discerning the Spirit in *Samson Agonistes:* The Dalila Episode

ALAN RUDRUM

It is only by a blind confidence in the reputation of Milton that a drama can be praised, in which the intermediate parts have neither cause nor consequence, neither hasten nor retard the catastrophe.

—Samuel Johnson

Where a mortified heart is, there also is a heart quickened to the life of God, and the more fit for duty, both within and without. The chief service of God is inward; and this inward stands especially in repentance, which first consisteth in the change of evil habits and qualities of the soul, ere new be put in.

—Richard Rogers

Samson Agonistes, the major poem of Milton's we must try to understand without the prompting of a narrative voice, might be held to exemplify the postmodern view that "meanings are unde-cidable."[1] Certainly some of the attention it has received seems to fall within the political agenda attributed to postmodern criticism, for example the view that pacificism is good, nationalism and war evil.[2] In this essay I confront certain critical positions of recent years: that Milton portrayed Dalila as being as right in her way as Samson in his; and that in publishing *Samson Agonistes* with *Paradise Regained,* he intended us to read it, by contrast, as a study in false heroism; to see Samson in fact as deluded and finally acting willfully rather than according to reliable promptings from the true God.

While some of these critical positions might be identified with postmodernism, they have generally been urged within the framework of the Western rationalist tradition, in which relevance of fact and cogency of argument are held to be decisive. The generality of Milton scholars have refrained from announcing that they would rather be interesting than right. In putting a case for traditional interpretation of *Samson Agonistes,* that is, as the drama of Sam-

son's regeneration, I am indebted to scholars with whom I disagree
but whose work I have found stimulating. Blake's saying that "opposition is true friendship" is never more true than within field
such as literary criticism and history in which validity of argumen
can rarely reach arithmetical rigor. In the course of writing thi
essay, I found myself perhaps less interested in the particular argument being developed than in the question of what condition
would have to be met in order for it or any other critical argumen
to gain universal acceptance. In other words, how does a criti-
who knows himself to be in the right persuade his colleagues t
abandon their contrary positions? I am still working on this important question, but for the moment can only say to those stil
inclined to disagree that "If they will but purge with sovrain eye
salve that intellectual ray which God hath planted in them," ther
they will come to a better mind.[3]

My argument that the poem is a drama of regeneration will res
principally upon a single episode, that of Dalila. Its central positior
within the poem correlates to its centrality for correct understand
ing. A relevant question we can put to it is one increasingly voicec
by undergraduate readers, who are less likely (where multi
culturalism is the norm) than those of earlier times to have beer
raised within a Christian context of instruction and biblical study
They ask why, if it was right for Samson to act on behalf of the
God of Israel, it was not equally right for Dalila to act on behal
of Dagon. This question has not always been directly addressec
by critics who have taken Milton's dramatization of Dalila as thei
subject. Milton's intention that we *should* consider it may be par
of the reason why the Dalila of his poem is Samson's wife, which
she is not in the biblical account. Husbands and wives have mutua
obligations, but those obligations have not always been symmetri
cal. That they *should* be may be arguable; in practice they have
not. In the marriage service of the Book of Common Prayer, for
example, the vow of obedience of wife to husband has persistec
down to our own time. Since Milton's anti-Laudian stance migh
be thought to invalidate such a citation, it should be added tha
Milton's dislike of fixed forms of liturgy did not entail his rejectior
of what, in the Book of Common Prayer, was biblically based. The
point of Milton's characterization of Dalila is that it enabled hin
to dramatize certain important principles, based on ancient Jewisk
and seventeenth-century European matrimonial law, and, at a
deeper level, on Milton's understanding of God and of our righ
relationship to him.[4] We reach the deeper level, of God's law, by
taking seriously, for interpretive purposes, the stratum of humar

law just above it. Of course, in theocratic societies, human laws are related to those societies' perceptions of the matters to which laws pertain; it is no surprise that matrimonial law in Hebrew and early modern societies should reflect the perception that God created man higher in the scale of being than woman.

If we accept the modern perspective that men and women are equal, standing on the same rung of the ladder of nature, and combine it with the traditional Judeo-Christian view that we must put our duty to God above our duty to all human beings whatsoever, then we might well see Dalila as morally correct in allowing the priests and elders of her tribe to persuade her to put Dagon before both Samson and Samson's God, the God of the Hebrews. And we could brush aside queasy questions such as "Should she not have left him first, explaining her position?" with the casuistry that if her allegiance to Dagon was to be acted out, then deception was necessary. Something that might alert us to the dubiousness of this view is the fact that it rests upon a combination of an ancient perspective with a modern one, essentially a picking and choosing designed to yield the result we happen to like. It should be clear that Milton did not intend us to understand the proper relationship between Samson and Dalila in such a way, and while we are entitled to think about the subject matter of the poem in our own terms, and decide that Milton's take on it is unacceptable to us, we are not entitled to pretend that our own terms are likely to yield the meaning that Milton intended. For that, we need to stay within Milton's terms of reference, which is not to say that it is necessarily easy to determine precisely what those were.

A study of the Dalila episode may help us to understand *both* why Dalila was not entitled to facilitate actions hostile to Samson as he was to undertake actions hostile to her people, the Philistines; *and* why Samson should be seen as a true hero rather than a false one. Such a study, I suggest, represents the kind of approach we need to take if we are to validate the recently much-disputed interpretation of *Samson Agonistes* as a drama of regeneration.[5]

One question to consider is, What were Dalila's obligations toward Samson? If we are to avoid a mere freewheeling detour on the subject of husband-wife relations, we need to situate that question within its relevant context or contexts. Two such contexts may be allowed: that of the society in which the Samson story received its canonical recension, and that of Milton's time, place, and known viewpoint. An archaeologist I consulted said that it would have been obvious, in the Hebrew context, that Dalila, in marrying Samson, renounced her god and society and owed fealty to his society and his God—so obvious that it would not have been worth writing down. The point is also taken as obvious by Arnold Stein: "A wife leaves, for her husband, both parents and country. And this human law was not abrogated by any other natural law, or law of nations, or national law (except the unpublished one, with the multiple blank lines, called 'public good')."[6] When Samson speaks of her "Treason against" him (391),[7] he is speaking accurately: treason is the act of betraying, or delivering up to an enemy, one to whom allegiance is owed, as, in the words of the *Oxford English Dictionary,* "of a master by his servant" or "a husband by his wife." This definition covers Dalila's case, considered in the context of the Judaism of the Hebrew Bible, or in that of Milton's England. Late twentieth-century dislike of male-dominated societies is irrelevant to an understanding of Milton's poem on this particular, and crucial, point. Critics of *Samson Agonistes* who sympathize with Dalila, seeing her as psychically torn between her husband and her nation, are in my view misunderstanding, though they project accurately part of what modern readers might justly see as the significance of the poem for today's readers. To use E. D. Hirsch's terms, they are operating in the realm of "significance," rather than in the realm of "meaning."[8]

However, we can go beyond this, and in a direction which might tend to mollify those who feel that Milton should have known better than to accept the masculinist assumptions of his time. Suppose that there had been full legal and practical equality between husbands and wives among ancient Hebrews and early modern Europeans. How then might we judge the issue between Dalila and Samson? I suggest that if there were no basis in human law, we could judge on the basis of God's superiority to Dagon, or vice versa. In that case, proponents of *Samson Agonistes* as a drama of regeneration would need to show that Dagon is a false god, one of the *bugiardi dei* of *The Divine Comedy.* The question is, then, how do we know that Dagon is a false god?

During the 1994 Milton Seminar on *Samson Agonistes,* at Duquesne University, a participant remarked, "Dagon is Dagon, and God is God." There was a general murmur of assent, which left me wondering if such unanimity would have been achieved had everyone there articulated his or her understanding of that statement; it also left me thinking, not for the first time, that consideration of Milton's intention in the Dalila episode should not be foreclosed by too easy an acceptance of this truism. Certainly modern political consciousness raises questions of what it might be like to teach *Samson Agonistes* to a class composed of descendants of the followers of God and of Dagon. However, Milton is not our contemporary and did not participate in the historical consciousness of modern times.[9] While we might legitimately read the poem, and the biblical chapters relevant to it, with an awareness of vistas of enhanced historical re-cognitions, such readings should not be treated as if they might have been Milton's. To put it crudely, we might condemn Milton for this apparent lack of sympathy for the Philistian ruling classes slain at the conclusion of the drama; but we should beware of treating our own response as a direct result of Milton's intention. To see this is to acknowledge both the principle that the intention of the author cannot legitimately confine the reader (the poem may well open up for us insights of which the author was unaware, and which he would not have intended had he been aware) and the recognition that Milton is likely to have understood his subject matter in terms closely related to, if not absolutely derived from, the Protestant hermeneutic principle of *sola scriptura*.[10] As Ralph Chillingworth says, "The Bible, the Bible only I say, is the religion of Protestants."[11] John R. Knott, Jr., writing on the early anti-prelatical tracts, refers to "an underlying reason for Milton's stance in these tracts . . . his sense of the Bible as a force transforming England. Milton's arguments for . . . presbyterian church government are less significant, finally, than the complex of attitudes toward the Bible that emerges in these tracts." Knott goes on, in a passage highly relevant to our understanding of *Samson Agonistes* "Although these attitudes are modified in Milton's subsequent prose and poetry, important continuities are to be found, especially having to do with a dynamic sense of the operation of the Holy Spirit."[12]

To return to "Dagon is Dagon, and God is God": in a small book on *Samson Agonistes* published more than twenty-five years ago, I wrote, "We should not gloss over the ethical issue between Samson and Dalila by inertly accepting that Samson's God is the true God, and Dagon a false god."[13] A good deal of subsequent criticism falls into the gap between that passage and John Carey's remarks in his brief book on Milton, published in the same year, on the immorality of Samson's slaughter of the Philistines.[14]

I would argue that the Dalila episode is not so much about men and women as about human beings and God; or rather about an understanding of the nature of God that is crucial to our relationships with him and with each other. This understanding may be summed up by stating that God's freedom, his not being tied to "his own prescript" (*Samson Agonistes* 308) is the ground and guarantee of human freedom and of human responsibility. At this point I take issue with Joseph Wittreich, who suggests that because Samson repeatedly disregards God's laws, the only way of redeeming him for heroism would have been "to argue for God's suspension of his own laws."[15] Of course the chorus does say that God is not bound by his own prescripts; such arguments are, according to Wittreich, implicity rejected by Milton himself when he argues in *The Doctrine and Discipline of Divorce* that he wants to be "able to shew . . . the waies of the Lord, strait and faithfull as they are, not full of cranks and contradictions, and pit-falling dispenses."[16] While it is reasonable to look in Milton's prose for interpretive aid, the words of the chorus at this point cannot be so readily disposed of, and especially not by a piece of polemical prose almost certainly written many years earlier. Milton was as opportunistic as other polemicists, as Thomas Corns has shown.[17] Moreover, he must certainly have been aware that the Hebrew Scriptures implicitly make much of God's freedom by showing him working in ways that strict Israelites would have found unorthodox; there are a number of cases in which the proprieties of a theocratic, male-dominated society were violated. Since Wittreich makes his point against the words of the chorus in terms of Samson's earlier sins, it should be said that both Judaism and Christianity exhibit heroes and saints who have been great sinners; we need only to recall King David and Saint Mary Magdalene. The tradition could hardly have done otherwise than admit Samson's sins; it also admitted that he was punished for them, as Milton and the other republicans thought of the Restoration as punishment for their sins that delivered them into the hands of idolators.[18]

It is precisely the perceived freedom of God, his not being bound by his own prescripts, which endows his human worshipers with freedom. It is not merely because he is worshiped in an image that Dagon is an idol, but because, his will being coterminous with that of the priests and elders of Philistia, he has no transcendence. As presented in *Samson Agonistes*, God is not God merely on the general ground that he is the God of the Israelites as known through the Hebrew Scriptures. He is God (and not an idol) because his will cannot in all circumstances be known by consulting tradition, or Scripture, or the priests and elders of Israel. This is both a biblical and a seventeenth-century radical Puritan perspective. From the latter viewpoint, even if there had been no scriptural warrant for Samson's apparently transgressive behavior, in attending Dagon's games, there was a seventeenth-century English position, found among the Quakers: George Fox, in "summing up the argument for women ministers," said, "and if there was no

Scripture, Christ is sufficient."[19] The words "and if there was no Scripture" clearly imply that Fox meant the Christ within our hearts, not Christ as he can be found in the words or actions of Scripture. Christ so conceived is no different from the "rousing motions" (1382) felt by Samson. It is worth recalling here John Knott's statement that "Nineteenth-century readers of *Christian Doctrine* exclaimed over [Milton's] Quakerism," along with Knott's comment that while such reactions may be extreme, they testify to Milton's real affinities with radical Protestant thinking.[20]

The crucial passage is in lines 850–61, where Dalila says to Samson:

> thou knowst the Magistrates
> And Princes of my country came in person,
> Solicited, commanded, threat'n'd, urg'd,
> Adjur'd by all the bonds of civil Duty
> And of Religion, press'd how just it was,
> How honorable, how glorious to entrap
> A common enemy, who had destroy'd
> Such numbers of our Nation: and the Priest
> Was not behind, but ever at my ear,
> Preaching how meritorious with the gods
> It would be to ensnare an irreligious
> Dishonorer of Dagon.

From a biblical or early modern perspective, it is of course part of the case against the magistrates and princes of Philistia that they were here failing to honor the fact that, in marrying Samson, Dalila had renounced fealty to Dagon and to the nation into which she had been born. The point is made by Samson himself:

> Being once a wife, for me thou wast to leave
> Parents and country; nor was I their subject,
> Nor under their protection but my own,
> Thou mine, not theirs: if aught against my life
> Thy country sought of thee, it sought unjustly,
> Against the law of nature, law of nations,
> No more thy country, but an impious crew
> Of men conspiring to uphold thir state
> By worse than hostile deed, violating the ends
> For which our country is a name so dear;
> Not therefore to be obey'd.

> (885–95)

However, we are for the moment pretending that this was not the case, and that Dalila had the right to consider the Philistian leaders' case against her husband. On those terms, it may well seem reasonable that in a theocratic society, in which the laws of the deity are taken as the statute book of the kingdom, magistrates, princes, and priest should combine to bring home to Dalila what her duty was. But there is a deeper consideration. Ask how Dalila knew her duty, and the answer is clear: the magistrates, princes, and priest told her. Put the question another way. How did Dagon make his will known to Dalila? He made it known through the magistrates, princes, and priest. In this respect Philistia bears a striking resemblance to the Roman Catholic Church as viewed from a radical Puritan perspective, or to the secular power in its relation to the established church in post-Restoration England. Milton's hostility to Roman Catholicism rested on his belief that it represented a reconstitution of pagan idolatry; and there is abundant evidence that in the years after the Restoration, Roundhead politicians regarded, and spoke of, the restored monarchy as an idol.[21] And how, at bottom, are idols to be recognized? "Their idols are silver and gold, the work of men's hands. They have mouths, but they speak not: eyes have they, but they see not."[22] The point is that if we draw a circle that represents the will of Dagon, and a circle that represents the will of the magistrates, princes, and priests of Philistia, those circles will be coterminous. In other words, Dagon has no transcendence; he is merely an objectification of the will of the ruling classes of Philistia. As Arnold Stein put it, "Philistia is institutionalized morality. The princes and magistrates represent, not surprisingly, the convenient good, which also represents them. The priests, like their god, represent public good. There is no gap between the two orders of morality."[23]

Certainly it was generally true that for the Samson of Milton's poem, the laws of Israel were also held to be the laws of God. But it was not true in an absolute sense. The regenerate Samson of the poem's ending acknowledges the general truth of the proposition by refusing to go to the games of the Philistines:

> thou knowst I am an Ebrew, therefore tell them,
> Our Law forbids at thir Religious Rites
> My presence; for that cause I cannot come.

> (1319–21)

However, he later acknowledges that the law was not true in an absolute sense, remarking of God,

> Yet that he may dispense with me or thee
> Present in Temples at Idolatrous Rites
> For some important cause, thou needst not doubt.
>
> (1377–79).

Shortly after this, he begins to feel the "rousing motions" (1382) that lead him to change his mind: "I with this Messenger will go along" (1384).

Not only may God's purposes be achieved through apparently transgressive human behavior (we know well enough that he can bring forth good out of evil); the important point here is that his champions as well as his enemies may exhibit apparently transgressive behavior. Blair Worden has recently shown that this is not only a biblical but a seventeenth-century radical perspective and that the apparently transgressive behavior might include deadly violence, as in Samson's case.[24]

Nearer the beginning of the poem Samson marks the distinction between the inner voice and the promptings of the devices and desires of our own hearts. Speaking of his parents' displeasure at his marriage with the "daughter of an Infidel" (221), the woman of Timna, Samson remarks that "they knew not / That what I motion'd was of God" (221–22); he, unlike his parents, "knew / From intimate impulse" (222–23), seeing it as potentially enabling the work to which he was "divinely call'd" (226). There is no indication here of Samson repudiating his former sense of the intuition of the divine will; when, however, he speaks of his marriage to Dalila, he says, "I thought it lawful from my former act" (231). We should note that Samson's *intentions* in this second marriage were unchanged; he was "still watching to oppress / Israel's oppressors" (232–33). But he made the mistake of acting by analogy. He had no "intimate impulse" but merely thought it lawful from his former act. In the first instance there was an apparent violation of God's law, in the second a real one.

The distinction between the inner voice and the promptings of the devices and desires of our own hearts is central to what has been called the "crucial question" in interpreting *Samson Agonistes:* whether Samson hurled down the pillars because he was divinely propelled or because he was self-motivated.[25] There is more than one level of answer to the view that the words "of my own accord" (1643) represent an admission on Samson's part that he does not act by divine commission. Taking Occam's razor to it, we need only to quote the phrase in its immediate context,

> Hitherto, Lords, what your commands impos'd
> I have perform'd. . . .
> Now of my own accord,
>
> (1640–43)

and say, with J. Martin Evans, that "of my own accord" stands in opposition not to "divine command" but rather to Philistine command.[26] This is quite sufficient to answer Wittreich's point.

However, it is worth saying, beyond this, that the phrase occurs in a speech, reported by the messenger, in which Samson addresses the lords of Philistia. It should not therefore be treated as omniscient author commentary. Samson is under no moral obligation of frankness toward his enemies, in this place any more than when he gave an explanation for his apparent change of mind in submitting to the Philistian command to attend Dagon's feast: "Because they shall not trail me through thir streets / Like a wild Beast, I am content to go" (1402–3).[27]

Furthermore, while "by one's own unsolicited assent; of one's own spontaneous motion" is the usual meaning of the phrase "of one's own accord" (and the sense Samson intends the Philistian lords to take), Milton is here thinking, as he so often does, philologically. He knew as well as any other writer of the time how to write in English while thinking in Latin and would have known that the verb "accord" means literally to "bring heart to heart" and therefore to reconcile oneself with another.[28] Words that are meant to be interpreted by the Philistian lords in their common sense are dramatically ironical enough, referring in their hidden meaning to Samson's own individual empowerment through reconciliation with God.

A full discussion of this topic would call for more comprehensive consideration of Milton's text, for closer critical questioning of works in which very different readings have been presented, and for wider contextual survey, for example, of contemporary discussion around discernment of the Spirit.[29] Fuller discussion along these lines would, I am confident, strongly support an argument for interpreting *Samson Agonistes* as a drama of regeneration and of Samson's rehabilitation as God's champion. However, this is an essay, not a book. The brief points that follow are a mere selection of those that might be made.

First, would Milton have cared to distinguish so clearly between the natures of God and of Dagon, giving Dagon the characteristics of an idol, if he had intended us to see God's champion as ultimately self-deluded? Would he have distinguished so clearly between the inconsistency of Dalila, in her very self-presentation, and the agonizing sincerity with which Samson attempts to speak truthfully of himself and of his situation, if he had intended us to see them as morally equivalent?

Then, we might consider whether our overall knowledge of Milton really precludes the view that he could approve of the slaughter of the "choice nobility and flower" (1654) of Philistia. Is such a view so unthinkable of the author of *The Tenure of Kings and Magistrates?* Within our overview of Milton, can his dismissal of warfare as "the only Argument / Heroic" (*Paradise Lost* 9.28–29) count for so very much, especially when the manner of Samson's last days and death can so readily be seen as exemplifying "the better fortitude / Of Patience and Heroic Martyrdom" (*Paradise Lost* 9.31–32), and when our overall knowledge includes the fact that "Milton's writings had always displayed an appetite for vengeance?"[30]

We need to consider the tone of the entire poem. Is the repentant Samson that we hear likely to be presented for our ultimate rejection? Can the ending, so consonant as it seems with the healing function of tragedy, really be inviting us to consider and reject? Is it likely that Milton intended *Samson Agonistes* to be so very thoroughgoing a self-destroying artifact?

We should question too whether an entire work, as long as this, is likely to depend so heavily for its meaning on juxtaposition with another work, as *Samson Agonistes* is said to do in relation to *Paradise Regained.* Where else do we find such extreme dependence except for the relation between certain works and the Scriptures themselves?

Further, the view of Samson as an ultimately failed hero appears to take its rise from a strong antipathy to war and to violence generally, which may be related to the antiwar protests of the 1960s. As a newcomer to North America at that time, I took no part in such protests; but I did teach *Samson Agonistes* as a work which implied the moral right, and in certain circumstances duty, to take part in acts of civil disobedience. As a drama of the inner light, that is what it means. In radical Puritan understanding, the right of civil disobedience included the right to perform violent acts. Philistia, conversely, as a totalitarian state, could concede no right of even nonviolent civil disobedience, any more than could Nazi Germany or the Soviet Union. Writing close to the fiftieth anniversary of the first sightings by the Western troops of the European camps of the Holocaust, I consider it worth saying that there have been wars at least arguably worth fighting, if that in Vietnam was not. The treatment of "dissenters" and "nonconformists" in post-Restoration England may pale in comparison with the Holocaust, but we should not forget that thousands of Quakers were imprisoned, and hundreds died in its jails.[31]

In the treasury of Santa Maria della Salute in Venice, there are two paintings that clearly answer to each other.[32] In one, Samson is pulling down the pillars, in an image that recalls strongly many others of Christ carrying his Cross; in the other, Jonah is forcing open the jaws of the whale. Both images may be related iconographically to those depictions of the Harrowing of Hell in which Satan lies crushed and impotent beneath the door that the power of Christ has thrown to the ground. It is worth recalling what those familiar words, "the Harrowing of Hell," refer to: the rescue and release of those who had been within the grip of absolute evil. I submit that Milton's view of the matter, in which the "choice nobility and flower" of Philistia may be taken as representing the repressive and tyrannical alliance of Church and State in post-Restoration England, does not call for us to sympathize with those who "only set on sport and play / Unwittingly importun'd / Thir own destruction to come speedy upon them" (1679–81). One wonders whether, by the time *Samson Agonistes* was published, even the Earl of Clarendon would have disagreed.

Notes

The epigraphs are from Samuel Johnson, *Lives of the English Poets,* ed. George Birbeck Hill (1905; reprint, New York: Octagon Books, 1967), 189, and Richard Rogers, *A Commentary Upon the Whole Book of Judges* (London: Printed by Felix Kyngston, 1615), 618.

1. Jacques Derrida, as cited in John R. Searle, "Rationality and Realism, What Is At Stake?" *Deadalus: Proceedings of the American Academy of Arts and Sciences* 122 (fall 1993): 77.

2. Searle, "Rationality," 56.

3. John Milton, *Of Reformation,* in *Complete Prose Works of John Milton,* 8 vols., ed. Don M. Wolfe et al. (New Haven: Yale University Press, 1953–82), 1:566.

4. This is to take issue (on this point only, it should be said) with Stella P. Revard, "Dalila as Euripidean Heroine," *Papers on Language and Literature* 23 (1987): 291–302.

5. See John Carey, *Milton* (London: Evans Brothers, 1969); Irene Samuel, "*Samson Agonistes* as Tragedy," in *Calm of Mind: Tercentenary Essays on "Paradise Lost" and "Samson Agonistes,"* ed. Joseph Wittreich (Cleveland, Ohio: Press of Case Western Reserve, 1971); Joseph Wittreich, *Interpreting "Samson Agonistes"* (Princeton: Princeton University Press, 1986).

6. Arnold Stein, *Heroic Knowledge: An Interpretation of "Paradise Regained" and "Samson Agonistes"* (1957; reprint, Hamden, Conn.: Archon Books, 1965), 172.

7. John Milton, *Samson Agonistes*, in *John Milton: Complete Poems and Major Prose*, ed. Merritt Y. Hughes (New York: Odyssey, 1957). All references to Milton's poetry are to this edition and are cited parenthetically in the text.

8. E. D. Hirsch, *Validity in Interpretation* (New Haven: Yale University Press, 1967). In the preface, Hirsch refers to "the crucial distinction between meaning and significance," xi; it is central to the work as a whole. In this essay, I have tried to use the words "meaning" and "significance" in accordance with Hirsch's usage.

9. See Hans George Gadamar, *Truth and Method*, trans. Joel Weinsheimer and Donald G. Marshall, 2d rev. ed. (New York: Continuum, 1994), xxiii–xxv. Gadamar warns that "the perspectives that result from the experience of historical change are always in danger of being exaggerated," xxiv. See also the second chapter, "Precritical Interpretation of Biblical Narrative," of Hans W. Frei, *The Eclipse of Biblical Narrative: A Study in Eighteenth and Nineteenth Century Hermeneutics* (New Haven: Yale University Press, 1974).

10. Gadamar, *Truth and Method*, xxxiii.

11. Ralph Chillingworth, *The Religion of the Protestants* (Oxford, 1638), as quoted by Patrick Collinson, in *The Religion of the Protestants: The Church in English Society* (1982; reprint, Oxford: Clarendon, 1984), viii.

12. John R. Knott, Jr., *The Sword of the Spirit: Puritan Responses to the Bible* (Chicago: University of Chicago Press, 1980), 107.

13. Alan Rudrum, *A Critical Commentary on Milton's "Samson Agonistes"* (New York: St. Martin's, 1969).

14. Carey, *Milton*, 138–46. This chapter is titled "The Outmoded Hero: Samson."

15. Wittreich, *Interpreting "Samson Agonistes,"* 69.

16. Cited in ibid., 70.

17. Thomas Corns, "Some Rousing Motions: The Plurality of Miltonic Ideology," in *Literature and the English Civil War*, ed. Thomas Healy and Jonathan Sawday (Cambridge: Cambridge University Press, 1990), 110–26. See also Thomas Corns, *Uncloistered Virtue: English Political Literature, 1640–1660* (New York: Oxford University Press, 1992).

18. See Rogers, *A Commentary*, 736–37, and Blair Worden, "Milton, *Samson Agonistes*, and the Restoration," in *Culture and Society in the Stuart Restoration*, ed. Gerald MacLean (Cambridge: Cambridge University Press, 1995), 134.

19. George Fox, as cited in Geoffrey F. Nuttall, *The Holy Spirit in Puritan Faith and Experience* (1946; reprint, Chicago: University of Chicago Press, 1992), 156.

20. Knott, *The Sword of the Spirit*, 122.

21. Worden, "Milton, *Samson Agonistes*, and the Restoration," 118. Worden cites, as references to idolatry in the poem, lines 13, 441, 453, 456, 1297, 1358, 1364, 1378.

22. Ps. 115.4–5 (King James Version).

23. Stein, *Heroic Knowledge*, 171.

24. Worden, "Milton, *Samson Agonistes*, and the Restoration," 132–33.

25. Wittreich, *Interpreting "Samson Agonistes,"* 355. In his review of *Interpreting "Samson Agonistes,"* J. Martin Evans (*Review of English Studies* 34 [February 1988]: 109–11) identifies Wittreich's nine references to Samson's acting of his "own accord": 74, 75, 120, 143, 154, 155, 171, 355, 363.

26. Evans, review of *Interpreting "Samson Agonistes,"* 111.

27. Lines 1369–72, spoken to the chorus, may be taken as Samson's true position:

> *Samson.* Where outward force constrains, the sentence holds;
> But who constrains me to the Temple of Dagon,
> Not dragging? the Philistian Lords command.
> Commands are no constraints.

28. I owe this point to Diane Kelsey McColley, who pointed out the significance of the etymology of "accord" at the Milton Seminar on *Samson Agonistes,* Pittsburgh, 15 October 1994.

29. See especially Nuttall's *The Holy Spirit.*

30. Hugh Trevor-Roper ("Milton in Politics," in *Catholics, Anglicans and Puritans: Seventeenth-Century Essays* [London: Secker and Warburg, 1987], 280), as cited by Worden, "Milton, *Samson Agonistes,* and the Restoration," 126.

31. For a discussion of the terms "dissenter" and "nonconformist" as used in the period, see N. H. Keeble, *The Literary Culture of Nonconformity in Later Seventeenth-Century England* (Athens: University of Georgia Press, 1987), especially 41–44. The eleventh edition of *Encyclopedia Britannica* gives the figure of four hundred deaths among the imprisoned Quakers.

32. They are attributed to Palma *il giovane* (1544–1628).

Contributors

DIANA TREVIÑO BENET is associate professor at the Gallatin School of New York University. A past president of the Donne Society and the Milton Society of America, she has written on Milton and other seventeenth-century authors and topics. She is also contributing editor for "The Elegies" in *The Variorum Edition of the Poetry of John Donne,* forthcoming from Indiana University Press.

DAVID J. BRADSHAW chairs the Department of English at Warren Wilson College, where he teaches English and Classics and also serves as lecturer for the North Carolina Shakespeare Festival. He has published essays concerning Homer and Sophocles, John Webster, and Virgil and Milton. Currently, he is working on a book concerned with Milton's emulation of Virgil.

CHARLES W. DURHAM, professor of English at Middle Tennessee State University, is codirector of the biennial Conference on John Milton and coeditor of *Spokesperson Milton: Voices in Contemporary Criticism* and *Arenas of Conflict: Milton and the Unfettered Mind.*

RICHARD J. DUROCHER is associate professor of English at St. Olaf College. He is the author of "Milton and Ovid." His articles on Milton and the classics have been published in *Milton Quarterly, Milton Studies, Modern Philology, Studies in Philology,* and *Comparative Literature Studies.* Currently he is working on a new book entitled *Milton and the Sacred Earth.*

J. MARTIN EVANS is professor of English at Stanford University. His most recent publication, *Milton's Imperial Epic: "Paradise Lost" and the Discourse of Colonialism,* brings together his passion for Milton's poetry and his interest in travel literature. Also author of *"Paradise Lost" and the Genesis Tradition, "Paradise Lost" IX–X,* and *The Road from Horton: Looking Backwards in "Lycidas,"* Professor Evans regularly reviews books on Milton for the *Review of English Studies.*

CHERYL H. FRESCH is associate professor of English at the University of New Mexico in Albuquerque, where she is also the director of Undergraduate Studies in English. Most recent among her publications on *Paradise Lost* is "'Whither thou goest': *Paradise Lost* XII, 610–23 and the Book of Ruth," in *Milton Studies* 32.

ALBERT C. LABRIOLA, professor of English and Distinguished University Professor at Duquesne University, is editor of *Milton Studies* and volume editor for the "Songs and Sonnets" in *The Variorum Edition of the Poetry of John Donne,* forthcoming from Indiana University Press. Since 1974, he has been secretary of the Milton Society of America.

KARI BOYD MCBRIDE teaches in the Women's Studies Department at the University of Arizona. She maintains a web site on Aemilia Lanyer at http://www.u.arizona.edu/~kari/lanyer.htm and is the author of "Sacred Celebration: The Patronage Poems of Aemilia Lanyer" and "Remembering Orpheus in the Poems of Aemilia Lanyer."

DIANE KELSEY MCCOLLEY is professor of English at Rutgers University, Camden College of Arts and Sciences. In addition to numerous articles on Milton, she is the author of *Milton's Eve, A Gust for Paradise: Milton's Eden and the Visual Arts,* and the forthcoming *Poetry and Music in Seventeenth-Century England.*

ELIZABETH MAZZOLA is Wegman Assistant Professor of English at the City College of New York. Her essay on "Apocryphal Texts and Epic Amnesia: The Ends of History in Spenser's *Faerie Queene*" was awarded the Spenser Society's 1996 Isabel MacCaffrey Award. The present essay is part of a larger project on Renaissance historiography.

MARY F. NORTON, assistant professor of English, is the director of Graduate Studies in English at Western Carolina University, where she teaches Milton and seventeenth-century literature. She has published in *Milton Studies, Milton Quarterly, Arenas of Con-*

flict: Milton and the Unfettered Mind, and is working on a book on chaos theory and Milton.

KRISTIN A. PRUITT, professor of English and department head at Valdosta State University, is codirector of the biennial Conference on John Milton and coeditor of *Spokesperson Milton: Voices in Contemporary Criticism* and *Arenas of Conflict: Milton and the Unfettered Mind.* She is also a member of the executive committee of the Milton Society of America.

STELLA P. REVARD is professor of English at Southern Illinois University, Edwardsville, where she teaches English and Greek. She is the author of *The War in Heaven, Milton and the Tangles of Neaera's Hair,* and numerous articles on Milton, classical literature, and Renaissance poetry. In 1997, she was named Honored Scholar by the Milton Society of America.

LAWRENCE F. RHU is associate professor of English at the University of South Carolina. He is author of *The Genesis of Tasso's Narrative Theory: English Translations of the Early Poetics and a Comparative Study of Their Significance,* another essay on Tasso and Milton in *Poetry and Prophecy: The Beginnings of a Literary Tradition,* and numerous essays on Renaissance literature.

ALAN RUDRUM is professor of English at Simon Fraser University. He is author of critical commentaries on *Paradise Lost, Comus,* and *Samson Agonistes,* as well as of *Modern Judgements on Milton,* and editor of the *Complete Poems of Henry Vaughan, The Works of Thomas Vaughan,* and *Essential Articles: Henry Vaughan.* He has held a number of research fellowships, including a Killam Research Fellowship and Visiting Senior Research Fellowship, Jesus College, Oxford.

LOUIS SCHWARTZ, associate professor of English Literature at the University of Richmond, has published essays on Milton in *Milton Quarterly, Milton Studies,* and *Arenas of Conflict: Milton and the Unfettered Mind,* and is working on a book-length study of literary representations of catastrophic childbirth in sixteenth- and seventeenth-century England.

CLAUDE N. STULTING, JR., is assistant professor of English and Religion at Furman University. He is currently working on a book concerning the sacramental dimensions of the prelapsarian books of *Paradise Lost*.

JOHN C. ULREICH is professor of English at the University of Arizona, where he teaches the English Renaissance (especially Milton) and the Old Testament. He has published on Milton, Spenser, Sidney, the Old Testament, C. S. Lewis, and Owen Barfield.

Index